TREASURE EXPRESS

TREASURE EXPRESS

Epic Days of the Wells Fargo

BY

NEILL C. WILSON

ILLUSTRATED

The Rio Grande Press, Inc.

GLORIETA, NEW MEXICO · 87535

First edition from which
this edition was copied supplied by
INTERNATIONAL BOOKFINDERS, INC.,
P O. Box 1
Pacific Palisades, Calif., 90272

A RIO GRANDE CLASSIC
First published in 1936

ISBN 0-87380-157-1

First printing 1987

The Rio Grande Press, Inc.
GLORIETA, NEW MEXICO · 87535

Preface

This title is a companion book to our previously-published (1986) *Silver Stampede; The Career of Death Valley's Hell-Camp Old Panamint.* In that title, we did not have and could not locate any pertinent biographical data on author Wilson, but we have some now.

Neill Compton Wilson was born May 25, 1889, in Minneapolis, Minn., the son of Walter John and Evelyn (Kneisly) Wilson. He married Gladys Patch May 15, 1920, and has a daughter Nancy Jane, and a son Bruce Neill. The family made their home in Sebastopol, Calif.

Author Wilson was a reporter, an editor, a rancher, all followed by a career in advertising. He served with the U. S. Army in 1918. He was a prolific writer on a free-lance basis after 1944, with a number of books and short stories to his credit. His brief biography in *Contemporary Authors* states that he wrote a history of the Wells Fargo Bank, an illustrious and famed institution well-known to Western history fans and of course, to American history altogether. Our research could not determine when Mr. Wilson died.

Like our earlier edition of *Silver Stampede,* this book is a dandy tale of treasure-carrying stage coaches during the hectic days of the California gold rush (1849/1859). Well-researched and beautifully-written, author Wilson brings to life a time and a place that is gone forever. Here is a capsule history of the nation's greatest gold rush; here are tales ". . . ` of men and mice", of good luck and bad, of bad men and good men, of fortune and disaster. Writer Wilson brings back the nostalgic days of yesteryear, when the cry of *'gold'* echoed around the mountains and around the world! Another time. Another Place. Read. Enjoy.

Robert B. McCoy

May 1987
La Casa Escuela
P. O. Box 33
Glorieta, New Mexico 87535

TREASURE EXPRESS

Epic Days of the Wells Fargo

BY

NEILL C. WILSON

ILLUSTRATED

NEW YORK

THE MACMILLAN COMPANY

1936

PRINTED IN THE UNITED STATES OF AMERICA
NORWOOD PRESS LINOTYPE, INC.
NORWOOD, MASS., U.S.A.

THE OLD STAGECOACH

Drums the rain and sears the sun.
Now its hardy course is run,
And the vines and meadow grasses
Draw it to oblivion.
Rusts its iron, rots its leather,
Parts its hickory, peels its paint,
And the steeds that swung together
Gallop far and faint.

U. S. Mail and brave Wells Fargo!
Dancing harness, screeching brakes,
Reinsman bold, superb, loquacious,
Sawed-off shotgun disputations,
Miners, gamblers, dames flirtatious,
Dusters, pokes and wideawakes—
On by winding purple canyons
Over granite crests you rolled,
Storm and battle your companions,
Glitter in your hold.
Where is now that gallant cargo
Of the days of old
When the West, to jingling traces,
Bounced and skimmed on thorough-braces—
Rocked and banged through sun and shadow
Up the trails of El Dorado?

The Old Stagecoach

Veteran of the craggy passes,
From their oat bins in the sky
Call your vanished six. Prince, Beauty,
Lady, Star, Nell, Lightning! Ay,
Back, you wheelers, swing-span, leaders!
Now, by foothill oaks and cedars,
Spring for pine-clad heights and rutty,
Sinks of sage and alkali.
Box aclink and stout defended,
Roll, O coach refreshed and splendid!

Nay. The odyssey is ended,
Charge delivered, waybill filed,
Passengers and whip descended,
Concord long outstyled,
And the grand old rubbish yields
To the fingers of the fields.

CONTENTS

ILLUSTRATIONS

Illustrations

I

SO IT ALL BEGAN

In the year 1848, when a workman chanced to spy yellow glint in a mountain river, California had six or seven thousand Nordic settlers. These had already considerably upset a placid Mexican régime. They had hoisted the bunting of freedom in the cattle-raising coastal valley of Sonoma; they had seen the flag of the United States raised at Monterey and San Francisco; their settlement at the Bay even had two newspapers. But in the main the land was about as vacant as the moon. A land without coins, clocks, calendars, post offices, or roads.

With his back to the great central valley, green under January rains, Jim Marshall knelt to inspect that curious substance in the bottom of his mill race. Coldly it gleamed —the spark that was about to blast Elysium into bedlam.

Word of the find reached John A. Sutter's baronial fort on the Río Sacramento. Native Californians yawned; they had heard of the gilt before, down San Fernando way. Why bother, señores, when life was already so satisfactory? Word also reached San Francisco, where a little newspaper was making up the pages of a special edition intended for Atlantic Coast readers. The editor casually included "gold" in the new land's resources, but declined to grow passionate about it.

But the report interested other San Franciscans. These slipped out of town, made their way across the bay which separated their peninsula from the mainland, and let out their horses. Returning, they marched into barrooms, ordered the best and wettest, and for payment slapped down the evidence. Sam Brannan, who owned a newspaper, ran through the streets shouting: "Gold, boys! From the American River!"

Seeing was believing. Bartenders ripped off aprons. Merchants shut shop. Sailors went over the side. The few printers dropped their type and kicked the pi into the corner. The little *Californian* produced a single page, announcing suspension. "The whole country from San Francisco to Los Angeles, and from the seashore to the base of the Sierra, resounds with the sordid cry of 'gold! *gold!!* GOLD!!!'—while the field is left half planted, the house half built, and everything left but the manufacture of shovels and pickaxes."

Down from the Sierra foothills came the first important wave of the new wealth. It came to purchase tools and provisions and cared nothing for the price. A quarter-million dollars' worth of yellow grains and flakes reached the seaboard in two months. Six hundred thousand more in the next six weeks. From rancho and pueblo every form of conveyance—*carreta*, calash, spring wagon—was lick-larruping for the "diggin's." A man named Weber, at Weber Creek, took out $50,000 in a few days with the aid of some wondering Indians. At Dry Diggings, near the site of Marshall's discovery, a man named Wilson gleaned about $2,000 directly under his doorstep. One man, working a piece of ground measuring only a few square feet, picked up nearly twenty pounds of gold in the space of twenty days. Major Reading, a pioneer ranchman on the upper Sacramento, climbed the knotted mountains at the head of the valley and took out $80,000 along the Trinity River in six weeks—moving on when he found himself too closely crowded by men from Oregon.

The instinct of a publisher dies hard. The *Californian* managed to recapture a printer or two. Soon it was recording the amazing scene. It told of dirt, carried in wagons two or three miles to water, washing out at the rate of $400 a load. Five exceptional loads produced $16,000. By midsummer some five or six thousand amateur miners were feverishly plying knife and pan along the Mother Lode, where average luck was said to be $100 a day and the fortunate were picking up $10,000 and $15,000 a week. From the spot where Marshall found his first flake, worth about fifty cents, an ever widening circle of strikes had been made until claims by the hundreds had been located along one hundred and fifty miles of the Sierra foothills.

This was local fervor. The Atlantic states were months distant by land, seventeen thousand miles and thirty weeks by sea. But the word spread. Kit Carson galloped eastward with it in army pouches. Mormon settlers heard the news and tossed it independently beyond the Rockies.

Gold!

The news caught the nation in fitting mood. The times

were ripe for a mighty surge westward. War with Mexico had lately ended. Victorious troops, blooded by adventure, had marched home in no humor for humdrum return to plow or counter. New lands for old. New lives for old. "Just address me at the mines, Ma." California!

First ships got away in November, '48. With February, sixty vessels departed New York. Seventy prows in the same month drove outward from Boston and Philadelphia; little New Bedford dispatched eleven. "We are on the brink of the Age of Gold!" cried Horace Greeley in his New York *Tribune*. "We look for the addition, within the next four years, equal to at least one thousand millions of dollars to the general aggregate of gold in circulation and use throughout the world. This is almost inevitable."

Twenty or thirty thousand overlanders by spring of '49 were gathered along the Missouri. Before them stretched a thousand miles of prairie. Beyond, stony mountains. Beyond those, God knew what. Barrens and unexplored fearfulness, certainly. But these companies were gay. Cares had been shed. Not one in ten would find fortune at the placer diggings, but who could ask fairer odds or a more glorious gamble? "How's the grass by now, boys, out yonder on the Platte?" "Fetlock-high!" "Giddap!"

Up Nebraska's long river, across Wyoming, into South Pass cleft in stupendous sterile mountains, and out upon the fateful floor of the unknown basin moved the continuous train of bellowing oxen, straining mules, cantering horsemen, swaying wagons—the grandest parade, and not the least tragic, in history. Others took the southwest course, following the caravan trail worn broad by Santa Fé freighting. Across Texas and New Mexico streamed yet more thousands; across Nicaragua; across fevered Panama.

> Oh, Susanna, don't you cry for me—
> I'm off for California with my washbowl on my knee!

So they hurried into the sunset, those marchers of '49, with their shovels and blankets, their hopes and enthusiasms, their youth and their primal cussednesses. Life was intensified. The sun had never been so radiant. Pull, you sweaty bullock! The track—where's the track? Is that the track? But it's white—white with salt; white with bones. No matter. We'll cross those sands and we'll burst those mountains. On for California!

Arriving by land or by sea, they made for the placers. They filled the manzanita vales and azalea hollows with their whoops. They set up tents and brushwood shacks; the more clear-sighted set up saloons.

By the end of '49 the number of them was thought to be around one hundred thousand: wholly male, footloose and obstreperous. Buckskinned frontiersmen from Oregon, South Americans, Chinese, Hawaiians mingled with swarthy Mexicans openly aggrieved at such interloping; mingled with men from every country of Europe and every state of the Union. Seldom in the world's slow turning had so many different kinds of men been drawn to one spot for so single a purpose. Other stampedes would follow, to Australia, the Pacific Northwest, the Rocky Mountains, the wide deserts. But this was the modern world's first great treasure rush since the days of the Conquistadores. In one year California, lately a wilderness, would be a populous state.

At San Francisco, where recently half a dozen ships had been a rarity off the wharfless shore, '49 brought half a thousand. They came from every frontage on the seven seas. Forty thousand passengers that year entered the port of tumult by water. Two hundred windjammers lay deserted at one time, a tangle of idle spars—crews gone for the mines. All the vessels that came were not sky-raking square-riggers, and all were not ocean steamships. The year before the rush, a "floating palace" was launched at New York for excursion duty on the placid Hudson River. The owners of the luxurious *New World* got into financial difficulties and in '49 the sheriff came to her wharf with papers of attachment. The broad-beamed paddleboat was gone. It was suggested that she was off somewhere on a week-end picnic. But the sheriff waited in vain. The *New World* did not return from her picnic. Windows boarded up and hold and decks stocked with fuel, she was making straight out the Narrows for the Atlantic, bending south, and flipping blue water behind her in a nervy charge for the far tip of South America. When next heard from she had rounded the hemisphere and was at Panama—a godsend and a surprise to a mob of gold-seekers who had crossed the Isthmus to its Pacific side and were waiting clamorously for any kind of transportation onward. After sixteen or eighteen thousand miles of varied steaming, Captain Ned Wakeman and his extraordinary river boat entered the Golden Gate and passed onward to do shuttle duty between San Francisco and Sacramento City. These were dauntless times.

Other craft, equally valorous, preceded and followed.

Stockton, burg of sacking built on mud, became the base town for the "southern" diggings, and its boats did a river traffic of $50,000 to $100,000 a day. Sacramento City fifty miles north, a canvas town built about a levee, did even better. It served the Mother Lode belt in the region surrounding Marshall's pioneer discovery. Marysville up the Sacramento River served the "northern mines." Down at San Francisco, the eight-score adobe houses of a few months previous grew to six hundred structures, mostly frame, to two thousand, to four thousand; the population, from four hundred and fifty-nine souls, including Indians, to six thousand, fifteen, thirty. "The busiest port on earth!" Jangling dance hall and whooping gin mill obliterated any memory of Mission bell; though by October of '49 life had become sufficiently stabilized for the *Daily Alta California,* a merger of the two elder weeklies, to urge its readers to "persuade some of the respectable families that have daughters to settle in life, to come to California and build up the society, which without woman is like an edifice built on sand." The oracle further discovered: "There is something in the climate, we of course except San Francisco and the Valley of the Sacramento, which predisposes one to contentment."

Meanwhile, out yonder where the Mother Lode foothills rose against the Sierra granite, canyons were being churned with a spirit that was the very reverse of contentment.

The merchant was there with boots and shirts at monstrous prices, flour at $600 a barrel, liquor at $50 a gallon, remedies at one dollar to ten dollars a pill and purge. The gambler was at hand with his polished boots, fine hat, and supple fingers; the horse thief, with his pistols; the Cantonese, with his pigtail and his "washee." For the favored minority the Snowy Mountains continued yielding up new gold in flakes, pellicles, and chunks. The story of it all has been told and retold, but when will it ever stale?

What days they must have been!

II

RISE OF THE EXPRESSES

"Put me down, Alex! One from my sister and six from my girl."

"Me, too!"

"*Me!*"

The youth with pantaloons stuffed into boots, pistol belt at slope, and whiskers making hammock for his nose writes them all down. Two dozen miners on Mokelumne Bar, half a hundred in Jackass Gulch, a score each in Murderers' Gulch, Bloody Gulch and Rattlesnake Flat—and he is on his way. He will bring back the mail: for a measure of gold per letter.

At Stockton or Sacramento City he puts up his horse and fights for a place in the first down-bound launch. The boiler manages to hold together. Twenty-four hours later, San Francisco pushes its sand hills through the morning fog. Up the littered trough called Clay Street he rushes for the post office.

Long queues of men stand before this shanty. They will be here all night. Places near the head of the line are worth a golden ounce or a mortal fight. A side-wheeler, weeks out from New York, has been sighted off the Golden Gate. The courier seeks the rear of the shanty,

9

plucks out Postmaster Geary, offers his services, and is sworn in as a clerk. With a pair of helpers he ransacks the arriving mail bags; by morning he has abstracted several hundred missives addressed to his clients.

Getting back upstream is no easy matter. Somewhere along the Embarcadero the resourceful courier finds a ship captain who will part with a skiff. Clearly the skipper is a newcomer, or he would want its weight in gold for the craft of pine. He names his price—$300, and the craft's capacity—eight or nine men. The new proprietor retails places on its thwarts and gunwales to twice that many passengers for an ounce of gold dust each, with the privilege of doing their own rowing up the hundred miles of bay and river and "eating themselves." The owner-captain sits on his mail bag and steers. Thus returns in style to his base town, one of the West's first letter express-men. He sells his small argosy at a handsome profit and probably pays it all out on a four-day board bill for his horse. Yes, this is El Dorado.

When he bursts through to the Mokelumne Bars, Jackass Gulches, Jimtowns, Mud Canyons, and Greenhorn Slides of his mountain territory: "Six from your mother, Baltimore, and only one from your girl. . . . Nothing for you, Provincetown. She must have took up with the drugstore feller that stayed home. . . . Three for you, Brattleboro. *At* sixteen dollars each. I'm starting back for another mail tomorrow."

News from home, boys! *News from home!*

The whiskerandos of '49 may have liked to consider themselves rough, tough, and boisterous; but scratch the surface, and every mother's son among them was unutterably homesick. Memories of home cooking and the girl in gingham grew more poignant with each passing day. A thousand yellowing diaries and letter packets have come down the decades to reveal this aspect of the Argonaut. "Address me at the mines, Ma," had been spoken lightly enough, with little thought for the vicissitudes those letters

LETTER EXPRESS

would encounter before one in five of them ever reached delivery.

In February of '49 one William Van Voorhees arrived at San Francisco as the first United States Mail agent. Washington knew nothing of the job it had sent him on. He was instructed to establish post offices in five towns. They were far from the mines. Most of the immigration was scurrying like ants over a great range of country remote from all former trading centers. To leave his dig-

gings and go down for letters meant a long, arduous trip
for the miner—and perhaps no claim when 'he got back.
With native gold or high wages beckoning to all, who
would carry the mail at government pay? Meanwhile,
from mothers and sweethearts of half the world, those
letters came pouring. They piled up at the entry port, and
later with equal lack of system at the few inland post
offices. Here was a problem officialdom could not solve.
But private enterprise could. Whether Alex Todd was
the first of the mountain letter-expressmen, he soon had
competitors. All developed from letter men into treasure
expressmen when the miners began entrusting them with
bags and cans of gold dust to take down for safe-
keeping.

Just behind Todd in the southern diggings rode W. T.
Ballou. Bill Ballou slashed Todd's bonanza rate to a
quarter-ounce per letter, or about four dollars. The
mining country lacked scales. So Ballou equipped himself
with a sewing thimble. With this domestic engine he
leveled off his fees just as they came virgin and shining
from the creek beds.

Jim Tolles was mining farther north. Fortune had
smiled on many, but turned the back of her neck to him.
He, too, conceived the occupation of community courier.
He journeyed down from the Feather River country.
Shortly before Christmas, 1849, returning from San
Francisco, he debarked from the river boat at Sacramento
City. Young Tolles had no horse, but he had willing
legs. He elevated his sack of letters to his back and set
out across country. By night he wrote up his diary:

Today it rained continually and the wind blew hard. I walked from the city up to Frémont and was very much fatigued, having to go through brush and water, traveling thirty miles. Two wolves kept a short distance ahead of me.

Meanwhile Todd was finding the goddess of Fortune no shy maiden. He covered the whole range of gold-bearing uplands behind Stockton. At each camp the principal merchant was his agent. Merchants enjoyed the distinction. It made their huts focal points for additional excitement. Todd rode far, but managed to be at San Francisco for the steamers. When the *California, Oregon, Panama,* or *John L. Stephens* was sighted through the heads, he rowed out and bought up old New York *Heralds* from the passengers at a dollar a copy. He retailed these for eight dollars each at the mines, and a single ship sometimes provided several hundred copies.

Opening an office at Stockton, Todd installed an iron safe. Still the personal expressman, he continued setting forth into the hills with two pack horses laden with letters and papers, and returning with them freighted with yellow dust. For lodging the gold in his safe Todd exacted one-half of one per cent per month, together with the privilege of lending like a banker. If the depositor preferred individual storage, Todd doubled the fee. He expanded, took partners, sold out, successively reëntered the lively occupation; finding time as well to be paddled for one hundred and twenty miles up the Columbia River and the Willamette, and to open Oregon's first expresses at Portland and Oregon City. A superlative business!—until California fires nine times cleaned him out, clerks decamped

with $40,000, $50,000, and $70,000, and competition
cut the rates to a dollar, to four bits, and finally to two bits
a letter.

Throughout the treasure lode country this evolution was
in progress, of volunteer post-riders turning into treasure
carriers and, in some cases, into bankers. Others never
went in for such large affairs; they remained lone travelers
of the trails to the end of their era, though their careers
took them to the firry ravines of British Columbia, the
limestone mountains of Montana and Colorado, or far
out into the alkali glare of the sagebrush basins. By horse,
by mule, and afoot these messengers were everywhere
breaking trails, breasting floods, confronting wolves and
coyotes that looked like wolves; braving Indians, grizzlies,
and that most temperamental of hazards, the river steamboat; carrying letters, toting and guarding treasure, tying
the remotest camp with "civilization." S. D. Brastow,
struggling through snow with two thousand letters to
stormbound miners high beyond the mountains at the
north; Pilsbury Hodgkins, his saddlebags stuffed with
mail, riding his white mule over the trails from the
Stanislaus to the Merced, while the miners yelled, "Here
comes 'Chips'!"—Chips, whose service did not end until
forty-two years later, with his family around his pillow
and the veteran messenger muttering, "The express has
gone wrong!"; Charley Schaeffer, who believed that no
river could stop him, no snow could pile too deep for him
to cross. But when it had been raining for days and every
gully was running bank-full, Charley set out once too
often. He made the up trip from Shasta in safety until

three miles from Weaverville. Several days later a rescue party found his pack mule across Brown's Creek, express and letters intact. Charley Schaeffer's broken form was far downstream. He would ride no more.

The Langtons, with "Ma" herself frequently at the six-horse reins, took up the errand trade along the Yuba. Brown, a messenger of the southern diggings, was shot and killed by an employee. Burns, one of the earliest traitors to his profession, made off with the entrusted pokes of his Tuolumne clients. The new calling had its lapses. But it met an imperative need, and it grew. "Mr. Taylor, express proprietor, who left this city [Sacramento] on Saturday evening last, for Colusa and Shasta City, arrived before eight o'clock last evening, on his return trip, making the entire journey in six days. The distance is nearly 400 miles." This was the stormy spring of 1852, when floods were drowning men in their cabins and bridges and ferries were gone. Yet "Mr." Taylor, by galloping and swimming, had maintained his pace.

The energies of the express riders were not all expended on delivering the mail. On a summer evening in '51 a small party of Indians fell in with two packers who were making their way across the Siskiyou uplands for one of the small mining settlements. The braves traveled with the white men for a brief way, pretending friendliness. But when within four miles of Young's ranch they drew nine-inch knives and attacked the pair. One white man, Jacob Bender, just had time to yell a warning to his partner Welch when he fell with a severed jugular. Welch saw his companion done for and fled on foot for dear life, abandoning all property to the aborigines. A big buck, his feet flinging gravel, set out in pursuit. Welch crowded on with all he had and, realizing that it was not enough, slowed his pace to save breath and let the hostile red man gain on him. As his pursuer pounced, Welch slid home his own sharp knife, and then continued on to the ranch. He found the place in a state of armed defense—to the extent of the two guns it possessed—and a general attack hourly expected. Welch volunteered to help garrison the little outpost. At this juncture appeared A. E. Raynes, rider for the upland express firm of Cram, Rogers & Co.

Raynes' sweep of territory involved an immense mountain area at the north and northwest of the state. His pack was heavy, and his accouterments included a rifle and plenty of ammunition. Seeing the state of affairs, he volunteered to fetch help from Tompkin's Ferry, two miles below. After regular Leatherstocking adventures, the express messenger reached the ferry, but only to find its four occupants murdered and Tompkins, the ferryman, a pincushion for arrows. Indians had crept up at daybreak, crawled under the tents, and dispatched the inmates pretty much as they slept. From this grisly scene Raynes picked his way delicately through the underbrush to the house of a family named Blackburn, stepping over the body of a white man in its dooryard. Here, while Mrs. Blackburn kept the two rifles loaded, her husband was single-handedly continuing the war between whites and reds that began on the coasts of Virginia and Massachusetts three centuries before and had not yet found its end. Only his perfect training as a threader of the wilds enabled the ex-

Post Office, San Francisco, California. A contemporary representation of the crowds daily applying at that office for letters and newspapers.

Where Wells, Fargo & Co. succeeded Adams & Co. in the three-story "fortress" at California and Montgomery Streets, San Francisco.

press messenger to reach this present scene of active battle. He was warmly welcomed by the defender; Blackburn had beaten the Indians off several times and had accounted for four of them before their last retreat. Raynes pushed on, got help, and raised the siege.

The same week, but well to southward, saw Captain Caldwell setting out on the Monterey-Santa Barbara horseback trail with his pouches of mail. This was idyllic country, the heart of the old Spanish region where for half a century a man had been able to ride the hills without a care, sure of cordial welcome, board, bed and a fresh horse at any rancho. Captain Caldwell had left the white adobe walls and archways of Mission Santa Ynez behind him and was threading the live oaks and smoky-blue wild lilacs of the Santa Ynez mountains when he noticed two Indians following. The letter-bearer had no fear of these lowly people. But the alien rush had swept away the old amenities. Three or four shots rang out. Captain Caldwell pitched from his horse. The Indians left him where he fell.

In this June, 1851, there were still but thirty-four post offices in all California's 158,000 square miles. But the mail was going up and the gold was coming down. Individual couriers and organized local expresses were threading every ravine. In many cases the letter and gold-carrying professions were closely allied with the simple business of mule-back freighting, and up-bound mail bags often traveled in quaint company. Centering at Stockton on the San Joaquin River, Marysville on the Sacramento, Shasta at the Sacramento Valley's head and Crescent City on the northwest coastal edge, the professional mule-packer was said to be employing seven or eight thousand mules, managed by at least a thousand men. Staunch, stocky Mexican mules in trains of forty or fifty, the white bell-mule or bell-mare leading with a merry jingling, up the narrow trails they moved. Winter rarely stopped them, though they met desperate conditions. Packers on the trail to remote Yreka were frequently plundered of their whole trains by the Indians. A way had to be blasted with shotguns frequently enough between Crescent City and Klamath or Rogue River points. For 120 miles wound this trail, miles on miles of it passing through gigantic redwood forests dense with ferns twelve to fifteen feet high, in the depths of which hostile eyes and pointed weapons could be sensed uncomfortably. The saga of the pack-mule freighter has never been told, and many of its secrets are lodged under the ferns and rhododendrons of the Pacific redwood country.

With these pack trains or quite independent of them rode the letter and treasure expressman, and sometimes he did not ride, but walked, or flew on skis. The latter method brought forward some mighty men, such as "Zack of Downieville," Granville Zachariah; W. P. Bennett, in later years manager for Wells Fargo at Virginia City; and J. A. "Snowshoe" Thompson of Placerville and Carson Valley. Up and over the five, six and seven thousand foot summits they moved, carrying a hundred pounds on their seasoned shoulders, performing prodigies of valor in sunshine or storm.

A. T. Dowd was one of these "back-pack" mountain

expressmen. He pushed long skis up and over the ridges framing Calaveras River. There was one dim glen on his route which Dowd never approached without a thrill of pride and wonder. As a game hunter for a gang constructing a mining canal, he had pursued a big grizzly through forests of balsam fir, cedar, sugar pine, yellow pine and dogwood until the bear led him between two

particular trees. When Dowd perceived those stalks he forgot the bear. Here, eighty miles back of Stockton, 4,500 feet above the sea, were the first-found of California's Sequoias. Each brown, fluted trunk was wide enough to hide a cottage and their crowns seemed lost in the sky. Beyond the first pair, Dowd saw a tree still bigger. He stepped off its circumference, refused to credit his own count, laid down his hat for a marker and stepped it off again. A hundred feet around. Beyond, ranging up the canyon, Dowd saw more such columns, and more, and more. He returned to his companions, told his adventure, and received the hoots and jeers such nonsense merited. Chance had selected April Fools' Day for him to spring that one. Thirty-two couples later danced a cotillion on the stump that had been Dowd's major tree.

Traversing the sides of yawning gulfs, clambering ridges whose tall pine trees were reduced by snows to tasseled bushes, moving their long solitary way far from human succor or habitation, the back-pack expressmen winter after winter brought the human touch to each sequestered shantytown, each nest of snowbound miners. J. B. Whitey for one grew weary of these mid-winter labors on foot, and concluded that if mules couldn't carry him, dogs could. He started his Dog Express in '57, running thirty snowbound miles that terminated at Quincy, county seat of upland Plumas. The dogs were a Newfoundland-St. Bernard cross and four to a sledge pulled several hundred pounds with barking eagerness. No storm ever stopped them. This and the other expresses early built and lastingly maintained a reputation for getting through, come hell, storm, Indians or high water.

So, from the beginning, the phenomenon of the expresses runs like a golden thread through the epic of the West. The gold thread soon becomes entwined with a silver. The pair are early braided with a crimson. The three bright strands form a cord leading to many a remote fastness and isolated camp, wasteland long since turned to commonwealth and booming town long since become ghost-tenanted hamlet. Assiduous historians and express-frank collectors have tracked down and listed hundreds of these one-man, two-man and more highly organized outfits that served the early gold-seekers, and concede that the list will never be complete. The expressmen are gone to their Valhalla and only some mention in a yellowing newspaper, or a tattered envelope bearing their hand-stamp, remains to remind of the breed who bore news and letters upward and nature's valuables downward from the heights.

It is to be doubted whether these pack-mule couriers had ever heard of Henry Wells, the Fargos, the Livingstons, Adams, Dinsmore or John Butterfield, express potentates back in the Atlantic states who were soon to give a new plot to the treasure-carrying drama.

Shaped to an altogether different task were the express companies then existing in the settled eastern states. There the industry had developed just about concurrently with the railroads. In 1830, when California was still a part of Mexico and its handful of settlers had no method of travel save silver-bridled mustang, creaking oxcart, or occasional trading brig, iron rails had been laid near Baltimore. In ten years, those thirteen miles of Atlantic coastal strapiron had grown to two thousand miles of rail. Short, incoherent little railroads were fussily charging everywhere, spelling doom for the turnpike stagecoach and creating a brand-new problem. Who would now do the countless services performed by the vanishing stagecoachman? Who would carry parcels for my lady from country to town, match silks to her sample, or bring back to her squire the proceeds of a draft? The challenge had been answered by a body of typical Yankee opportunists. As the admiral-like coachmen abdicated, young men of energy—railroad conductors, canal-boat clerks, hotel runners, anybody with vim and hustle—began bustling about the country with leather gripsacks that presently became stuffed full of assorted commissions. Among them was Alvin Adams, a Bostonian.

In 1840 Adams was carrying parcels and commissions in his hat. Eight years later, when the undistinguished Jim Marshall in far-away California was stooping over to see what glinted so curiously in his mill race, Adams had attained to the beaver-fur topper of a successful magnate and was rather grandly directing Adams' Eastern Express, Adams' Southern Express and Adams' Western Express from No. 18 in red-brick Wall Street.

Meanwhile a tall young steamboat runner from New York's Duane Street wharf, "Stuttering" Wells, had gone into the express business in Albany. Henry Wells was smart, agreeable. He carried anything and everything that would earn a fee between Albany and Buffalo, not scorning fish and oysters. In 1843 his business was carried in one trunk. But the business, like that in Adams' hat, outgrew its first container. Another messenger was added on the Albany–Buffalo run, one William George Fargo. This was still in the decade when in distant California there were not 12,000 people, and of the few who knew it was El Dorado not one cared.

Business rivalry brought Wells full-tilt into a formidable adversary. This was John Butterfield of Utica, a mail contractor and the proprietor of most of the stage lines still running at the core of the Empire State. Butterfield was a man of sweep and vigor. His interests were ultimately to include freighting across Panama, steamers on the Great Lakes, telegraphs, and control of a railroad. More important to romance, he was to become president of Butterfield's Great Southern Overland Mail across half the continent.

Looking each other over now and squaring off for battle, Wells and Butterfield may have sensed destiny. They concluded to join forces instead. They'd join and expend their competition on Alvin Adams. Other interests joined the attractive combine. Wells emerged as head of this consolidation, which was known as the American Express Company. Fargo was secretary, and Butterfield, the capable stageman, was line superintendent.

Then it was that, far out West, occurred the discovery which lit the fuse to the national explosion, the California gold rush.

Alvin Adams was making money, and the stampede for far shores did not particularly interest him. But it did interest young Daniel Hale Haskell, a clerk in his Boston office. Haskell saw the tall Cape Horners fill their sails and set gloriously out, crammed to the gunwales with seekers for the Golden Fleece. He drank in all the fabulous tales, and he read Horace Greeley. There was gold out there, gold pouring down from the mountains and rushing for the sea, and where there was gold there were expresses. Gold expresses. The phrase set his clerkly pulses leaping. Perhaps he noticed pieces such as this in the New York *Sun,* indicating the place that was waiting out West for such a favorably known name as that of Adams:

The closing of the California Mail affords an opportunity to advise our readers in the Gold Region to observe great caution in making their remittances to friends in the United States. We learn that parties have gone out to California for the purpose of selling drafts on New York, New Orleans, Baltimore, Philadelphia and Boston, in exchange for gold dust, and although such drafts may be perfectly good, and probably are, we would be disposed to make strict inquiries into the character and standing of the drawers before we took them in exchange for gold.

A characteristic of the expressman is intrepidity. Another is persistence. A third is speed. Intrepidity took the clerk to his beaver-topped employer. Persistence took him back after each rebuff. Speed saw all details attended to and himself on board the steamship *Panama* when she sailed in September of '49 for San Francisco.

The principal proprietor of Adams' Eastern, Southern, and Western expresses considered that the hazards of a new land were all against Haskell's enterprise. Though he reluctantly contributed capital and a New York connection, Alvin Adams made it sternly known that Adams and Company's California Express was but the merest stepchild of his house. Haskell didn't care. He was off for El Dorado, with the goddess of Fortune on shining clouds leading the way.

On November 1st the Pacific Mailer rounded Clark's Point under Telegraph Hill, bringing 45,000 letters, several bales of newspapers and 320 passengers. There it lay, the fantastic city of the rainbow's end, asprawl on the

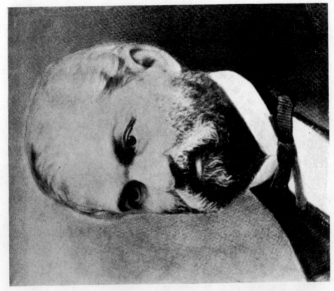

WILLIAM G. FARGO

HENRY WELLS

oak-wooded tip of its peninsula. Blue sky scarfed with fog; bay-ringing mountains scarfed with redwoods; deserted ships by the hundreds at idle anchor; pandemonium ashore.

Haskell landed with the rest, saw with amusement the lines at the post office, rented an upstairs office in a shack on Sacramento Street, and in seven days announced:

Express for New York, Boston and the principal towns of the New England States, Philadelphia, Baltimore, Washington, etc. Gold dust bought, also forwarded to any of the above places and bills of exchange given in any amounts. Letter bags made up and forwarded by special messengers in each of the steamers.

Here was naught of the eastern expressman's modest advertising—"purchasing goods, collecting drafts,—orders of all kinds,—small packages safely delivered." The western expresses were keyed to more thumping music: to the carrying of priceless mails through any hazards; to the transport of heavy treasure for which men would gaily stake and ruthlessly snatch lives.

Back in New York, headquarters of the American Express were at No. 16 Wall Street, close to Alvin Adams. Its magnates soon beheld shipment after shipment from the new Golconda entering opposition portals. The consignments of virgin wealth arrived in leather bags, heavy and authoritative, and in massive ore-boxes packed dense with the luscious fruitage of underground vineyards. From the far-away Mother Lode by pack mule and stage, down the Pacific by sidewheel steamer, over Panama to the steamers of the Atlantic those treasures had come.

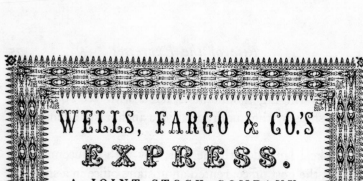

WELLS, FARGO & CO.'S EXPRESS.

A JOINT STOCK COMPANY,

CAPITAL, $300,000.

DIRECTORS:

HENRY WELLS. WM. G. FARGO. JOHNSTON LIVINGSTON,
JAMES McKAY, ELIJAH P. WILLIAMS, A. REYNOLDS,
EDWIN B. MORGAN, A. M. C. SMITH, HENRY D. RICE.

JAMES McKAY, Secretary. EDWIN B. MORGAN, President.

Having made advantageous arrangements with the U. S. and Pacific Mail Steamship Companies, for transportation, we are now prepared to forward

GOLD DUST, BULLION, SPECIE, PACKAGES, PARCELS, AND FREIGHT,

Of all kinds, to and from

NEW YORK AND SAN FRANCISCO,

Thence to Sacramento, Marysville, Nevada, Shasta, Stockton, Sonora, Columbia, Mokelumne Hill, Portland, Oregon City, and all the principal towns of California and Oregon.

OUR REGULAR SEMI-MONTHLY EXPRESS is despatched from San Francisco on the 1st and 15th, and from New York on the 5th and 20th of each month, **by the Mail Steamers,** in charge of our own Messengers, through to destination. **Connecting at New York** with the lines of the American Express Company. to Buffalo, Cleveland, Cincinnati, Louisville, St. Louis, Detroit, Chicago, Galena, &c., and Toronto and Hamilton, C. W.; the Harnden Express, to Boston, Philadelphia, Baltimore, Washington, Mobile and New Orleans; Pullen, Virgil & Co.'s Vermont and Canada Express, to Whitehall, Burlington, St. Johns, Montreal and Quebec.; Davenport & Mason's New Bedford Express, and Livingston & Wells' European Express.

We are at present running **Daily Expresses** to Sacramento, Marysville, Auburn, Ophir, Yankee Jim's, Rough and Ready, Grass Valley, Nevada, &c., &c.

We connect at Sacramento with **HUNTER & CO.'S Daily Express** to Placerville, and all parts of El Dorado County ; and at San Francisco with **TODD'S Daily Express** to Stockton, Sonora, Columbia, Mariposa, Moquelumne Hill, &c.

A **Semi-Monthly Express to Oregon,** by the Mail Steamers.

Gold Dust, and Gold and Silver Coin and Bullion, bought and sold.

Deposits Received, Collections and Remittances promptly made.

SIGHT EXCHANGE

For Sale, on New York, Boston, Buffalo. Pittsburg, Cleveland, Cincinnati, Louisville, St. Louis, Detroit, Chicago, Galena. Milwaukee, and **Forty** other principal towns in the Atlantic States. Also on Toronto and Hamilton, Canada West, and Montreal and Quebec, C. E.

Our Express Lines in California and Oregon are not yet complete, but will be extended as rapidly as the public convenience may require.

WELLS, FARGO & CO., 114 Montgomery St.

46

AN ADVERTISEMENT OF 1852

The continuing auriferous display at the house of Adams averaged $300,000 to $600,000 a month. Finally it brought down the legs of the chairs next door with a bang.

In the winter of '51 Wells, Fargo and Company was organized. By May it was ready for business. On July 1st the San Francisco *Alta* advised Pacific Coast readers in a modest three inches of space:

WELLS, FARGO & CO.'S ATLANTIC AND PACKING EXPRESS, a joint-stock company . . . is now ready to undertake a general Express Forwarding Agency and Commission Business; the purchase and sale of Gold dust, Bullion and Bills of Exchange; the payment and collection of Notes, Bills and Accounts; the forwarding of Gold Dust, Bullion and Specie; also, Packages, Parcels and Freight of all descriptions, in and between the city of New York and the city of San Francisco and the principal cities and towns in California . . . energetic and faithful messengers furnished with iron chests for the security of treasure and other valuable packages accompanying each Express upon all their lines, as well in California as in the Atlantic states.

They will immediately establish offices at all the principal towns in California, and run messengers on their own account for the purpose of doing a general Express business. As soon as arrangements are completed, notice will be given.

On June 30, 1852, Samuel P. Carter as general agent for California arrived at San Francisco on the steamship *Oregon*. Ten days later R. W. Washburn arrived on the *Tennessee* to conduct the banking department.

The curtain was up on a rousing drama. Though its stage was limited at first, extending only to the Sierras, successive acts in the six-decade spectacle of boot and spur, shotgun and whiplash, blizzard and sudden battle, were to take place on a stage two thousand miles square.

Meanwhile, up in the mountains, the independent saddlebag expressman continued his solitary course, threading trails on the cliffsides drawn by the deer, the wolf, and the jackrabbit.

III

THE CONCORD COACH ARRIVES

ON June 25, 1850, the arrival of a mail by sea was still an event of enormous commotion at San Francisco. Said the *Alta:*

The rush at the Post Office, yesterday, was tremendous and the struggling, pushing, pulling, hauling, growling, grumbling was really amusing to a disinterested spectator. Notwithstanding there was a good deal of impatience manifested there was a vast deal of patience also, and rather more forbearance than is usually exhibited in such a crowd. Nothing but the desire to receive intelligence from relatives and friends at home could possibly induce persons in this fast country to stand in line for hours and hours in all the heat and dust.

Perhaps the pushing and pulling and the tedium of standing in the heat and dust were partially recompensed by a rather novel sight. Men from the mines in their red or blue shirts, ladies—the few there were—in full-skirted tarlatans and straw bonnets, pigtailed Chinamen moving under basket-hung poles, and bartenders in their doorways must have stared with interest. Splendid as a yacht, confident as a sixty-gun frigate, up Clay Street, northward into Montgomery and around the Plaza it curved. The six spanking bays that drew it were harnessed two and two.

Their navigator sat proudly on his box. Ash spokes spinning, leather fore and rear boots rocking, landscaped panels and damask-lined curtains glistening, the vehicle swept through streets that had just been blackened by a town-wide holocaust.

The Concord coach had come.

Elsewhere those products of a New Hampshire wagon factory were in retreat before spark-belching locomotives. But in the raw West new strikes were everywhere calling and the demand was for instant movement. Into this insatiable demand for transportation the vehicles from Messrs. Abbot, Downing & Co.'s plant moved with something of the air of predestination. Their makers had foreseen neither the gold rush nor the terrain involved. But to an extraordinary degree they had developed the equipage for it all. This first-arriving of a long line of stagecoaches was to be followed by scores, by hundreds. For three or four decades, the chief instrument of public transportation in the wilderness was to be this leather-slung contrivance. Romance and chivalry were to ride in its interior. Valor was to sit its box. Peril and tribulation were to lurk in its path. Violence was to leap for its step. It was bouncing for Sacramento now, and tomorrow would be spinning for Mariposa, Sonora, Hangtown, Bottle Springs, Shirt Tail Canyon, Piety Hill, Brandy Flat or Secret Diggings. By next spring it would be rocking on its steerhide springs from Shasta Butte City to Pueblo de Los Angeles. In a few more years it would be scaling the naked Sierra Nevada. Soon enough it would be lashing out for the Rocky Mountains and the far-lying prairies. A hundred, a hundred and fifty miles a day would be reeled off by those bounding wheels. Eluding arrows, outracing cloudbursts, rumbling and lurching over the two thousand miles that lay between the Pacific Ocean and the great rivers, it would be carrying mail, carrying express.

The appearance of the West's first Concord did not immediately suggest quite all that to the throngs in San Francisco's unpaved streets. The editor of the *Alta* dismissed its coming with forty words, though he admitted with homesickness that "it was a splendid turnout altogether and carried us several thousand miles, over the hills and far away." The attention of the port was gripped at the moment by its sumptuous steamships and its really marvelous clipper ships, several of which at that hour must have been winging their way around the Horn with more Concords in their stomachs.

Perhaps young Daniel Hale Haskell was one who stood in the crowd that day and saw the Concord make its proud tour of the town square. Haskell was finding this port of gold all that his dreams had painted. The metropolis was growing by leaps. Wealth was tumbling down from the placers, and he was shipping it onward at a handsome profit. The nationally known name of Adams was a lodestone that drew much patronage. Haskell soon moved out of the original second-story shanty office into a Montgomery Street structure rented from one Isaiah Woods. In a few weeks the new location required enlarging. Then it required enlarging again. It thrust out lean-tos, bays, annexes. It was the headquarters of the town for public tidings, for eastern newspapers, for the sale and forwarding of dust, for the importation of all sorts of goods on which Adams & Co. collected seventy-five cents a pound, with special charges on many items—twelve dollars for a book, three dollars for a daguerreotype. If these charges were immoderate, so were the times. A carpenter who turned contractor and made a fortune enlarging the boom town's housing facilities discovered that Adams & Co. required seven per cent of his stake for transferring it from Pacific port to Atlantic.

Inland branches of the house were established at Sacramento and Stockton. From there they crept afield. Connecting expresses were beaten down and bought out. Equipped with scales and a safe, each outpost of Adams & Co. nailed to its office doors an official table of values for the gold output of the camp or district. At these prices it stood ready to swap spot cash for dust. Wherever Adams & Co. hung out its sign, there a camp boomed. High interest, high profits, and much forwarding kept its mule trains moving incessantly down the mountain grades for the river towns, where laboring steamboats chugged with rich consignments for the metropolis. With feeders, Adams & Co. presently lay over El Dorado's Drytowns, Fiddletowns, Columbias, Last Chances, and Horseshoe Bars like a funnel, collecting the newly won gold and discharging it into its vaults at the entry port.

Not that Adams had its way without a battle. Every inch was disputed by local rivals; by pioneering competitors who might lack something in capital but nothing in stubbornness. Steamboats were chartered and fired until bright-red boilers quavered. Horses were lashed to the breaking point. Wagons were sent careening down any short-cut at every risk of smash-up. Bluff and bluster were exuberantly employed. Among hard-fighting organizations still very much in the field were Reynolds-Todd, succeeded by C. A. Todd; Newell and a dozen others in the southern mining region; Hunter, Birch, and a score in the area back of Sacramento and Placerville; "Langton & Brother's Treasure Package and Letter Express" up the foaming Yuba; Gregory, Dodge, Haven, Miller, Berford, Freeman. To all of these Adams was the common "opposition." The times and this uproarious commercial warfare developed an indomitable strain of express carriers, riding hell-for-leather with no thought for anything save getting their burdens through.

On a July evening, as the *New World* ended her down trip from Sacramento and touched her wharf at the metropolis there was a typical scramble between the two expresses Freeman & Co. and Gregory & Co. for the honor of making first delivery of Sacramento newspapers to the San Francisco news offices. Both set out together. Said the *Alta:*

When near the Plaza, Mr. Adams [of Freeman & Co.] was precipitated to the ground by the falling off his horse, and Gregory, pressing hard behind, dashed into the confusion of man, mail and horse, and was very quietly and gently landed among the ruins. He jumped up and won the race—Mr. Adams being prevented from "going in" and winning by an injury inflicted on the leg in falling. . . . We cannot but admire the manner in which these two expresses endeavor to serve the public.

A cloudburst almost state-wide in its proportions fell with fury on a hundred communities in March of 1852. Hall & Crandall's stages could not even negotiate the sea-level flats between San Francisco and San José. Elsewhere, melting snows rushing down from the higher mountains swelled the already abnormal rivers. Sacramento City was a lake, the roofs and upper stories of its houses sticking out like islands. All the mountain camps were marooned. Thirteen miners of a company of fifty in a canyon of the American River were drowned trying to save a flume. Bridges went down. Streams were maelstroms of crashing logs and boulders. Ferries vanished. After days of heavy rain an Adams messenger left San Francisco with copies of eastern newspapers, just arrived by the *Tennessee*, for inland editors. The Stockton *Journal* on the following Tuesday acknowledged receipt of these dispatches

by an unparalleled piece of enterprise. Adams & Co.'s messenger started on the *Bragdon* [a river steamboat] on Sunday afternoon, and when off the mouth of the San Joaquin, left her, and with two others proceeded in an open boat. They arrived in Stockton on Monday night, after rowing the entire distance—120 miles. They were 24 hours in the boat . . . and placed the intelligence in Stockton half a day in advance of the regular conveyance. The performance of such a feat redounds as much to the energy and enterprising spirit which direct the affairs of Adams & Co. Express, as it does to the determination and endurance of the men who accomplished it. Thomas Cornell, Sebastian Ellis and Peter Wichelhauan are the names of the hardy fellows who were in the boat.

The waters went down, and stagecoaches, stage wagons, and freight wagons once more rolled on.

Down at San Francisco, half a dozen conflagrations in quick succession had demolished and redemolished the young metropolis. After each catastrophe it rose anew, wiped the ashes from its face, adjusted its draggled dress, and held wide its apron for the gold pouring down from the mines. Poor today, rich tomorrow. Stranger, have a drink!

Through these storms and cataclysms two business establishments of the seaport town stood like twin Gibraltars.

Haskell's Adams & Company had soon outgrown the shanty of Isaiah C. Woods, and negotiated with Mr. John Parrott for a magnificent edifice, three stories high and fortress-thick. Mr. Parrott imported its huge building cubes from China, whence they arrived cut and numbered, it is said, like laundry parcels, and were reared by Cantonese sons at the corner of California and Montgomery streets. When the celestials struck for more pay, they got it; no one else could read the laundry marks. Double doors and window-shutters of the financial keep were of malleable iron a quarter-inch thick. Over three of the seven Montgomery Street lintels rode the inscription, "Adams & Company, Bankers and Express." Over the other four, "Page, Bacon & Company, Bankers." Into the frowning portals of the granite structure with its two important tenants passed the bulk of El Dorado's daily gold harvest, to be trundled forth bi-weekly and sent a-voyaging.

Across Montgomery Street, Mr. Sam Brannan's new four-story Express Building flew the flag of an enterprising contender.

Wells Fargo had entered without fanfare and was continuing to build without any particular hullabaloo. But

its eastern sponsors were veteran assemblers and forwarders. Behind their young western venture was plenty
of capital. More important, behind it was plenty of spirit.
Soon after it opened, the San Francisco *Herald* was reporting:

It is only during such tempestuous weather as that of the past
few weeks that our people can fully appreciate the services of the
admirable express lines that, having their center in this city, radiate
to all parts of the state and world. The roads throughout the interior have become almost impassable morasses, rivulets have
swollen to running streams, and brooks to roaring torrents. Yet
in the face of the obstacles and beset by the pitiless storm the
energetic and ever faithful expressman plunges forward on his
mission, bearing to the miners in the most remote ravines tidings
of their families and friends far away. . . . The recent important intelligence of the presidential election gave opportunity
for the display of great enterprise and daring on the part of the
various companies here. Wells Fargo, a firm which has gained
rapidly in public favor and is now fully and successfully established,
made extraordinary exertions to supply the press here with the first
news. . . . They succeeded. . . . In addition, they are ever
prompt and often in advance in furnishing us with news from the
most remote towns of the interior.

The genius and hurry of the invaders had already
brought some semblance of roads into the new land where,
a half-dozen years before, the only "highway" had been
a mule path through coastal valleys connecting the Mis-
sions. For long, however, the coaching and freighting
roads were mere unfenced routes across the flatlands and
appallingly narrow scratches through the mountains. But
despite mud, dust, precipices, narrow turns, ruts, and

"chuck holes," the newcomers intended resolutely to "git thar." Blasting and filling, corduroying and planking, they pushed their lanes for travel into the wilderness. In its first half-dozen years El Dorado achieved river ferries and a hundred or more bridges, though the former long remained adventurous and the latter decidedly hilarious. When a vehicle came to a bridge the passengers painfully separated their arms and legs, got down, walked across, climbed up, and squeezed back in again. On up-grades or in deep mud they got out and pushed; from the summit, with wheels chained and brakes set hard, everything slid gaily downward.

James E. Birch, a Rhode Island stageman, was a pioneer importer of stagecoaches into the gold country. Birch had arrived with the Forty-niners at the age of twenty-one, and in September of that distinguished year was piloting a rude ranch wagon between Sacramento and the Coloma diggings. It cost two ounces, or $32, to ride with this youth behind four Mexican mustangs controlled by a bull whip. Frank S. Stevens inaugurated another chapter of coaching history when he established, in '51, his Pioneer Stage Line, Sacramento to Placerville (Hangtown)—the line which, a few years later, was to be the luxurious link of the Overland Mail from Sacramento as far as Virginia City.

A stage-going traveler, leaving Stockton in '52, describes a typical early morning start:

The driver climbed to his seat; then the team began to make its appearance; each animal securely held by two men; two animals were secured to the tongue; six more were then hitched up three abreast. The lines were passed up to the driver. While all this was going on, it became evident to the passengers that a band of wild mustangs were being harnessed to speed us on our way, which they faithfully did. A line of men stood at each side of the team until the last tug was secured and the last ribbon passed up to the driver. I then heard him call out, "let go." The stage appeared to leap from the ground and cleave through the air like a railroad train. . . . On reaching the foot of the mountains the passengers all alighted and walked. It would have been unsafe to have walked behind or on either side, as the team scratched their way up that fearful grade; the air appeared thick with stones flying through the air like a hail-storm.

By '53 the nondescript wagons of the stage roads were disappearing in favor of the thorough-braced type of vehicle—the body cradled on longitudinal leather straps for momentum and balance. In '54 Hugh Splicer was up over the summit of the Siskiyous with two Concords pulled through the wilderness from Oregon. At the start of '54 Jim Birch consolidated three-fourths of all the stage lines in California, with Sacramento as headquarters, and from that town a dozen lines of three to a dozen stages, each mainly Concord coaches, went whirling off daily for every section of the state. Ten, fifty, a hundred thousand dollars in the boot. Sixty miles and seven hours to go. Sixty miles and five. Away with all coaching feats of older lands! Over good roads, bad roads, or no roads at all, young California and the West—men, mail, and express—were awhirl and away. Until whistle of locomotive should be heard, and long thereafter, the valor, romance, and treasure of El Dorado rolled on yellow coach wheels behind eager horseflesh.

With acknowledgments to Mae Helene Bacon and Wells Fargo Bank & Union Trust Co.

Some old-time shotgun messengers and stage drivers of the Shasta run.

Standing: Left to right—

Joseph Henry Bacon, Charles Laird, Hank Giddings, Frank Hovey, Daniel R. Haskell, Jerry Culverhouse.

Sitting: Left to right—

Ab. Giddings, Daniel Masten Cawley, who drove the first and last stagecoaches over the Siskiyou Mountains.

Taken in Yreka, Siskiyou County, California, about 1884.

Through these first years the express courier rode singularly safe from highwaymen, though for robberies committed upon other travelers there were twenty-four convictions prior to 1855, numerous lynchings, and any number of unscotched acts of private brigandage. Trails were solitary. Camps and townlets were far apart. Wealth was casually guarded. Gold, $50,000,000 to $80,000,000 a year, was still being torn from the prolific hills. Yet the earlier '50's saw entire fortunes in raw gold go down the trails in leather sacks and wooden cases with less interference than was often to await a Wells Fargo box thirty years later that had nothing in it but a cheap silver watch, $50 or a money order.

While the Tom Bells and Black Barts were waiting for their cues, a different type of bandit leaped to saddle. Joaquín Murieta was slender, soft-voiced, silky-mustached, with gold braid on his jacket and a plume abob in his hat. With a gay señorita in boy's clothes riding at his stirrup, he cantered through four industrious summers that began in 1850. No express robber was he, but he raided the gringos' settlements with a large band, broken with executive skill into numerous detachments. He ranged from southern California to its center. He overwhelmed ranchos, pounced on lone travelers, garroted isolated miners. His unpleasant lieutenants, Valenzuela and Three-Fingered García, could not resist Chinamen. They galloped after these with slow-looping reata, caught them by swift-jerked noose or with hand wrapped in their queues, and snapped back their throats for the knife. The legislature of 1853 appropriated large rewards to Joaquín's extermination. The band was trapped, and Murieta's head and Garcia's hand floated for years in alcohol in Natchez's arms store and museum at San Francisco, where the leader's long black hair and his lieutenant's three finger nails are said to have continued to grow—to the consternation of beholders.

Survivors of the Murieta band managed for some years to carry on the bloody tradition. Hispano-Californian ranchmen hailed them as patriots and liberators, and though Anglo-Saxon sheriffs pursued them with large heartiness and blazing guns, the hills provided snug retreats and fast, fresh horses.

The comparative immunity of expressmen to all this was soon to draw to an end. But in his first six years the western messenger with his treasure express, whether he traveled on four hoofs, on two feet, or on four wheels, in general met with little armed interference. With his "pepper-box" pistol slung at hip, knife in belt, half-wild horse between his thighs, and a pouch or two at his saddle, he was too speedy for the freebooter, or too lucky, or too popular, or just too soon.

IV

ON A PEAK IN DARIEN

BELLS were ringing in Panama town. Its old wall, built as the Conquerors built, was bright with people. Panamaian burghers in straws and wrap-arounds; pot-bellied, naked little wrigglers; mothers clasping babes, men-of-affairs clutching fighting cocks, all had mounted under sultry dawn to the thirty-foot parapet. Among them were a few Americans. Their red shirts no longer brave and their blue jeans sprung and dissolute, these aliens looked forth from under their sugar-loafed palm-leaf hats with little curiosity. The gold rush had landed them this far and marooned them, or borne them onward and washed them this far back. Yet habit, or the bells, or the pleasant hour drew them too to the wall.

The bay was radiant with September sunrise. Forth and out between those wooded, mountainous little islands, Pizarro once had sailed to search out and hurl down the empire of the Incas. Into this bay, for centuries, tall ships had returned. The broad Spanish road behind the town, the rocky stairway it became up and over the mountains, was worn deep by the ceaseless traffic of merchandise, altar cloths, cathedral paintings, blessed images, and long files of prelates, officials of the Inquisition, and

Portobelo-bound mule trains laden with the gold and silver of Peru; laden with pearls and precious gems. Panama the opulent, first colonial city on the American continents, knew its great days and its frightful. Finally, when Caribbean rum and the Indian girls had dealt with the Conquerors for three centuries, Spain's grip relaxed. Since the expulsion of the hidalgoes thirty years before, the capital of New Granada had retreated far in mildew. The trans-isthmian rush of the gringoes had brought tawdry revival. But the thick wall, built to resist buccaneers, was undercut by the ocean; houses sagged; and the bells were badly out of tune.

Yet now they were ringing. The Pacific Mail steamship, bringing freights, bullion and returning gold-seekers down from San Francisco, had just let go its rattling anchor between the sea wall and the islands. Cayucos were hoisting sail and making for the fuming sidewheeler. An army of muleros were bringing transport animals into picket line before Mosquera, Hurtado & Co.'s arcaded place of business.

Among those in flapping hats and faded jeans who had first watched the steamer's advent were a group now hastily vanished. These included J. G. Burch, a lawyer of sorts who had dwelt some time in the tropical town, though penniless and briefless; and an equally out-at-elbows Dr. Roberts. Some days before, Burch and Roberts had taken a walk together. It was evening, and the way led to the top of the ancient town-embracing fortification. Three long cannon, once brassy-bright, lay tumbled in the grass. The lawyer and doctor sat down on one of them. Dr. Roberts pointed in some amusement to the tarnished arms of Spain that still rode the lusty twelve-foot guns, and to their grandiloquent names: "El Flautero," the Flute Player; "El Persuador"; and "Ultima Razon," the Last Argument. From the guns the two rejects of fortune looked out to sea, and the doctor said: "We've got to get away."

"Yes," said the lawyer, who also was tired of mangoes, cock fights, creole girls, bells and heat, but who had stared from that parapet many times and found no answer.

After that the men talked in low tones that grew confidential. The next night they came again, bringing with them a Laban Manning, a Myron Saunders, a Thomas Summers, and a Dr. Berry. All were snatchers for the golden hem of fortune who had failed in their clutch and had drifted from the California diggings down to New Granada in an aimless effort to get home. Dr. Berry had originally made his way overland, meeting and marrying a respectable woman in the course of that prairie schooner journeying, and she was now maintaining a boarding house at San Francisco while he lingered in Panama, permanently "on the beach." Long colloquy was held by the six in the silent company of El Flautero, El Persuador, and Ultima Razon. Their plans were large. But an element still was lacking.

Manning undertook to supply this ingredient. He approached Thomas Cromwell, an enormously strong and very big black man, who was cook and dishwasher in a second-rate American hostelry. Cromwell was induced to take an evening stroll and invited to seat himself on the broad breech of the Flute Player.

"Thomas," said Manning, "do you want to go on a gold-hunting expedition?"

"Yes *suh!*" answered the cook.

"Wait a few days," instructed Manning, "and all will be arranged."

There had been robberies of the gold express in transshipment before. As early as December of '49 two cases of dust, brought down the west coast by the steamship *Oregon* and reshipped on the farther side of the Isthmus by the *Empire City*, were found on arrival at New York to be about seven hundred ounces light. Suspicion followed the clerk and the third mate of the *Oregon*, who had left their vessel in Panama. The looters were trailed together with the missing dust and picked up at the Philadelphia mint. And within quite recent weeks, this year of '51, three boxes of dust transferred over Panama and sent on to England had been stolen from the railway between Southampton and London. But all this was simple thievery. Burch, Roberts, Manning and their confederates were going in for something more. They were about to indulge the California treasure express in its first case of genuine, big-scale brigandage.

Only one or two pairs of eyes remained to see the screw-headed, wax-sealed boxes of gold lifted from the arriving *Tennessee* via dugouts and lighters to the backs of Mosquera & Hurtado's mules. These observant eyes stayed just long enough to count the boxes, multiply them by their standard weight, and conclude that sixty-nine thousand pounds in grain, nugget and leaf gold represented about $1,800,000—enough to get seven conspirators off the beach of the Isthmus and keep them off for quite some time. Satisfied of this, the watchers pushed on rapidly through dilapidated gardens and up the wooded plain behind the town.

After the usual turmoil of shouting, swearing, lashing of packs to aparajoes and fixing of saddles, the guarded train set out. Movement of gold over the path ahead was no novelty. Two centuries before, Henry Morgan, after falling on Old Panama and putting it to the torch, had passed this way with his hideous buccaneers, driving ninescore mules laden with rich stuffs and pieces of eight, and herding six hundred prisoners. For the past two years this miasmic path had also been the regular route between the two mosquito coasts for the gold dust brought by the Pacific Mailers. A substantial force of carabineers rode before and beside the Yankee treasure train.

For six miles behind Panama town the route ran through parklike country, with open glades and clear pebble-bottomed streams, and over the pavement and bridges of an old colonial highway. Then it began to climb. Close around was complete jungle, of vivid broadleafed plantains, sombrous mahogany, dead trees hung with orchids, the bright flutter of parrots, and the hot reek of rotting vegetation. The paving yielded to mudholes, sometimes half a mile wide, into which the pack train sank to its bellies. Now broken crates, bursted trunks and scattered litter, the débris of two years of tragic travel, came into evidence. Occasionally there was a dead mule to get around. Scores of foul birds rose and moved off with slow flapping. The way grew narrower, steeper.

Torrents had rushed through and gouged out what incessant hoofs had grooved. For this was the rain-barrel of the world. Over the brim of these deep, slippery chutes was the dense greenery of tropical forests. Into this bottleneck trail, inches in width, there approached every fortnight the grand total of all the gleanings of a Mother Lode hundreds of miles long and three thousand miles away. Just at noon the white bell-mare appeared, first of the long train of animals. Troopers whistling, muleros yelling, the van of the parade passed without interruption. Then in quick succession two salvos crashed from the thicket. "Come on, boys! We've got two mules!" shouted someone.

From one of the mules the cargo was quickly slashed. The amateur brigands also made a rush for the other mule, then halted in dismay at their bloody work, turned and fled pell-mell. A huge, grunting black man followed in their wake, calling to them occasionally, and floundering under the enormous weight of the wooden case on his shoulder.

News of the assault was galloped back to Panama. It arrived at a most unseemly time. The governor of New Granada, and all his fellow-citizens, were just settling to their customary siestas. But what the trooper had to say tumbled the governor from his couch, freightmaster Hurtado from his hammock, port captain Garrison of the Pacific Mail from his big cane armchair and the pigeons out of the belfry of the cathedral. Fifty musketeers of the national militia were shaken out of slumber and rushed up the trail. Meanwhile the train at the point of assault was in wild confusion. Three guards were prone. Two had been fatally struck and the other was riddled below the knees with buckshot. The rest of the guard, leaving the muleros to struggle with their frightened animals, had ranged themselves for defense against whatever new assault the leafage might be screening. When the militia arrived, followed far at the rear by the rotund governor on a mule, the robbers were in flight into the woods and still traveling.

Six of the fugitives were making better time than the seventh, for Thomas Cromwell was burdened with the solitary case of gold which all this furor and blood-letting had succeeded in abstracting. Cromwell perceived that he had been invited to this party purely to carry the gold. He toted it as far as he could, though at each step his legs sank deeply into mud and decay, festoons of vines yanked at him, and the box of wealth bit deeply into his shoulder. The sound of his companions thrashing through the growth grew fainter. Not at all certain now that the gold was as desirable as he had assumed, and overwhelmed with the thought that he might be left alone to the red ants, jaguars, alligators, howler-monkeys and leg-boring jiggers, the black man threw down his burden. His feet came out with more grace from the mud after that. He set himself to catching up with his co-conspirators, and succeeded so well that he overhauled and passed Summers and almost came within hallooing distance of the others.

The militia was now advancing into the woods, following the easily distinguishable trail. They came upon the box of gold which had already exacted two lives. They came upon Summers, who was caught to his hips in a quag, and they came on the huge black man, who was snared in a web of gaudily flowered vines. Cromwell was conducted to a glade and given a hempen fitting. To make him properly uneasy, he was told that Summers had already been hanged. With whitely rolling eyes, the black confessed, and divulged everything he knew about his accomplices; after which he was run up and left suspended by the neck for some moments on the theory that it might be a good lesson for him. The enormous strength of the man did not exclude his neck muscles, for when his excellency Governor Diaz reached that scene and had him cut down, the darky was still breathing. In half an hour he recovered sufficiently to walk.

Beyond and above all this rose the blue crest of the heights, on the other side of which lay the primitive villages Cruces and Gorgona and the winding descent of Chagres River to the Caribbean. If the way had been narrow before, it was threadlike now. Between robbery site and summit the trail passed between cliffs a dozen to fifty feet high. The cleft was often choked with big stones and here and there became so slim that a man on horseback could not keep his feet in stirrup. The pass was a fracture caused by some past convulsion of nature, a vertebral slip. It was the only opening in many miles through all that jungle between the eastern and western oceans.

To the fugitive brigands the route through the gap was too obvious for safety. In spite of torrential rains, clutching bogs, tripping vines and destroying heat, the uncaptured five elected to make for the other side of the cordillera by untrod courses. They moved by separate ways. There was now neither conspiracy to share nor loot to divide. There were only necks to save, and every man had his own view as to which was the most precious.

Due to the intense labor of bucking jungle, the bungling desperadoes were slow in making the crossing. Two of them, Manning and Dr. Berry, stumbled into Cruces, a town of two hundred huts, a few stone and frame houses, a calaboza and a single hotel of galvanized iron—the whole embraced by mist-shrouded hills and a river which sometimes rose four or five feet in an hour. Cruces was the point where Pacific-bound travelers left their canoes and whaleboats and struck by foot or muleback for the final pass. It was also the point where Atlantic-bound caravans shifted their cargo to the hands of the river boatmen. Here, therefore, the California-Atlantic express companies had their agents, and Agent Parisen of Dodge & Co. was awaiting the robbers' sure coming.

Agent Parisen and Alcalde Miranda were making a tour of Cruces' few eating and drinking places when they encountered Dr. Berry in the galvanized-iron French Hotel. In shreds and generally disorganized, the doctor had just traded his firearms for something more desirable, and was lifting to his lips the much-wanted drink. As the

searchers opened the door, another man, Manning, rolled
out of a hammock in an adjoining room and disappeared
for good through a back door.

Agent Parisen saw his prisoner locked into the calaboose and then returned to more habitual duties. The
mule train was discharging, and $1,800,000 was still
$1,800,000. Even as the serially-numbered cases were
being transferred to the waiting fleet of dugouts, two were
slyly dropped overboard. Agent Parisen's quick eye took
in the incident and the gold that had been panned from
California's streambeds was once more fished up—this
time from the bed of a Central American river.

On the bank of the green-flowing Chagres, certain
shiny backs were given appropriate treatment. Then the
steersmen mounted to the sterns of their thirty-foot cayucos. The oarsmen took up their chant. Out from the
brush one by one moved the woebegone white fugitives,
anxious to pay their penalties—anxious to pay anything
that would rescue them from the ocelot, the boa constric-
tor, the strangling fig and the foot-wide bat.

And onward for Chagres' outlet and the Caribbean
surf moved the glamorous cargo.

V

DICK TURPIN MAKES HIS BOW

On some leafy trail along the Mother Lode, in a sun-baked ravine of the rocky Siskiyous or in the broad shadow of a Sierra pine a gold expressman, coming down from one of a thousand diggin's with saddlebags well loaded, was suddenly confronted by a sinister figure.

The figure was long overdue and may or may not have been properly dressed for the part. Fancy presumes he had an enormous pistol in each hand, a knife at his belt, a mask or sack over his head and perhaps a shotgun in reserve behind the rocks. Precisely who he was or where he struck will never be known. For the first treasure courier to stand and deliver was much too concerned with immediate realities to attend to his place in history. Somewhere along the Mother Lode the first expressman to get robbed just rode up and got robbed. That is all that can be guessed about it.

The first big-scale assault on a western treasure train, the abortive affair of September, 1851, in the isthmian jungle back of Panama, introduced the new profession. But in the Mother Lode country where that gold originated, Dick Turpin's first entrances were hesitant, dim and confused. Through the eyes of one Hubbs of Downieville we seem for a moment to catch definite sight of him. Hubbs, on a quiet Sunday afternoon in October, 1851, was riding unarmed down Goodyear's Hill with about a pound and a half of gold dust in his charge. Nature prompting, he dismounted to compose himself a moment in the shade of a big yellow pine. As he later explained it, he had no sooner got himself established than a villain of size sprang out from behind the thick bole, seized his arms from the rear, pinioned them tight, and proceeded to commit larceny in Mr. Hubbs' pockets.

Mr. Hubbs was of medium height and quite taken by surprise; besides which, his feet and ankles were entangled in suspenders. In this mortifying posture Mr. Hubbs quite willingly offered himself up for the niche that was waiting for the first-to-be-held-up gold expressman. In confirmation of his story Mr. Hubbs was later able to show his clients the suspenders, the pine tree, and the direction his assailant took in fleeing toward Yuba River. He could also prove that his person no longer had the buckskin bags with their $400. But Mr. Hubbs was not permitted to stay on his historic pedestal. Granting that the yellow pine grows large—there was an entire hotel made of the boards from one tree, down at Nevada City —and that the usual full-grown specimen could have concealed even as big a brigand as he described, there were suspicions. Six weeks later the Marysville *Express* thus closed the incident:

Hubbs, the expressman, has unquestionably departed for the States, and loud and furious are the curses of the swindled. The amount is not large, but the victims are almost exclusively the poor fellows who have saved a few hundred, and started them, as they fondly hoped, to carry happiness to many a lone fireside. It was really painful to see one poor fellow who had sent his all (some $200) to his wife; the temptation to Hubbs was too strong and he has fallen.

Even so, brigandage upon other kinds of travelers was already a systematized business and was creeping closer to the bullion couriers. "A bandit band," reported the *Alta* for November 7, 1851, "numbering thirty, commanded by one 'Charley Smith,' has been discovered in Shasta Valley." And a few days before, the *Times and Transcript* at Sacramento had chronicled:

ROBBERS IN INDIAN COSTUME.—Mr. Free . . . informs us that on the 23rd ult. two miners were attacked near the base of Shasta Butte mountains, and about four miles this side of Shasta Butte City, by four robbers, who were dressed in Indian costume. Several shots were exchanged, and the men would doubtless have been killed and robbed, had it not been for the timely appearance of the party with which Mr. Free was travelling. The robbers fled to their horses, and escaped in the direction of Shasta. . . . It is supposed that the greater part of the stealing done in that section is by whites, who assume the Indian garb, even to wearing moccasins.

Down in the "southern mines," a little trunk containing $2,000 in dust was lashed to the rear boot of Dillon & Co.'s night stage from Sonora. The owner of the shipment, who was making a break for home, settled himself on the rear coach cushions where he could frequently touch the container. He yelled when he felt it slip, but before the coach could be brought to a stop the straps had been slashed and the gold had taken wings in darkness. Sadly the owner walked back for another year to toil under Table Mountain.

And at Mormon Island, a foothill camp, on an April night of '53, Agent Nichols of Adams & Co. had just gone to bed in his quarters at the rear when three men entered, asked for mail, confronted the clerks with cocked pistols, and trussed them up in deerskin thongs. Then Agent Nichols was routed forth in night garb, tied up, and "rolled" for keys to the safe. While four confederates watched outside, the visitors loitered for some time, read the newspapers, smoked Nichols' cigars, and after enjoying a pleasant evening left with $7,000. As this showed the "profession" no longer inclined to concede immunity to the expresses, Adams at once offered $2,000 for the robbers and a quarter of all the plunder for its recovery.

The summer of 1854 sees Robert Woods of Tomlinson & Woods, boss packers of Yreka, crossing Scott Mountain when a shot is fired at him from behind a rock. Does the assailant think Wood carries treasure? Or is he a thief after mules, or perhaps a private enemy? Woods cannot know. His riding mule is crashing to its knees. He scarcely has time to land on his feet, draw a revolver and return the compliment. To his satisfaction the fellow just visible over the rock leaps up, shouts, "I am a dead man," and proves it by falling headlong. Two others then appear with rifles, and Woods just does make his escape. He leaves behind him his saddle mule, lead mule, and $1400. But the property is his own.

At last, through a July twilight of 1855, John McMillan rides into the authentic rôle of a successfully attacked expressman. Messenger for Langton's Pioneer Express, he is riding the route of the lamented Hubbs. He bears $3,000 in Forest City gold dust, distributed in three buckskin bags. Unknown to him, and therefore undisturbing to his reverie, three fates lurk ahead. They are appareled in black coats, dark-colored pants and low-crowned black "California" hats.

As McMillan moved through the purpling dusk on his steady-going mule these figures emerged from ambush, snatched his bridle, put a gun to his chest, dragged him down, blindfolded him and tied him to a tree. It was twenty minutes before McMillan worked loose, to find his $3,000 gone. The outraged messenger reported a blurred and dancing memory of a lean-faced man of about twenty-five, beardless, five and a half feet tall; a shorter man, red in the face, chunky, of the same age; a short dark Latin youth with a whacking bowie knife; and a fourth figure that lurked in the chaparral and kept well out of sight. None had been masked.

Two months later two arrests had been made, and a confession wrung from one which cleared up not only the Langton holdup but the Adams office robbery at Mormon Island. But just then the chief of the two arrested malefactors—his name was George Walker—filed off his irons with a tool mysteriously obtained, rushed past the jailer who brought in his supper, slammed and locked the cell door on that official, and departed. Two weeks later the second ruffian broke out of Marysville's jail and rejoined his comrades. It was hard to catch rogues in those days, and still harder to keep them caught—which explained in part the rising popularity of Judge Lynch.

In December of 1855 the messengers of Wells, Fargo & Company and Rhodes & Whitney were traveling together on horseback from Weaverville to Shasta. Some distance in advance rode a merchant of Weaverville, named Clifford, and his partner. Jingling along easily through the bushy trail, the pair in the van were halted by two men. Others closed in behind. Clifford was pulled from his horse. There was search of his saddlebags and curses at the lack of booty. "I thought these express fellows carried something handsome." The two merchants had marched into a trap evidently intended for the messengers. Clifford's partner did not wait to be manhandled. He flung himself from his horse and ran down the gulch. Three pistol balls followed, one piercing his shoulder. The shooting caused the steeds of the approaching expressmen to wheel and bolt. It was some moments before they could be turned about and spurred to the scene. The waylayers fled. Their horses could be heard crashing through the downhill underbrush.

As later information proved, the attack on McMillan, as well as the raid on the stage office at Mormon Island; the shooting of Clifford and near-waylaying of Wells, Fargo & Co. and Rhodes & Whitney, and larger events to follow, were all a part of the work of an organized gang headed by Walker, a certain Bill Gristy, and the formidable Tom Bell, though the leaders were often miles away and operated through many far-scattered detachments.

The gang of Walker, Gristy and Bell was now ready for bigger coups.

Early morning stir in front of Yreka's Lafayette House on Miner Street. Mules stamping, straps slapping, diamond hitches tossing over leather saddlebags. " 'Bye, Sam! 'Bye, Larry! Look out for Tom Bell and the Injuns! Take a look at the volcano down there near Red Bluffs. They say she's a-smokin'!"

Men of the Klamath diggin's liked to ride with Brastow. He was a first-rate specimen of the pack mule mountain expressmen who pioneered trails, breasted storms, carried communication upward and fetched downward to the valleys the wealth of the mines. Brastow had just sold out his independent business and now rode for Rhodes & Whitney, whom Wells Fargo would soon take over. On this March day of '56 he was about to strike south with a treasure-laden string which Wells Fargo would take in charge at the foot of the mountains.

Seventeen thousand dollars, stowed in heavy bags, was lashed by Packer Delass to a capable mule. Two passengers, one of them old man Hickman of Batterton & Hickman, Yreka provision merchants, swung to saddle. When the cavalcade set out it carried total dust and coin amounting to $26,000.

Up Wagon Valley, over a snow-sheeted ashen plain rode the party. Shasta Butte, long extinct tosser of these ashes, held its cold torch two vertical miles aloft. South of Callahan's ranch at the end of Greathouse & Slicer's stage line from Oregon, the roadway became a mere track marked by blazes on trees and heaped-up stones. On the third morning out, at the base of Trinity Mountain, the party rose for the last half-day of its journey. The sun was just coming up over Lassen's Butte and the distant Sierras when the party rode full tilt into a circle of cocked rifles and leveled shotguns.

Five men disputed the way. They were grotesquely habited. Red undershirts and drawers had been pulled over their clothing. Their heads were hooded in red blanket-cloth slit for eyeholes. Strapped at each red demon's waist was a brace of sixshooters and an eight-inch knife. The surprise was complete. While four plunderers covered the travelers, a fifth relieved them of their weapons and trussed their hands behind them. They were led half a mile off the trail and tied to trees.

One marauder jeered Messenger Brastow. "I've been waiting for you for three months. I lost $30,000 by Adams & Co., and you express fellows are going to pay it." To show no personal feelings, he let the messenger retain $40 of private funds.

Brastow retorted: "I'll follow your trail and get the express money back if it takes all my life."

The freebooters turned the pack mules and drove them off with yells.

Larry Delass was the first to work his arms free. No sooner were the four men back on the trail than they heard the robbers again approaching. While the lately plundered quartet crouched hastily in cover, the band rode by without the stolen animals. The looters, headed by

George Walker, had removed their masks and were chatting cheerfully.

The travelers from Yreka reached Shasta village on foot by mid-afternoon. Sheriff's parties searched for two days. Twelve miles north of the place of robbery at the head of Clear Creek they came upon a dump of saddles and blankets. Here the brigands evidently had divided the booty and turned the stolen animals loose.

Brastow rose to be superintendent of Wells Fargo at San Francisco, and by repeated visits made good his pledge to spend the rest of his life looking for that stolen express dust. Some was quickly recovered, but the rest still is somewhere under logs or stones on the breast of Trinity Mountain.

VI

STEAM AND LATHER

STRUGGLES of the expresses for supremacy continued to be the sporting event of the day. They were encouraged by the newspapers, for such rivalry meant speed in getting the latest newspaper exchanges from other towns. For the expresses, victory meant free renown; and for the public it meant free steamboat racing, free horse racing, and generally enjoyable free commotion.

Yet there was a bill, and it was the public that paid. In the previous January the *Alta* had felicitated its readers: "The new year dawns upon the navigation by steam of all the navigable waters in the State. . . The white sail of the laggard launch is fast disappearing from our rivers; the wooded shores give back the din of splashing paddles, and the scream of the steam alarm startles the solitary haunts of man and beast, while its piercing cadence floats along the night air, awakening the lone Indian from his sad reverie . . . And this is indeed the 'age of steam'!"

But it was an age under precarious control. A perfectly paralyzing number of paddle-boat explosions, occasioned by faulty boilers and the stop-at-nothing rivalry of competing expressmen, were about to put the lives of travelers into desperate insecurity.

It was the *New World* that sounded the overture to

the overdue symphony of disrupting boiler iron and sky-hurled machinery. Coming down from Sacramento, while boiling through the waters of the lower bay ahead of the *Henry Clay* and *Wilson G. Hunt*, the hard-driven vessel blew the cap off her steam chest, killed a fireman and a passenger, and flung three passengers overboard. Charles Youmans, the clerk of the boat, was badly scalded while checking his sacks of bullion. This on June 3, 1851. In September:

"The *New World* and *Confidence* came down from Sacramento under a high press of steam last evening, and we understand that many bets were pending on the fleetness of the two steamers. The *Confidence* arrived at Benicia a few minutes in advance of the *New World*; but the latter was first at her berth in this city. We are informed that a passenger, coming on board of the *Confidence* at Benicia, accidentally fell overboard, and thus delayed the steamboat some minutes. We trust this steamboat racing will not be persevered in, for if it be, we shall very soon have some horrible catastrophe to chronicle which will chill the community with horror." So warned the *Alta*. But the age was at keen edge and public delight egged on the racers. When one expressman was pitted against another on a rival boat his fellow-travelers took sides, not hesitating to back their favorite with their dust and abet him with their sweat. On an up-bound trip, when the vying *Senator* and *Confidence* both grounded, they were poled and rope-hauled off with great energy, all passengers assisting—the *Senator* and Adams' messenger winning by a few minutes.

Into the fog-laden air went the pieces of a boat named the *Sagamore*, while she was getting up steam at her San Francisco dock. The engine was transferred to another hull with new boilers and the assemblage became the *Secretary*, running between San Francisco and a tidal fork of the north shore. On April 16, 1854, the *Secretary* left her Pacific Street wharf with sixty-five passengers. Her rival, the *Nevada*, got away fifteen minutes later. It soon became evident that the *Secretary* was crowding on all steam possible. Still the *Nevada* drew closer. Twelve miles out, the two crafts were abreast and about a hundred yards apart. Then there was a stupendous roar as one of the *Secretary's* boilers let go. Fragments came down on the *Nevada* and a brick was hurled through her pilot house. Among the *Secretary's* thirty dead was engineer Bessie, who had been saving choice firewood for days for this trial of speed. "We are informed," reported the *Secretary's* owners ruefully, "that a few minutes before the explosion the Engineer had an oar across the lever of the safety valve, fastened down; and that the oar was bending with the upward pressure of the safety valve." In the same week there came from Oregon the news of the blow-up of the steamboat *Gazelle* on the Willamette River, killing twenty and injuring twenty-five.

The toll exacted by defective iron and human recklessness is lengthy. Bad roads and prolonged rains often made winter staging virtually a form of navigation, so liquid grew the mud, and particularly was this true on the flat country between San Francisco and the capitol at San José. Preferring genuine boating to the four-wheeled imitation, most passengers traveled to the end of the bay by steamer. But the *Jenny Lind* strained for a note too high and flew apart with a loss of two-score lives. A single autumn day of the same year provided a double-header. Just as dawn was gilding the San Joaquín River, the *American Eagle* was moving down-bound from Stockton with fifty-three passengers and a cargo which included barreled brandy on her deck and gunpowder below. With a roar and a geysering rush of steam her boilers flew apart. Five dead, four missing, many hurt. The boat was completely turned to kindling fore of its wheelhouse and the skipper's berth was cut cleanly in two, pitching its occupant senseless to the afterdeck. The brandy, igniting, then turned the whole into a holocaust. In the afternoon the steamboat *Stockton*, up-bound for that port, blew apart, hurled her captain overboard, killed her engineer and wrought great injury to nine of her passengers.

Not every explosion could be attributed to express-man's rivalry. Folly and bad engineering played the chief part. But the times, to which the expressmen were a mirror, demanded speed and action beyond the abilities of steamboat builders and skippers safely to provide.

Still the furious express races continued, by every form of transport. "Adams & Co., first with the up-river news, and just two seconds afterward came Wells, Fargo & Co.'s messenger last evening" was a casual acknowledgment in the *Alta* for high-spirited journeying that had consumed hours of furious effort. "SULLIVAN STEAMBOAT EXPRESS. —By the enterprise of Jerry Sullivan, of the newspaper agency in San Francisco, the steamer *Young America* was chartered on Sunday night, and arrived in this city yesterday morning at 8½ o'clock, bringing a large quantity of Atlantic papers and some thirteen bags of mail matter, to the great accommodation of our citizens and those of the interior towns." This in the Sacramento *Union*, which found Jerry a great benefactor, at no expense to itself. On another occasion: "J. W. Sullivan, of San Francisco, with his usual promptitude, dispatched a steamer on Saturday evening, about 9½ o'clock, with newspapers and other matter for this and northern towns, which arrived yesterday at 11 A.M." Again, "Jerry Sullivan chartered the steamer *Leviathan* and started early in the morning from San Francisco for Sacramento, but at the mouth of the Sacramento River the boiler gave out, and Sullivan was obliged to make use of the *New World* in order to get away from his uncomfortable position." On the next arrival of an Atlantic mail, Jerry traveled by horseback.

The river-boat *Pearl*, with 101 passengers, left Marysville on a particularly bright morning of June, '55, and was opposite the mouth of the American River close to Sacramento when H. Keefer, messenger for Adams & Co., handed his letter bag to James McBride, the Wells Fargo courier, with the request that he take charge of it for a moment. "I want to go aft and get my treasure box," said Keefer.

Just after he departed, a terrific explosion rolled up the forward deck of the vessel and flung it far out over the bow. Spectators on the shore declared that they saw a dozen bodies soar fifty or sixty feet into the air, some nearly falling on the far shore. The wheel house and forward deck of the vessel rained down as matchwood. McBride, with sixty-one other passengers, had disappeared. The mail bag he was holding for his rival was afterward found in the river. Keefer, the Adams messenger, found himself unhurt.

At the ensuing inquiry, one of the deck hands gave particularly expert testimony on the subject of explosions; he had been on the *Helen Hensley* when she sprang into atoms at her Jackson Street wharf the year before. In the case of the *Pearl*, water as usual had been allowed to get too low over the fires. A young man who put out in a skiff, some hours after the disaster, located and brought up the Wells Fargo box, containing bullion worth $6,500, and subsequently the Adams box with 823 ounces, worth $16,000 more.

On February 5, 1856, the steamboat *Belle* left Sacramento on a foggy morning for Red Bluffs up the river. The *Belle* was a 75-ton stern wheeler. Her captain as a rule was not in a hurry. It was said of him that he would stop anywhere along the route, picking up parcels and making himself generally accommodating, and once waited at a farmhouse river-landing while a farm wife's eleven eggs, destined for Colusa, were being augmented to twelve by a pensively laboring hen. That the good craft *Belle* was frequently bested by stagecoaches ashore and even by heavy mule teams was not news to her master. But on this occasion he had among his passengers Robert A. McCabe, mountain messenger for Rhodes & Co. between Shasta and Yreka, and Charles Bowen of Wells Fargo. And they were in a characteristic rush, being paced by an Adams messenger ashore.

The captain permitted himself to be induced to press his boilers. Still the messengers had visions of a hard-spurred horse showing his heels to their prow. The trees of the bank, dim through the mist, glided past all too slowly. They urged the indulgent captain to crowd on yet more steam. Forty passengers were at breakfast, which was being served below at two long tables, when the deck split open from stem to stern. Fifteen lives and $100,000 in valuables joined the cots, chairs, tables, kitchen miscellany and general cargo that went up and showered down in inextricable confusion. McCabe died with his treasure, overwhelmed with debris. Bowen lived to brave new hazards.

Into three decades the disruption continued: the *Washoe*, with a sickening release of seventy-five lives, flying to pieces on the river just below Sacramento; the *Sophie McLane* following a few weeks later. The *Senator*, after rescuing innumerable victims of shipwrecks and explosion on the waters of San Francisco Bay, was relegated finally to the Columbia and Willamette rivers. She let the water in her own boilers get too low and one day in 1875 came floating past Portland with many injured, many lost, and only the upper part of her cabin visible.

Charley Youmans, who had helped to open the ball while clerking on the *New World*, was again trapped in '66 when, as messenger for Wells Fargo on the little train running from the bay shore for Petaluma, his engine exploded. Engineer, fireman and station agent were killed and Charley lost his teeth and was badly scalded.

On duty or off, it was in the messenger's blood to beat the opposition. In the summer of 1851, Pilsbury "Chips" Hodgkins was given holiday leave and set out for San Francisco. Shortly before the boat was to cast off at Stockton, a stage arrived from Sacramento with papers from the East for Adams & Co., but none for Reynolds, Todd. This went through Chips' innards like a knife. His beloved company would be a joke throughout the camps.

Adams & Co. had been specially prepared for the mail steamer when it arrived at San Francisco two days before. Their chartered river boat was ready with steam up. Quick time was made to Sacramento. From there a stage had flung up clouds of dust all the way into Stockton. Reynolds, Todd & Co. were seemingly helpless until the regular river steamer should arrive with their consignment.

Chips saw the Adams rider whisk out of town and head for editorial offices in the uplands. All thought of vacation vanished. Time for wits and action had arrived. Chips bolted for the local Adams office, checked his pace at the door, strolled innocently in and bargained for spare papers. Joe Miller, Adams' agent, did not recognize him, so began to count the extras off. Chips leaned casually on the counter and tried not to look too happy. Just then a stage driver for Adams, and, unfortunately, a friend of the schemer, clumped into the office and sang out:

"Hello, Chips, what you doing here?"

Miller stiffened at that word "Chips," snatched back the papers and stuffed them underneath the counter.

"We have no papers to spare," he said, and Chips walked out.

He went to a friend, who agreed to buy up the papers for him. This time Miller was gulled into counting them out and handing them over for a fancy price. A moment later the friend met Chips at the back door of the Reynolds, Todd agency, where a horse was saddled and waiting. The two hundred papers filled both saddlebags. Chips swung onto the horse, tied the sleeves of a long-tailed coat around his waist, so that the skirts swung over the bags—and the race was on.

It was near midnight when he overtook the Adams courier and said:

"Good evening, sir, you are traveling late."

Adams' rider explained that he was hurrying to the camps with papers twelve hours ahead of the opposition. Chips expressed admiration for such dash and go, adding that he too preferred traveling at night to avoid summer heat. They rode on together until dawn, when Chips found an excuse to slip from his companion and go around a hill. From there on to the camps he scuttled through every short cut known to man or rabbit. At Jamestown he changed horses and made for Sonora, where he distributed papers about the town, sent some on to Mariposa and other camps and gave the remaining few to the Adams agent. Then he looked after his weary horse, went to breakfast, took a seat on the hotel porch and waited for the Adams rider. At eight or nine o'clock that individual arrived, his horse shimmering with sweat. With a shout the man swung off the heaving animal and waved his bags of New York *Heralds* and *Tribunes*.

But Sonora looked up absently from over the tops of the papers that Chips had brought in at six.

Chips Hodgkins ended his riding days in 1857, having meanwhile passed to Wells, Fargo & Co. along with the rest of Reynolds, Todd & Co.'s appurtenances and good will. He became a steamboat messenger, handling millions in gold dust. In 1866 Chips took his treasure on board the *Julia* at her Stockton wharf and had just laid his hand on the railing to go below when her captain exclaimed, "Something is wrong!" At that instant the explosion came. Five fellow-passengers were shot up through the hatches and killed outright, and six fatally maimed. Eighteen months later the reconstructed *Julia* again blew up, with consequences yet more tragic.

During the thirteen years Chips made the river run his vessel often grounded, sometimes necessitating the finish of the run by rowboat. If low water didn't strew hazards in front of the courier, high water did. There were occasions when the rowboat not only carried the gold express, but rescued settlers out of second story windows.

At the end of 1852, Adams & Co. were making spectacular plans to outdo all previous feats of speed and enterprise. When the mail steamer arrived with word of Pierce's election as President, its messengers were off.

Ten hours later the news was in Stockton. Six hours after, it was in Sonora, borne to that hill-hugged camp by six streaking relays of saddle horses. At another tangent

Adams' horsemen were whirling for Weaverville. The 330 miles were made in thirty hours, with Adams' men racing a stop-at-nothing opposition all the way. But these conquests crumbled the following December. Accepting President Pierce's Congressional message as a torch to carry, rising young Wells Fargo had it in Weaverville in time that broke all records, and the casting of it into Stockton and the camps beyond was accomplished by extraordinary efforts with backs and oars up a hundred miles of tide and river current, followed by sensational horsemanship.

Despite occasional defeats, grander and more opulent grew Adams & Co., forwarders and bankers. Its ramifications reached up to Oregon and out across the Pacific. From its strong portals passed the bulk of the splendid express freights for New York and other cities of the Atlantic; for Canton and other Asiatic ports. Ever expanding, by early '53 it was pushing its offices into the gold camps of Australia. Given a little longer, it would engirdle the earth.

Isaiah Woods, who had ceased to be Adams' landlord to become its managing partner, was the driver seemingly born to handle the wild horses of this chariot of commerce. Haskell, rich in three or four years, had more or less abdicated. The ambitions of the two men, eyed from the opposite side of the continent, proved too dizzying for Alvin Adams. From the Haskell-Woods enterprise on the Pacific he and his associates concluded to withdraw. Haskell valued the Adams name too highly to let it go without struggle. He succeeded in inducing the elder magnate to remain as a special partner with limited liability. Haskell and Woods, now chief proprietors, planned even grander exploits.

When suddenly, after five years' brilliant dominion, all smashed.

VII

REMME'S GREAT RIDE

Louis Remme, stockman, had just completed a profit-
able drive of cattle up the inland valley. A score here,
a dozen there, he had traded his steers and cows for clinking gold. The gold, $12,500 of it, was on deposit with
Adams & Co. at Sacramento City. Now Remme was sitting down to a leisured breakfast in Marius Bremond's
restaurant adjoining the Orleans Hotel.

Marius put a copy of the *Daily Union* in his hands.
Newspapers in the fifties did not shout all they knew from
page one. Before the stockman got far into his journal
he had caught the news from the dining room's queerly
excited chatter. Fragments of it were crashing about like
crockery. "Page Bacon's cleaned out." "Adams too.
Looks bad." "They say Woods has skipped."

Three days before, which was February 17, 1855, the
steamship *Oregon*, Captain Allan McLane, had arrived
through the Golden Gate heavy with mail and passengers
and fairly alist with news. The news concerned the failure
of Page, Bacon & Co. of St. Louis. This was not only the
largest banking concern west of the Atlantic seaboard,
but its main branch was at San Francisco and was the
largest bank on the coast. Moreover, Page Bacon for some

years had been next-door neighbor of Adams & Co., and between them was believed to be more than a physical bond.

Remme tore open his newspaper. The story had just come up from San Francisco by river boat. Page Bacon's downfall had started a run on its branch. Other banks had been sucked in. All was seething, boiling panic. Wells Fargo seemed to have the public's confidence, but there was grave doubt as to whether the other banks and expresses would ever reopen their doors. Rage and dismay were particularly acute concerning Adams. The house had ramifications everywhere, it was the poor man's shield and lamp, and the shield had turned to paper and the lamp gone black. Managing Director Woods' wild flight was subject to only one interpretation. In every town, hamlet, camp where Adams had set up gold scales and forwarding service, its clients had been robbed, looted, swindled or made the victims of some egregious financial nonsense that had cleaned them bare.

Remme came to his feet. The stockman was a small man, about five feet eight, weighing about 155 sinewy pounds and bearing the blood of French-Canadian voyageurs in his veins. That $12,500 in good $50 gold slugs, on deposit in Adams' Sacramento branch! In a few strides he was shouldering through to the counter at 46 Second Street, outside of which a roaring, milling crowd was gathered. He demanded his money. "You will have to see the receiver," Adams' cashier told Remme, intimating that the line was going to be long and the waiting considerable. Remme thought rapidly. Should he dash for

Marysville and try to cash his claim there? But the news just arrived from San Francisco must be already at Marysville. He could guess the scene with accuracy: the excited, jamming populace, the shouts for torch and rope, the closed doors, the smashed windows, the locked or empty vault, the cries to high heaven of anguish and despair and indignation. Grass Valley then? Georgetown? Placerville? The news would be ahead of him everywhere. But his savings out of five years' labor! Then Remme stopped short. Portland!

Adams had a branch there, surely. It couldn't have heard the news yet. There was no railroad, no telegraph. But Portland was seven hundred miles away and the steamer from San Francisco would be sailing next morning. Nevertheless, Remme walked to the river levee. Should he go on down to San Francisco and take that steamer? If so, he would arrive at Portland simultaneously with the bad news. Again there would be the milling crowd, the shuttered windows, the locked doors, the sheriff's notice.

A stern-wheeled river paddler, the successor to the *Belle,* was just starting for Knight's Landing, forty-two miles upstream. Even as it drew its gangplank in Remme made up his mind. He jumped for the boat. At Knight's Landing he got a horse from Knight himself, the baronial ranchman; rode to the head of Grand Island, swapped for a fresh steed from Judge Diefendorf, an old friend, and set grimly to the long north trail.

He had friends on ranches and in towns here and there up the valley. The Marysville Buttes were swimming in the violet of sunset when he made his third or fourth change of mount, paying a bonus plus a blown horse where necessary, and spurred on. Ten o'clock, ten hours from Sacramento, and he galloped into Red Bluffs. Five minutes later, sandwich in hand and fresh steed between his knees, he was off again. Twenty miles farther a camp fire gleamed in the dark. "Who's there?" "Remme, stockman. I'm after a thief, and I want a fresh horse."

Stockmen and freighters were natural allies. The teamster helped him to shift saddle. "Cut, now! You can leave it to Comet's Tail!"

Two hundred miles above Sacramento the valley floor bumps into the pedestal that supports fourteen-thousand-foot Mount Shasta. In darkness the rider swept through Shasta City and sleeping Whiskytown. Dawn found him breakfasting at Tower House on Clear Creek. Straight above rose the craggy columns, the rosy quartz and gilding granite of Old Bally, its feet in dense carpets of cedar and pine. Across the creek loomed tall bare mountains which, as he well knew, rolled away to the north in a labyrinth of interlocking ranges, deep gorges and faded, broken summits. Here at Tower House all semblance of a road ended. In the uplands beyond, no wagon wheel had yet drawn crease. But the trail was a familiar one to the cattle drover. All that day he rode, climbing and swinging back around bold headlands, and as he rode he left springtime far below. Snow whirled in the higher canyons and a wind howled on Trinity Mountain, setting its tall firs and tamaracks creaking. It was under night-black forests that he reached Trinity Creek. Here no money would buy a horse, but a good-natured miner lent him one and provided supper. "Hope you catch that thief you're after. Fetch him back on my horse, and I'll help you hang him."

Remme reached Scott Valley in six hours, where he slept till noon. To eastward the soaring dome of Shasta loomed like a big white lamp. Far out at sea the folk on the busy little *Columbia* were probably looking also at that lofty radiance. Thought of the *Columbia* tin-kettling its slow way northward sent the rider's spurs deep. The steamer had two companies of soldiers on board, one to land at Humboldt Bay and tame the Indians, the other to garrison the mouth of Rogue River. Though he did not know of it, these stops by the "opposition" would be in his favor.

Beyond Callahan's, Remme found slightly easier going. Lindsey Applegate had brought six wagons down from Oregon that far in '48. Easier going—the rider felt he could stand some. Seventy hours out from Knight's Landing, he stumbled into the mining community of Yreka. A big drink of brandy in the Yreka Hotel and State House on Miner Street, where there were cheers for his enterprise and a fresh horse borrowed from Horsley & Brastow's Mountain Express, and he was on again for the Oregon valley. Four hours later, ascending the long rise eleven miles north of the Klamath River, he came to the cairn on Hungry Creek marking the California state boundary. "Thank God for Oregon," sighed Remme.

The Modoc Indians were on the warpath between the Klamath and Rogue rivers. Remme rode carefully. In

the Grave Creek hills they had committed frightful dep-
redations. Remme galloped down the frozen valley floor
of Bear Creek, took coffee at Jacksonville, and again
snatched two hours' sleep. Then, on a fresh steed, he
crossed the Rogue River by means of the pioneer ferry.
Just eight hours out of Jacksonville he ascended the bank
at Dardanelles and hired a strong horse from a stout Irish
farmer named Kavanaugh. Walking this horse under a
bluff near Jump-Off Joe, he suddenly bent low and drove
in his spurs. A ball had whizzed by his ear. Five more
Indian rifles spoke. At Cow Creek, the Indians out-
paced, he walked his mount carefully to avoid the quick-
sands. Then through picturesque Round Prairie, where
Roseburg stands today, and onward to Winchester village
on the north fork of the Umpqua. At Joe Knott's tavern
he again snatched some rest. Twice so far he had lost the
trail and been forced to retrace; five times his horse had
played out, and he had been forced to dismount and lead.
One hundred and ninety-five miles yet to go! The sky
was cold and leaden. It changed to a darker hue as he
entered the beautiful valley of the Yoncalla. Great rain-
drops were falling now. But Remme, who had outridden
blizzards and Indians, did not flinch before the Oregon
mist. At the cabin of a tall, hale pioneer by the name of
Jesse Applegate he again told his story, now familiar in
ranch houses and camps for nearly five hundred miles.
Sure, help yourself to a fresh mount! Remme turned his
jaded steed into the corral and waved farewell. Now it
was raining harder; the trail was a bog; Pass Creek a quag-
mire. Cougars howled in the somber forest. At eight

o'clock that night he saw a light. "Woo-hoooo!" Thus properly announced, any man was welcome in the cabins of the wilderness. A cup of coffee and a fresh mount, and he was on.

Just before daybreak he entered the little city of Eugene, where John Milliron sold him a nag for $70 and allowed $65 for the horse he had just ridden in from Coast Fork. He crossed the brimming Willamette at Peoria. The day was now mild and clear. The white cones of the Cascades towered against a radiant blue sky. This was the fifth day of his ride and Remme had so far allotted himself just ten hours' sleep.

All that night the stockman continued riding. At midnight he saw a light in a cabin and rode up to the window. A young lover within was just putting the all-important question. Remme did not tarry to learn the answer. Breakfast at the lower end of French Prairie, a fresh horse for five dollars to take him to Oregon City, which was reached at half past ten, and noon of that sixth day found him at Milwaukee, where the ferryman's son got him across the swollen Willamette once more. And by one o'clock he had reached Portland town and was putting away his horse at Stewart's stable.

"Is the steamer in from 'Frisco?"

"No, but she's fetchin' in here today."

"Where is Adams & Co.?" the traveler then asked, with a stab of sweet relief.

Dr. Steinberger, the agent for the banking-express house, was just taking down his shutters after returning from lunch. "Can you," a mud-spattered stranger asked

him, "cash a certificate of deposit for me on your San
Francisco bank?"

"Regular charge is one-half of one per cent for all sums
over a thousand dollars. How much you got?"

"Twelve thousand five hundred," said Remme. "I'm
a cattle buyer and I need the money."

The certificate was in good order. It was signed by
W. B. Rochester, the agent at Sacramento. Dr. Steinberger
chuckled at the easy profit of $62.50 acquired by the trans-
action. He set forth ten stacks, twenty slugs to the stack.
Forty pounds of gold. "—Eight, nine, ten," he counted.
Remme took the gold to his hotel, saw it locked in the
safe, and then came back.

"You'd better save yourself," he remarked with real
affection.

"Eh?" asked the doctor.

Just then a cannon thumped out on the river. The
Columbia was announcing her arrival. Before her skipper,
could get his lines ashore, Purser Ralph Meade had leaped
from the gunwale and made for the Adams establishment.
Meade had $950 on deposit there, and a constable's writ
attached it for him. No other depositors got anything.

Four years later the valiant Remme, with a real bunch
of cattle this time, started south from Rogue River for
Yreka. The passes of the Siskiyous were blocked with
snow. The cattle became difficult to handle. They milled
and bolted. Fruitlessly Remme tried to make his way out
by way of Sam's Valley through Cottonwood. The fleecy
flakes fell faster and faster. Farther strayed the animals.
The dogged blood of his French-Canadian forebears, the

blood that in 1855 had made him ride 665 miles in 143 hours of total time, ten of which went for sleep, at an average gait of five miles per hour through rains and storms and mud, still drove Remme on. In vain he sought to turn and extricate his cattle. The snows fell deeper, the drifts piled higher. In the spring some mountaineers found him. Indomitable Remme, fighting hard for his stake, had answered the last round-up.

While Remme was making that tremendous bid for the safety of his deposit by riding the long north trail, other horsemen had streaked east, south and north. Justified now were those tremendous races which had trained and tested mounts and couriers. Wells Fargo was riding, riding as never before, riding to forestall others to its branches with the news of its own grim crisis. At Placerville the concern faced a heavy run, but for a substantial period met all claims. At Marysville it was forced to close, but at Grass Valley, Auburn, Nevada City, Sonora, and Stockton it confronted the run head-on with bulging bags of specie. Everywhere it paid claims cheerfully as long as funds lasted, maintaining confidence. At every point its express business continued as usual.

While these events were transpiring in valley and foot-hill, Lassen's Butte at the north end of the Sierras blew off the top of its ten-thousand-foot volcanic cone. The upheaval was tremendous and the shards flew wide, but could not add a ripple to the general maelstrom which at San Francisco sucked down two hundred business houses in a single little seaport of forty thousand people. Haskell some years after appeared at the almshouse, stricken and half crazed; he was admitted, and there he ended his days.

Two days after Adams' foundering, Wells Fargo agencies reopened their doors at Sacramento, Placerville, Auburn, Nevada, Dotan's Bar, Coloma, Diamond Springs, Grass Valley, Sonora, Yankee Jim's, and Rattlesnake Bar. On the fourth day it resumed banking at San Francisco.

The financial waters went down. The sun of prosperity returned. On the surface of the lately churned seas floated the complete wreckage of virtually every rival to the house of William George Fargo and Henry Wells.

The first three years had been spent in conservative building. Now the hour for expansion had arrived. The company's capital was increased, and by August forty-two offices lay between Panama, Honolulu, Portland, and the Sierra Nevada. By November the offices numbered sixty. By 1857 they had extended to Bellingham Bay and Vancouver Island on Puget Sound and numbered seventy-eight.

In the closing month of this year of stormy doings John Parrott's Granite Block was observed to be once more swinging back its quarter-inch iron shutters. Had Adams resumed? No, nor evermore would in the western theatre. Wells, Fargo & Company, successor to its prestige and inheritor of its opportunity, was permanently moving into that fortlike building.

VIII

THE STAGECOACH HILARIOUS

THROUGH this era the Concord coach rolled judg-matically, carrying passengers and treasures with increas-ing go and precision over the mustard-yellow plains and piney slopes.

Comfort was hoped for, but conquest was the object—conquest of fearful roads in any weather. Its front wheels were three feet high, its rear wheels five. Its weight, unloaded, ranged up to twenty-five hundred pounds. On twin keels of oxhide it rolled over the granite waves like a galleon. Another thorough-braced vehicle, called stage wagon or "mud wagon," was also present. Lower to the ground, canvas-curtained, less curvesome, it comported it-self with reduced majesty but unreduced utility.

The coaches were built to accommodate nine inside—three facing forward, three backward, and a triad in the middle—and a half dozen more on the deck, above and behind the driver and his two companions. But a stage-coach, like any other accommodation vehicle that ever moved, was somewhat of an accordion. An observer for the Butte *Record* at Oroville noted, one day in 1858, "A stage from Shasta passed through town yesterday, about one o'clock, with an enormous load. The coach was one of the biggest size. We counted thirty-five persons on and inside of it, besides the driver and one Chinaman."

A gentle clergyman who voyaged to the gold shore in '55 made a stagecoaching tour of the more accessible camps and recorded his emotions. He had already observed, on the arrival of his ship at San Francisco, that "the dock was black with people and carriages as we came up. Express Agents came off in little sail-boats—caught the news (to us 23 days old), and flew back to dock, where post riders put their horses to their speed, to reach printing offices, &c." Now he had reached the Mother Lode. The place was Auburn, the month was August, the weather was malignant, and "on starting, a large rough man got my seat on the outside of the stage; though the agent at Sacramento and here told him it was pledged to me as an old man and an invalid; and he refused to get off unless taken off by force. It was of no use for me to try to get my right; for the passengers were all of the same sort—miners armed with revolvers and knives, and would have taken his part; and the Agent of the Stage Co. dared not interfere. So I had to get inside, where the heat and dust were awful. I never rode more uncomfortably than I did from that time till 11 o'clock at night." The Rev. Mr. Sessions perceived that here was a vineyard for resolute laboring, where manners needed to be taught possibly ahead of godliness.

The coach inside contained seven. Outside, three unhappy gentlemen had the pleasure of dangling their legs over the boot, receiving the full benefit of the dust. Seven or eight others hung theirs over the sides, while I with several others fixed ourselves

Turk fashion upon the top. . . . Railroads and steamboats are all very well if a person wants to be rushed through on business—but for comfort and pleasure give me the old Coach, when the day is fine, and the road hard, when the teams at the changes come up fresh, and the horses go to their collars with a will and make the bounding stage rattle on the solid ground—when the boxes talk, and the passengers converse, and the driver feels in a jolly good humor—oh, then give me the old Stage Coach; and for music, the crack! crack! of the merry lash, and the whir-r-r-r-l-l-l-l of the flying wheels.

So exulted a panegyrist in *Hutchings' California Magazine* for 1860. But the day was not always fine, the road not always hard; and as for comfort, there would arise occasions:

"Look out!" from the driver . . . but ere we have time to perform his bidding, over goes the coach and out we go, all rolling downhill together . . . picking ourselves up very carefully, stretching each arm and leg, and then with a good will "right" the coach, gather up the distributed baggage, pack it and ourselves in the stage again, and away we go . . .

And away they truly went. But the durability of the Concord was sometimes brought home in hardy manner, as to a coachload of passengers driven by one Colby one day on a smart grade in Nevada county. Narrow, as all mountain roads were, this road fairly hung by the grace of Providence above a steep declivity with Greenhorn Creek shouting rip-roariously over the stones below. Driver Colby was not surprised, at the most dangerous bend, to encounter an ascending wagon. It was in just such places that one would expect to encounter ascending

wagons. He directed his passengers to stay in or climb
out as they chose. One and all they chose to climb out.
Then the jehu attempted to cast his horses around the ob-
stacle. Everything went nicely until the lead bars caught
in a wagon wheel. With a shriek the animals went off the
grade, dragging everything with them. Colby leaped for
his life. Horses and stage went out of sight and those

THE STAGE

who stood above waited to see the whole concern land
in Greenhorn Creek three hundred feet or more below.
Instead, they beheld the four horses with the forewheels
still attached rise from ruin and make at top speed for
the head of the ravine. Up the slope clambered the
steeds, and then hightailed for home. A tree had caught
the coach thirty feet below and knocked it from its front
undercarriage, otherwise clasping it undamaged.

When the driver of the Meadow Lake stage got down,

one evening to fix his light before ascending the grade, his horses reared. The reinsman jumped to his box and grabbed the lines. To his discomfiture the animals took command and went up the slope as if attached to exploding firecrackers, leaving the dismounted passengers behind. Swift as the vehicle pounded up hill, however, the passengers took to their toes and adjourned the other way. A large grizzly bear had sent the horses into flight and was now ambling up the grade.

Once the Downieville stage, ascending the mountain above Goodyear's Bar, encroached too closely upon the outer verge. The road gave way, the vehicle dropped and rolled a hundred feet, and the passengers climbed out a window.

Times were not unknown when the safety mechanism would slip on a long descent. Then all the prowess of the jehu would be needed, as when, on Mount Hope hill above Marysville, a brake gave way, and the horses went dashing at full speed to the bottom. The hill was about half a mile long, and one of the most dangerous in the state; but through the skilful management of driver Clark, the horses were guided safely down the run. The stage was full of passengers at the time, and it may be assumed that for the moment all conversation ceased; but the wild drive ended in security and tongues freely wagged again.

Approaching San Andreas from Mokelumne Hill, driver Homer Smith attempted to engage the brake with his foot at the precise moment his vehicle selected to drop into a hole. The disappearance of the brake under his heel just as he thrust for it catapulted the reinsman straight of

his seat. Over him rolled the wheels. But stagemen were
made of stern stuff. "His wounds," mildly informed the
local journal, "will disable him from his business for a
short time."

The coming and going of the stagecoach, its bustle of
changing horses, the Olympian descent of its driver and
the ceremonial entry of that great man to the tavern bar
were a permanent mining town occasion. "On the arrival
of the stages from Sacramento on Thursday evening last,"
dispatched a correspondent at Yankee Jim's, a lively
settlement in the Placer county hills, "there was a grand
rush to the stage offices. The stages were crowded inside
and out, and many were anxious to see the newcomers.
. . . Speaking of stages, several of them go out and
arrive daily." This in 1857, when the novelty of a coach
arrival should have been wearing off. But its clamor
outlasted many a camp to which it brought the first deni-
zens and from which it bore the last away.

It was ever adjudged good form to laugh at the stagedriver's jokes, and otherwise concede the mighty man his
due. For he could enforce discipline. When the discovery of gold and silver beyond the Sierras sent the
great breed forth to new fields, one of the most redoubt-
able was Hi Washburn, who drove six spanking bays for
Wells, Fargo & Co. from Central City to Georgetown
in the shadow of Pike's Peak. One fine day there arrived
at the Connor House in Central City a young dude from
Philadelphia in whose being, according to his own opin-
ion, the wisdom of Solomon and the beauty of Adonis
were concentrated. This youth appropriated the seat on

the box without invitation, and began to enlighten Washburn and the outside passengers.

He informed them that he was disappointed with Rocky Mountain scenery, "and, by the way, driver, why can't you touch up these horses a little? Back in our Pennsylvania mountains, the coaches make marvelous time; they never break a rapid trot up hill or down."

Hi Washburn sat silent while the well-trained horses toiled slowly up the mountain, but he chawed his piece of plug in a manner boding no good.

On reaching the head of a long canyon, Hi pulled up and asked all but the tenderfoot to get inside. He then let his lines go slack, shouted like a Pawnee at his leaders and started down a four-mile hill as if all the demons of hell were after the outfit. The youth from the East tried to look unconcerned for a while, but when the coach began to careen like a ship in a squall, sometimes four wheels on the ground and sometimes two, each horse running for dear life, and Washburn yipping and hoorooing at every jump, the young man weakened. He implored Hi to stop that terrific speed.

"Speed, shucks! This is the way we always come down these hills," assured Hi, reaching to his pockets for his plug.

On arriving at Central, the authority from Pennsylvania left that coach, and returned to Georgetown on a pack mule.

When the last Pacific Railroad spike was driven, and the first overland trains passed through Reno, a party of gentlemen in the hotel at that place were remarking upon the dazzling wonder of it all. They were interrupted by a sun-browned individual who informed them that the iron horse had ruined many a good man and a most noble tradition, and he undertook to whip any man in the crowd who disputed it.

He was a dispossessed stageman.

Like the age of sails on the sea, the age of six-ribboned coachcraft then was closing. But as with its glorious contemporary, the clipper ship, the Concord was ending its day in a sudden shaft of afternoon sunlight that has gilded it with splendor.

Yes, they were a gallant race, those drivers of the dusty, steep, rutty, perilous grades of yesterday. Atlantic farms and post roads apprenticed them, the Sierra Nevada developed them, and from the Sierra Nevada they went forth to the Cascades, the Washoes and the Bitter Root; they manned the drivers' seats from the Bill Williams Mountains to the Black Hills and from the Red River to the Frazer. We strew a few of the names of the whip-cracking legion:

"Uncle" Jimmy Miller, who drove the winding roads out of Angels Camp, and was held up about as many times as any knight of the western lash; and that other Jim Miller, six feet of showmanship, who whipped from Virginia City to Austin, Nevada, and who, it is said, used to present himself in yellow overcoat and yellow pants striped down the leg, made to order by an excellent tailor and duly creased; who wore high-heeled shoes, red waistcoat, and sported a silver chain anchored to a watch that could have been used to block a wagon on Geiger grade;

Ben Wing, who lashed the Overland between Virginia City and Salt Lake, and who once had on board two deputy sheriffs and a captured horse thief. On Quaking Asp Hill in the Wasatch range the prisoner jumped down and bolted. As he fled down Echo Canyon, deputies Jack and Bill Coaster plugged him, then called for a shovel and looked about for a monument. Ben Wing shook his head. "These here papers say 'You are commanded to take the body of Richard Gardner to Salt Lake.' He's express matter and I'm agoin' to take him." "That means his live body, not his dead one," argued the deputies. "It don't specify so," responded Wing, "it says 'the body of.'" So they strapped the "express" carefully to the rear boot, continued for Salt Lake City, and whirled up to Wells Fargo's office followed by a hundred whooping men and boys, the corpse swaying and staring on its reception committee from its post behind;

John Reynolds, the "perfect reinsman," who, tale has it, whisked eight horses and a Concord containing twenty people over the twenty-two miles between Wilmington and Los Angeles in an hour and thirty-two minutes. When he spun to a halt before the Bella Union Hotel the harness was a wreck, one leader had nothing on but a collar and some of the passengers were in approximately the same fix, but Jim had fetched the Pacific Ocean several minutes nearer to Los Angeles;

"Pop" McCray, who gave up the buckskin lash for a ranch in Sonoma Valley, and whose birthday was the occasion of an annual pilgrimage by his admirers about San Francisco Bay for forty years;

OVERLAND MAIL ROUTE
TO CALIFORNIA.

Through in Six Days to Sacramento!

CONNECTING WITH THE DAILY STAGES

To all the Interior Mining Towns in Northern California and Southern Oregon.
Ticketed through from PORTLAND, by the

OREGON LINE OF STAGE COACHES!

And the Rail Road from Oroville to Sacramento,

Passing through Oregon City, Salem, Albany, Corvallis, Eugene City, Oakland,
Winchester, Roseburg, Canyonville, Jacksonville, and in California—
Yreka, Trinity Centre, Shasta, Red Bluff, Tehama, Chico,
Oroville, Marysville to SACRAMENTO.

TRAVELERS AVOID RISK of OCEAN TRAVEL

Pass through the HEART OF OREGON—the Valleys of Rogue River, Umpqua and Willamette.

This portion of the Pacific Slope embraces the most BEAUTIFUL and attractive, as well as some of the most
BOLD, GRAND and PICTURESQUE SCENERY on the Continent. The highest snow-capped mountains, (Mt. HOOD,
Mt. SHASTA and others,) deepest ravines and most beautiful valleys.

Stages stop over one night at JACKSONVILLE and YREKA, for passengers to rest.
Passengers will be permitted to lay over at any point, and resume their
seats at pleasure, any time within one month.

FARE THROUGH, FIFTY DOLLARS.

Ticket Office at Arrigoni's Hotel, Portland.

H. W. CORBETT & Co.,

PORTLAND, July 19, 1866.   Proprietors Oregon Stage Line.

(W. B. Carter, Printer, Front st., Portland, Oregon.)

STAGECOACHING POSTER, 1866

John Craddock, never late, never capsized and never held up, who drove the prickly Marysville-Shasta route though its first ten and most exciting years, so constantly on the road that for days he could not remove clothes or overcoat—snatching a few moments' sleep while sitting in a hotel chair ready to "go out";

A certain Ross, who playfully drove so close to an opposition coach out of Marysville that he sent it over a greasewood-covered bluff, and by this display of sportiveness so irritated a tumbled passenger that his hide was swiftly and mortally filled with quail shot;

"Curly Bill," mighty of physique, who once dragged an army officer out of his vehicle for insulting a lady passenger and who while yanking out the military man fetched the door-frame of the coach out with him;

Jared Crandall, first to toss coach and horse straight up the seven-thousand-foot granite wall behind Placerville; and who in a later day, grown old and stiff, was heaved off the box on his last drive when a forewheel hit a rut;

Bill Blackmore, who couldn't sleep in his bed without dreaming, sitting up, tugging at the blankets, and fairly pushing out the footboard as he hollered "Whoa!";

Curly Jerry Robbins, ambushed by Indians in '56, who opened the West's whole Indian-stagecoach drama by larruping seventeen miles from Pitt River to Hot Creek through whistling arrows, catching sixteen with his body and losing his coach, but saving his team;

Henry C. Ward, who served many years as driver and messenger on the Sonoma-Mendocino road, and who never let a swish of sudden lead deprive him of command of his horses or his treasure;

And that famous old-timer of a hundred names and routes, who dying, rose up in bed and shouted: "It's getting dark and I'm on a long downgrade, and I can't get my foot on the brake!"

Surely no more earnest eulogy was ever penned by the Virginia City *Enterprise*, that journal of many obituaries, than its comment of March 6, 1883, on the demise of the most famous driver of them all:

HANK MONK.—The famous stage driver is dead. He has been on the down grade for some time. On Wednesday his foot lost its final hold on the brake and his coach could not be stopped until, battered and broken on a sharp turn, it went over into the canyon, black and deep, which we call death. In his way, Hank Monk was a character. In the old days, before the leathers under his coach were soaked with alcohol, there was no better balanced head than his. There was an air about him which his closest friends could not understand. There was something which seemed to say that stage driving was not his intended walk; that if he pleased, there were other things, even more difficult than handling six wild horses, which he could do quite as well. In his prime he would turn a six horse coach in the street with the team at a full run, and with every line apparently loose. But the coach would always bring up in exactly the spot that the most careful driver would have tried to bring it. His eye never deceived him and his estimation of distance was absolute; the result which must be when leaders, swings and wheelers all were playing their rôles, with him an exact science. His driving was such a perfection of art that it did not seem art at all, and many an envious whip, watching him, has turned away to say "He is the luckiest man that ever climbed on top of a box."

It was not luck at all, it was simply an intuitive, exact calculation from cause to effect, and his whole duty ended when he fixed the cause. The effect had to be. He has often driven from the summit of the Sierra down into the valley, ten miles, in forty-five minutes. Other drivers have done as well, the only difference being that with others it was a strain upon the eye and hand and arm and foot; with Monk it was a matter of course. He was to stage driving what the German papers say Edwin Booth was to Hamlet, "It was not played, but lived."

Thus the Monks and the Washburns, the Fosses, Coopers, Joneses and Hamiltons; the Comstocks, Burkes and Scammons; the Scotts, Buxtons, Mayhews, Haworths and Sillses; the Curly Bills, Curly Dans and all the other Curleys, Bucks, Uncles, Jims and Pops—picturesque legion, they sat the driver's boxes of their Concords and with cunning hands and well-braced feet played on those instruments like master organists. With their cream hats, silver-ferruled whips, tall yarns, tall tumblers and good cigars, they were as appropriate to the times as ears to the burro, gay waistcoat to the gambler, or to the miner his boots and whiskers and cabin in the pines. They flourished in all their glory for about three decades, and after that with diminishing grandeur on the byways of a dozen western states. "Not many were church members," recalled Major Ben C. Truman, journalist and traveling postoffice agent of the Jingling Decades, "but they all read the Sacramento *Union* religiously and swore by Wells, Fargo & Company."

Beside them on the box, with more and more frequency as the years wore on, rode the George Hacketts, Jim Humes, Aaron Rosses, Eugene Blairs and Mike Toveys of that special fighting race—the shotgun messengers.

IX

THE STAGECOACH BELLIGERENT

A THOUSAND untoward doings shook the Mother Lode end to end in '56. At the bottom of much of it was an uncouth individual who went by the name of Captain Tom Bell. He was a considerable figure, with an auburn goatee and a bashed-in nose, and he grew in stature as each new victim came into town and recounted a painful meeting. A former army surgeon with a bit of education, Tom had ambitions. This was combined with a strong liking for mystic ritual. His large bands had hideouts, signs, spies; and the hills and hollows from Trinity River to Yuba were full of lamentations emanating from riders who were one by one mistreated.

Tom Bell was quite in line to project what may possibly have been the West's first attempted treasure-coach hold-up.

The event had been nearing, with or without a Captain Bell to direct it. On August 4th two men rode up in the night and ordered the driver to halt his coach on the Coloma road, within gunshot distance of where Jim Marshall had found his historic flake. They waved pistols and they wore masks, and they peered hard into the vehicle's murky interior. Seeing it illuminated by more burning cigars than they had expected to find, they apologized briefly, put spurs to their horses and disappeared.

Less casual was Captain Bell. He sensed the opportunities of a new profession and he planned strategically. Active roles were assigned to Bill Gristy, an ex-blacksmith of great strength and pugnacity; to Ned Connors who wore vast red whiskers; and to Jim Smith —first of a long line of stage-robbing Jim Smiths—who seems to have been a walking art gallery, so extensively was he tattooed. Had the early-time Napoleon of banditry been in Sacramento one autumn day of 1856, he might have read his Union with profit, for it said: "FORTIFIED EXPRESSMEN: It is stated that Langton's expressmen, who travel through the northeastern countries, now go armed with double-barreled shotguns. They will be hard customers for the highwaymen to handle."

The stage from Camptonville came booming down on schedule. Tom's spy system had told him there would be $100,000 on board. John Gear was on the driver's seat, Bill Dobson the "fortified" messenger beside him. Courageous, coolly confident of his hands and his horses, inured to skimming the edge of mountain abysses, accustomed to voicing the word authoritative and the word oracular, John Gear was a very representative example of the Sierra Nevada stageman. With one foot on the brake and the other on the express sack—express boxes being not yet invented—he drove his Concord down into the ford and up the opposite bank of Dry Creek.

At the farther bank there was a shout to pull up. John

Gear, with instantaneous appraisal, answered with a yell to his horses and a crack of whip. Bill Dobson the fortified one also went into action. His pistols crashed with a force that nearly took him backward off the stage. A broadside from the leafage raked the coach in return. Mrs. Tilghman, colored wife of a Marysville barber, crumpled inside with a bullet through her brain. Two male passengers beside her absorbed a peppering in face and leg. A third white man and a Chinaman departed the off side of the coach so fast that the record never after caught up with them. Driver Gear, swearing grimly, clung to the lines and guided his team, one arm drilled by a ball. Dobson was unhurt and still full of fight. Four of Bell's stalwarts fled. Bell, Gristy and another made a second effort farther down the road, found Gear and Dobson several army corps too many for them and galloped away. Gear's coach with its gold dust, its injured and its dead rolled in to a civic triumph at Marysville. Tom Bell was caught and lynched a month later.

Thus begun, open warfare on the stagecoaches continued as long as coach wheels rolled. Treasure vehicles with increasing habit carried shotgun guards as regular equipment; though with the multiplication of routes there could never be more than a fraction of the vehicles so guarded.

In the first two decades the hold-ups were usually a phenomenon of the downbound trips, the coaches then being most likely to contain a consignment of dust en route from the mines. As drivers had not yet learned caution, and the owners of the dust were often riding with it, there was always a good chance of a fight being put up. But the exhaustion of placer gold after the first big years, and the substitution of underground and corporation mining, began to tilt the direction of highwaymanship the other way. Not virgin bullion, which came down from the mining districts in heavy unwieldy bars, but coin upward-bound for the mining pay rolls became the shining target.

The method of attack took on a recognized pattern. The selected spot was usually at the top of a grade, with horses blown and moving slowly. Here a figure would emerge. The driver, shotgun or rifle leveled on his chest, would be ordered to toss down the express box. As the express company was well-to-do and always impersonal and not likely to suffer very drastically if the gun went off, whereas the driver was a poor man, not at all impersonal, the John Gear tradition was usually forgotten. Perhaps the driver took into account that both he and the highwaymen were permanent features of the scenery, quite likely to meet again. At all events, he complied. With the passing years he complied with more and more alacrity. Down went the box, clanging as it hit the earth; up went the jehu's hands; and—on some grades at least, such as that known as Funck's Hill above Copperopolis—the horses might almost have been called robber-trained. Certain roads, notably the Shasta, Nevada City-Grass Valley and Sonora highways, became so regularly patrolled by a variety of Dick Turpins that a small state's prison might very well have been dedicated to the captures effected on them. The single thirty-five-mile stretch above and

A typical pair of express messengers reasonably ready for business.

below Funck's Hill delivered up a harvest of twenty-one highwaymen between May, '76, and February, '85. This was something close to two-thirds of a highwayman per mile, or two and a third highwaymen per year, and the figures represent actual captures and convictions. They make no account of the numerous strikes and getaways that were successful.

On the whole, Dick Turpin in his successive incarnations was not very original. While he held his gun on the driver, a partner would line up the travelers, sometimes inviting them to lie face-down on the ground while he worked on the stoutly locked box with a hatchet. Then all would be motioned on and the roadside would absorb the dirty shirts and overalls of the fleeing pair.

Easy work. Never, after the first few years, was a house more divided against itself than a halted stagecoach on a lonely mountain road. In the decision for battle or passivity three interests at once developed: the interests of the owners of the line—represented by the driver; of the express company whose box was desired—represented by nobody unless an armed messenger was aboard, which could not be every time; and of the passengers. The driver, whose chief charge was his horses, with half a dozen ribbons in his hands was helpless anyhow. The passengers were also filled with equanimity toward any loss that might fall on the express company. Only the messenger, if one was present, had any desire for battle-and-defense. Should battle occur, the passengers would be right in the line of fire, packed in and useless. Their vote in the matter was foreordained. There was seldom

any opportunity to ask for it anyhow; for the first notice
of a crisis would be a hoarse order issuing out of shadow
or darkness, and the second would be a masked face and
gun-muzzle presenting themselves at the window.

Such a decision rested with Charley Bowen one starlit
evening on a Marysville-Shasta "fortified" coach, and it
had to be met in the fraction of instant that it takes to
swing a shotgun to hip and squeeze—or not squeeze—
its trigger. Charley was the messenger who had been
blown from the steamer *Belle* when she exploded on the
river four years before. He was still a resolute guardian
of Wells Fargo funds. On this night he had five robbers
in front of him and a lady passenger immediately to his
left. Shotguns in the hands of strangers are not dis-
criminating. Charley Bowen let the express box go, nor
protested when his gun was lifted from his hands and
the keys from his person. Sadly he watched the box
opened, saw $15,000 removed, and heard the robbers
remark to each other that the company was rich and could
afford the money. It was a doctrine that was to be
enunciated again and again as long as stagecoaches ran.

Nevertheless, there were often lively and unexpected
denouements when the order came to "put 'em up."
When the night stage of A. N. Fisher & Co., piloted by
"Mr." Oliver, moved down the foothill grade from
Sonora, two horsemen set stealthily in pursuit. Mr. Oliver
had a clergyman and his wife inside and a colored man
for outside passenger. None could be counted on to help
him in the approaching crisis which his ears detected.
When it came time to water the horses at a wayside resort,

Mr. Oliver selected a king-bolt from the kit box. The muzzles of his horses were deep in the trough when the pursuers came up. They rode into the light of the Concord's candle-lanterns and bumped heavily into the horses. That was enough. With a lusty wallop of the iron pin, administered from the elevation of his driver's seat, Mr. Oliver stretched one marauder in the dust. With the well-aimed charge of his juggernaut and four he bowled aside the other, who threw away pistol and fled. Mr. Oliver drove fast into Stockton, much perturbed about the rascals who had got rough with his horses. If they had merely asked for the express box he might have controlled himself.

The driver of the outward-bound stage from Hollister in the coastal hills was held up one morning in '74 and kept in a state of rigid perturbation by the customary "two bandits, one tall and his partner short," for two surprising reasons. One was that the taller of the brigand pair was epileptic and idiotic, a combination which might do anything to a shotgun trigger; and the other reason was that the short bandit, who frisked his person most impertinently with the snub nose of a blocky revolver, was a girl. She was about sixteen years old, the driver afterward recalled, and not bad-looking.

The driver had no passengers. He was suffered to go on, minus the payroll of the New Idria mine, and the more he thought about it the madder he got. When, on his return trip, the pair stepped out of the tall wild mustard at the same identical spot and ordered up his hands again, it was just too much. Drivers were expert with their long thong-tipped whips, and this driver was no exception. He brought it down with a smart crack, caught the leveled shotgun with its leaping fang, hurled that cannon high in air out of the astonished renegade's hands, and turned his attention to the lady. She was too startled to do more than stare. So the driver motioned them aboard, took over her snub-nosed revolver, and escorted Fred Wilson and Lizzie Keith to the Hollister jail.

At San Pablo, an early-time settlement on an elbow of the bay shore, there dwelt a Mexican desperado known as El Macho. One Sunday morning in 1858 the stage for Oakland set out, guided by driver F. J. Watts, its last passenger on board being a Mexican woman who had fled to its interior with many bundles.

Out of the front gate of his dwelling charged El Macho on horseback, chasing the stage and yelling imprecations. This annoyed Driver Watts, who liked to sit his box in peace and chew his bit of plug in philosophic quiet. When El Macho drew abreast, holding a huge pistol, and finally thrust it through the coach window and pulled trigger, Driver Watts was thoroughly dad-busted. Fortunately the gun did not explode. Watts called to desist. El Macho again snapped the gun, this time at the driver's breast. For the second time its cap was defective.

Watts was more than an able driver. He was one of that great American race who, through practice, were said to be able to spit over a stagecoach, four mules or a strong young pine tree from a sitting start. El Macho's discharge might be imperfect, but Driver Watts' was not. Straight into the gun-sighting orb of Señor Macho the

driver sent a deadly stream. Then he leaped from his
stage, ran into a hotel and got a shotgun. It was un-
necessary. El Macho, calling upon all his saints, was
head-down in a horse trough. An hour later he was
again stalking prey on the street of San Pablo and was
demolished by a weary citizen. Coach and runaway
mistress were by that time far on the road to Oakland.

Coursing down Geiger Grade one evening on the way
to Dutch Flat, a stage from Virginia City entered the
broad plain of Steamboat Springs. It was nine o'clock, the
August twilight had just deepened into black, the coach
was heavy with treasure and its passengers were heavy
with personal armament. Ten miles beyond the steamy
geysers, robbers yelled and opened fire. The driver
yelled and cracked whip, the passengers yelled and
cracked pistols, coachwheels bounded, horses galloped,
and three highwaymen were alleged to have bellowed
that they had been variously hit. A couple of the belli-
cose passengers also bore bloody smears and the coach was
well sieved when it rolled into the mountain village. This
in 1866.

These were fighting instances, and there were others.
The stagecoach could be belligerent. It could be hilarious.
It could be timid. It could be romantic. It could be
perfidious. It could be just about anything, and often
was; the most certain thing about it was that it was unpredictable. Nothing could be more indeterminable than
the actions of a coachload of people, strangers to each
other and moved by every impulse of greed, fear, trucu-
lence or private purpose, advancing through raw, vacant

country behind half a dozen spirited horses and suddenly coming full tilt on adventure.

And always thereafter, when disaster had struck the coach, there was the stir and clatter of a tremendous man-hunt.

X

STEVE AND HENRY

In the decade preceding the Civil War a shirt manufacturer of New Haven, Connecticut, lifted his attention from tails, bosoms, and cuffs to contemplate an invention in the hands of Tyler Henry, a Vermont mechanic. The object was a rifle. The world had rifles. But this was a rifle with attainments. With the aid of Mr. Winchester's finances those attainments were put on a modest production basis. The meat of Mr. Henry's invention was this: Unlike other rifles, the best of which loaded only seven cartridges at a time, through a hole in the butt, and lifted each missile rather laboriously into firing position, the new arm as finally fashioned carried fifteen extra cartridges in a tube under the barrel, tossed them into place by a back-and-forth swing of the trigger guard, and spat half-ounce balls at the clip of twenty-five per minute. The weapon weighed ten pounds, had a two-foot barrel, was handy as a pocketbook and came up to a man's shoulder pretty as a sweetheart.

The fame of the arm that could be "loaded on Sunday and fired all week" spread west. In 1866 one of the severely plain members of the Henry clan stood behind the cabin door of Steve Vernard, former town marshal, at Nevada City.

The southbound coach left North San Juan in the silver-powdered hours after a May midnight. "Look out for yourself," cautioned the agent of the Telegraph. Stage Company, "you might see ghosts."

"Reckon I will," responded Driver John Majors. "Snug inside, you Chinks? All a-bo-o-ard!"

Three miles north of Nevada City the "ghost" materialized. The Colt's navy revolver in his hands was solid. So were those of two companions who emerged beside him.

Driver Majors was philosophical. For human cargo he produced two unhappy Chinamen. One offered two dollars as his worldly wealth, which the bandits rejected. The other, after a successful bout with pie-gow and chuck-a-luck in North San Juan gambling dens, had entered upon his journey trussed in a money belt containing $400. As the substantial hands of the ghostly one slid down his ribs, the celestial put up a fight. It was necessary to knock him down twice and sit upon him before a brigand could cut the belt from his squirming person. Then the freebooters turned to the Wells Fargo box.

It was a doubly secured affair, the outside lid having a brass padlock and heavy hasp. This after a struggle was forced. The inner box was made of chilled iron. It successfully resisted all walloping.

"No use, boys," grinned Majors from the elevation of his driver's seat. "The express company must have been expectin' you."

"They're gettin' pretty damned smart. Next time we'll come better prepared."

With his Chinamen stowed inside and the box reclaimed, Majors saluted with his whip and drove on.

The day had only begun. Before it closed, Latta's Washington stage, a few miles away, had also been stopped and looted; and a single horseman coming on the brigands had escaped similar interception only by making a break-neck detour through the woods.

George Shanks, leader in these forays, had been a waiter in a Camptonville hotel. But waiting for tips had been slow. He had adopted an alias "Lewis" and an alias "Jack Williams" and had started out to gather wealth on an accelerated basis. There had been a Jack Williams hanged for highway work in '56. Consequently the successor to his name became known as "Jack Williams' Ghost." And, as ghosts go, this one was extraordinarily restless. It preyed upon Chinamen shuffling home single-file by dark trails from the fan-tan dens of Grass Valley and Nevada town. It held up white men traveling lonely roads. Of late it had been levying considerably upon stages. The business opportunities afforded in this line were lucrative; for Nevada County, lying against the western side of the Sierras with its feet in the plains, its head in the eight-thousand-foot clouds, was a wild tangle-land of oak and aspen, chaparral and chamiso, pine and fir, the hillsides and benches of whose shouting streams and plunging canyons were charged with yellow metal. In the main the attention of the "ghost" focused on that highwayman's paradise lying on the four-mile hillside between Grass Valley and Nevada City, where pickings were particularly choice, ambush easy, and a steep dive through chaparral down to the South Yuba River led to any number of hideaways. Here he assembled cronies. Through the spring of '66 his predatory pouncings and nimbleness at dodging bullets had become extraordinary. He appeared from nowhere. Into nowhere he dissolved. With continuing success he and his crew had become inexpressibly bold, finally pursuing a man named Smith into the heart of Grass Valley town and firing two shots at his heels. Smith had picked his feet high and planted them far to outrace that ghost.

"Jack Williams' Ghost" also exhibited a strain of sociability. One Saturday night, planting himself on the road leading from You Bet, he first halted a shuffling Chinaman. The victim yielded four bits. The Ghost then ordered the Chinaman to sit down by the side of the road. Victim No. 2 proved to be a German, No. 3 a Chinese, No. 4 an American who protested volubly, No. 5 a Swede—all of whom were robbed and made to sit side by side under pain of being pistoled. Victim No. 6 proved to be a local citizen named George Hilton, who had a reputation as a fighter, always walked armed, and had $60 on his person. But when Hilton saw the five in a row, sitting very quietly beside the road, he concluded they were all robbers waiting for him and put his hands up high. He too was then seated at the foot of the line and the robber departed, thanking them for their company and trusting the delay had not caused inconvenience.

On a subsequent evening, two men dropped into Nevada City and purchased liquors, cigars, and provisions. Robert Finn, known locally as Kerrigan, was a grim-looking citizen not especially to be played with but otherwise favorably enough known. George Moore, his companion, was a small man with a tender eye which was given to weeping whenever he drew from his breast pocket daguerreotypes of wife and children in the East. A man who had known him at Rough and Ready seven years before recalled that he even then had carried those pictures and turned lachrymose whenever he drew them forth, which was about third drink time. Moore had later disappeared, and with reason. He was lodging mainly in the penitentiary during this interval—though twice escaping.

Supplies purchased, Finn and Moore departed for a "claim" they had at some unstated point.

On the dawn of May 15th it was Cal Olmstead at the reins of the Telegraph stage who was ambushed at the top of the grade north of Nevada City. "Get down, Cal, and keep your hands up." Six passengers were also routed out. Two highwaymen kept them peaceable with cocked revolvers. One passenger, discovered to be armed, was relieved of his six-shooter, its caps removed, and the instrument courteously returned. "Gentlemen, we don't want anything from you, but we are after Wells Fargo's treasure, and we mean to have it."

Since the holdup of John Majors' stage the express company had substituted a stronger box. Though they had two sledges and a crowbar, the robbers for a moment were foiled. But only for a moment. From the fruitful bushes of the roadside they produced a can of black powder with the remark that they'd take the treasure or blow the stage into the Yuba River. Passengers also glimpsed, through the parted thicket, a complete blacksmithing outfit.

First blast rattled the coffer but failed to burst the lock. One of the passengers, Ned Hatfield, was moved to chaff.

"You've called me before and found I held a pretty good hand," said a masked man sternly: a remark which set Hatfield to thinking back swiftly over whom he had lately played poker with. "We'll give it another try, and if we don't succeed we'll come again. We are bound to have Wells Fargo's treasure. We are strictly 'on' it."

The second charge was generously proportioned. It was tamped down under the big brass padlock with earth. Hills and heavens danced to the detonation. The lock lay asunder. A buckskin bag heavy with gold was lifted out and swung over the leader's shoulder.

"I've got $3,500 in there," moaned Hatfield.

"Wells Fargo will settle with you. They always do."

Before departing, Jack Williams brought forth a flask and assuaged each discommoded passenger with a drink of brandy. Bag on shoulder, he then followed his mates into the brush.

When the wildly excited stage galloped into Nevada City, smoke of breakfast fires was rising and first shafts of sunlight were streaming down over Chalk Bluff Ridge.

These repeated robberies were a nuisance. Sheriff Gentry swallowed his breakfast and was joined by a posse of five volunteers. Needle-hunting, they called it, as they plunged into the chaparral leading down the fifteen-hundred-foot descent to the river.

Head-high and brittle, chaparral is an unbelievably snug cover for operators who would rather collect treasure by forced loans than by sweaty endeavor. It grows in somewhat scattered clumps in its search for ground water, leaving natural lanes whose windings and twistings offer a thousand choices of pathway for escaping men and a thousand bewilderments for their pursuers. Nevertheless two of the scattered posse uncovered footprints. These they followed for a mile and a half. The quarry had evidently headed downstream. One of the trackers went back for horses, with instructions to lead them to Black's Crossing a short way below.

The remaining tracker proceeded on foot with utmost caution. There had been late spring rains; the prints of the "ghost" and his comrades were tidily preserved. They led straight down to the South Yuba, a torrent bawling lustily of its recent birth in high Sierra snowbanks. Across the stream Myer's Ravine shot northward at an abrupt ascending angle.

If the South Yuba had a lot to say about its late sky nursery, Myer's Creek was positively rhetorical. It chattered and screamed between high, sun-concealing walls. The stream was at flood. Its bed was a choke of rocks, trees, brush, and logs. The solitary man-tracker, deafened by the tumult, moved up this cul-de-sac warily, slipping from boulder to boulder. Occasionally, just occasionally, there was scratch of wet hobnails on the granite in front of him. Tracks that would dry out and vanish in another quarter-hour. No time now to go back for help, and no way to deploy other men along those vertical walls anyway. . . .

A rock twenty feet high, splitting the torrent, rose ahead of him. Two or three trees formed a tassel at its downstream summit. About its base were other granite chunks, flung down in past cataclysm from the brinks above. Below the stream-splitting rock a yelling waterfall took a fifteen-foot leap, filling the ravine with spray. Good place to keep ammunition dry—and trigger handy.

Climbing doggedly with feet, knees, and one hand, Steve Venard reached the top of this fall. A half-shattered log led to the base of the islet. The man-tracker advanced over this bridge, stepped ashore around a granite block, and came full on Jack Williams' Ghost. The ghost was cocking and leveling a long .44 revolver.

Williams and Venard sighted each other at the same instant. And at the instant, Venard's rifle leaped to his shoulder. Also, at the instant, Venard saw Finn, alias Kerrigan, drawing bead on him from the summit of the islet.

No time to change targets. Venard drilled Jack Williams' Ghost directly and speedily through the heart. A flip of trigger-guard and another half-ounce cone of lead was in firing position, just where Tyler Henry had once pledged Mr. Winchester it would be. The second shot, dispatched before echo of the first had caromed off the cliffs, sped upward and spattered on the canyon wall, having entered Finn's skull below the right eye and toured his skull en route. A scramble for the top of the islet proved the third bandit vanished. Venard kicked leaves over the Wells Fargo buckskin bag which lay beside Finn's body, took new bearings on the ravine that still mounted by high, wet terraces in front of him, and set up its eastern face.

Bandit Number Three was doubling and twisting like a hare along the steep brush-covered hillside. Venard's rapid shot all but nipped him. The quarry turned at bay, full of fight, as its dust spurted in his face. The next shot out of the pursuing Henry explored his heart, sent his spirit winging and his person crashing downhill into the canyon.

The rest of the posse found Venard sitting on the buckskin bag, communing with his plain old, well oiled rifle. The odds had been three to one and the three had been under cover while he had advanced in the open; each adversary in that one high-blazing instant had held fair bead on him; yet here they were. Three dead men, two of them still clutching cocked revolvers, and one live deputy. But—four expended bullets. The Henry must be getting old. Steve Venard was regretful.

The stage had been robbed at 4:30 A.M. It now was noon. The treasure was back in express company keeping by two P.M.

The governor of California commissioned Venard a lieutenant-colonel of militia "for meritorious services in the field," and the express company made over to him its $3,000 reward money and, with considerable celerity, a brand-new, suitably inscribed sixteen-shot Henry. It had become fixed policy with the express management, when a man showed himself adept at gunning bandits, to present him with a fine rifle and its hearty compliments.

XI

REVERSING THE EMIGRANT TRAIL

In their first dozen years the Poker Flats, Rough and Readies, Hell-out-of-Noons, and Angels Camps of the Mother Lode produced $585,000,000 in gold. In its first seven years Wells Fargo alone conducted down from the mines some $59,000,000. But discovery was preparing to vault the Sierra wall. From the first, gold had been known in southern Oregon. Certain undisproved Spanish legends were then recollected concerning Arizona's Gila Valley. Presently color was found in pine-shaded British Columbia. Where reality was demonstrated, Wells Fargo pressed forward with the rest. It was one of the first establishments of each new camp. Its messengers were on all routes, its express coffers on every stagecoach, and on tinkling mule teams long before the trails widened into wheel tracks.

The men of '49 and '50, as they raced west, had regarded everything between them and California as just so much geography to be hurdled, dodged, and departed as rapidly as possible. The Washoe Mountains of "Western Utah" were all of that. Grotesque uptilts, they were boulder-strewn, sage-drab, sun-cracked. Their folds had little pasturage, their creek beds little song. Perhaps a few overlanders, seeking grass for famishing stock, had wandered into Gold Canyon or up Six Mile Creek just off the Carson Valley trail. But for the California-bound tens of thousands who came streaming over the intermountain plateau, up the green-fringed Carson, and on toward the Sierra Nevada, those Washoes were just lumps left over by the Almighty while he was fashioning real mountains beyond.

The Mormons were in less of a hurry. They turned seeing eyes up the rivulets that trickled off the Washoe height later called successively Sun Peak, Mount Pleasant, and finally Mount Davidson. What they found, six thousand feet above the sea and two thousand feet above Humboldt Sink, was yellow and granular. It was not in abundance, but there was enough of it to impel Brigham Young to summon home to Salt Lake his wandering Latter-Day Saints in fear that what they had found would make them too worldly. Ventured then into those shadeless hills other men, not Latter-Day or any other kind of saints, but weary souls who had found California too far, or evil souls who had found its vigilance committees too tough. They picked up a little gold, enough to make wages, and called their camp Johntown.

In '53 the Grosch boys, Hosea and Ethan Allen, puzzled over a peculiar muck which glued up shovels and ruined tempers. "A dark gray mass," they wrote home to Parson Grosch, their parent in Pennsylvania. "Resembles thin sheet-lead." It looked like "carbonate of silver." They slipped over the granite crests to Downieville for a secret assay, blinked fast at what they learned, returned to the Washoes, built a little furnace, and set to a systematic diagraming of the whole region. But Hosea Grosch died of blood-poisoning from a blow of a pick, and his brother, trying to cross the Sierra in midwinter, perished in a blizzard. Only Henry P. T. ("Old Pancake") Comstock, who had been left in their cabin as caretaker, knew—if anyone—what was jotted in their notebooks.

The citizens of Johntown and the other rag settlements about Sun Peak went on picking about for the scanty yellow glint. Ten years of dwelling beside the emigrant track had drawn to Washoe's settlements but four hundred souls. California, just over the abrupt wall, had acquired her hundred thousands. Sun Peak slept on. "Old Pancake," if he knew anything of the Grosch boys' secret, evidently did not know enough. While other residents plied desultory picks he squatted over his fire, eyes ranging the hills, tossing idly on the fry-pan his favorite and indigestible comestible.

Such was the situation when the 10th of June, 1859, shone on those ragtag diggers. Looking down over the shoulder of one as he pressed heavy foot to shovel were the towers of phantom cities; with the sucking uplift came whole sweeps of sagebrush turned into imperial states. But the miners grouped about the shovel didn't see all this. They saw only a load of that sticky gray muck. The stuff was the natural tailing of the Silver Lode, the latchstring to the treasure-vault of a hemisphere. Pete O'Riley and Pat McLaughlin did not know they had hold of the digit 4 followed by eight dizzy, dancing, crazy ciphers. They knocked the silver sulphide off their shovels and heaved it into Six Mile Creek.

Next day their tools rang on something: a ledge of quartz. It was the top of the Ophir mine, entry to the hillside fissure that in twelve years was to disgorge $145,000,000. At the surface it was worth $1,595 in gold and $4,791 in silver to the ton. Two sides of bacon and a gallon of whisky for each shovelful tossed out.

Six months later the folds of Sun Peak contained an anarchists' paradise of pushing, fighting, delving humans; "Old Virginny" Finney or Fennimore had fallen, smashed his bottle, and hiccuped "I christen this here town Virginia"; "Old Pancake" had clamped his name forever to the Comstock Lode; the discoverers had sold out for a song and departed; and the richest, whoopingest mining camp of them all had come to crown Washoe Hills and dislocate the monetary affairs of nations. Two years after, Nevada was a state. Within twenty years the Lode produced seven million tons of ore, one hundred eighteen million dollars in dividends, sixty-two millions in assessments, three gigantic booms, three titanic collapses, a whole new order of millionaires and paupers, and a Boot Hill stuffed with murderers, merchants, harlots, gamblers, innocent bystanders, and honest men inebriated and fallen down shafts.

Winter comes early to the Pacific cordillera. Scarcely had convincing word of the find reached San Francisco in the shape of bullion silver before flakes were falling in the uplands. They fell on what was left of the old Emigrant Trail, blotting out its weed-choked wheels, broken axles, discarded bullock yokes and whited bones. From the high crags, the high pines, the flakes swirled down. They filled the hollows to six, twelve, twenty feet.

With earliest spring the treasure-rush was renewed. In and through the toiling trains of freight wagons, plunging horses, struggling mules, smashed carts, and overturned dumps of blankets and provision boxes whipped the stage-coaches of the Pioneer Stage Line, Swan & Company, and other contenders. A stream of traffic about half as dense was playing over Henness Pass to northward, where Langton and the great California Stage Company were lashing through.

A shaft was sunk on the site of the discovery mine. Its four-foot quartz ledge widened to twenty. To forty. Men's eyes bulged. The report did not diminish as it leaped the leagues.

Early in the fifties and long before the Comstock Lode discovery, a celebrated reinsman named Jared Crandall had undertaken to drive up the Sierras from the California side with a Concord coach. In a fine June week, with benefit of little or no roadway save the ruts of emigrant wagons of '49, this enterprising whip had lashed a four horse stage triumphantly up and over the double granite crest and down into the sagebrush at the edge of Salt Lake basin. The line he was extending already ran coaches down on the lowlands between Sacramento and Placerville. Now it began providing a tri-weekly service up and over the Sierras to "Western Utah"—the present Nevada line. Crandall did not foresee the enormous strike that was to occur in the Washoe hills just beyond, or the tremendous traffic that was to result from it. His line passed through an intermediary to Louis McLane, the general agent of Wells, Fargo & Company, in a deal which must be regarded as one of the luckiest pranks fate ever played on that otherwise much-plagued corporation. The transfer marked the entry of the big banking-express company into the field of stagecoach ownership and operation, a field it was to dominate for a decade and a half from the Pacific clear to the Rockies and beyond.

Virginia City's first two-story building, Pearlman & Newman's store, was just going up, and Penrod, Comstock & Co., two of the "discoverers"— for "Old Pancake" considered himself one—were occupying a tent on Sutton and A streets when Dave Ward as Wells Fargo agent took up his quarters in a tent near by. A few months later the Wells Fargo Washoe Express was moving into its own two-story brick building on C Street facing Sun Peak, now renamed Mount Davidson. Pioneer Stage Company and Overland Mail Company had their offices in the same structure. Charley Sturm's Express Bar served choice refreshments in the basement. Below Charley's establishment was the vault into which bullion was locked, pending outward shipment; and beneath that was yet more wealth, of an amount unguessed, in the galleries and stopes of the unplumbed future.

As banker and expressman to the extraordinary West in this, its latest and most extraordinary phase, Wells, Fargo & Company sat behind stout fire-resisting iron shutters. To and away from that wooden-awninged porch moved a ceaseless human traffic. In and out through the throng

moved William M. Stewart and John P. Jones, neither a
Nevada millionaire yet, their hands reaching for Charley
Sturm's tall bumpers in geniality. In and out moved
Mills, Sharon, Hearst; moved Jim Fair, "Slippery Jim,"
practical miner and draw-poker player extraordinary;
moved four-dollar-a-day John Mackay, hands rough from
toil, whose hairy arms would presently hug something like
fifty million dollars. Across the dusty way were the
brokers' offices, their windows posting the latest quotations
on Comstock mines received by wire from San Francisco.
Soaring, plunging, leaping, swooping, a dollar a "foot"
on the vein today, a thousand dollars tomorrow, fifty cents
today, fifteen hundred tomorrow, up and down went those
reason-wrecking figures like cages in a mine shaft.

Three hundred and six million dollars, in less than
three decades, issued from those Comstock mine mouths
and rushed like lava for the sea. In the four decades following, a hundred million more. The United States passed
through money panic and returned to specie payment by
Washoe treasure. San Francisco capped herself with
Washoe-built hotels, office structures, palaces. The flaming walls and towers of 1906 were in no small part a
Comstock fire-dance performed beside the Golden Gate.
The nation had become spanned with telegraph wires built
with Comstock millions. The West had become criss-
crossed with Comstock-financed rails. Old Pancake, Old
Virginny, and their mates, like Jim Marshall before them,
drifted off forlorn. Suicides and ne'er-do-wells, upon
them the goddess of Fortune, wearing one slipper of
gold and one of silver, had smiled once and vanished.

With the tide of Washoe-bound stage travel steadily rising, the glory of the Pioneer Line and of stagecoaching in general now climbed to its briefly held zenith. Three tight-packed days and two wayside nights were in the earlier times required for the upward journey. This with improving roadbed was steadily whittled. The seventy-two miles from summit to Placerville, a drop of seven thousand feet, came to be flung behind regularly in seven hours including all stops. Special occasions produced special effects. W. H. "Shotgun" Taylor (name derived from a successful argument with a bullwhacker) twirled three distinguished editors and a Speaker of the House through fifty miles of downhill grandeur in considerably less than four hours, depositing at the bottom a speaker speechless and the editors numb from something more than writers' cramp.

The Pioneer Line's great rival, the California, continued to carry its Comstock-bound passengers by the other pass back of Grass Valley and Nevada City. Magnificent in equipment and daring in its schedules was the California. Since '54 it had dominated the coaching of the state. By 1860, along the 710-mile Sacramento–Portland route alone its stations were stocked with 500 silky-coated horses. Its lines radiated everywhere in the Mother Lode. High discussion raged in every tavern over the comparative merits of the two main routes to Virginia City. To argue horse speed was to promote a horse-race, and nothing to El Doradan or Comstocker could be more engaging. Result—cross-country steeplechases of bouncing stagecoaches, with mountain ranges for hurdles.

So over winding mountain shelves where a slide of six inches would seemingly send stage, horses, trunks, and passengers in a thousand-foot aerial dive for the piney depths; where angry stream-bed foamed below, and aloft the fir-tipped ridges swam in sunlight, the Sierra jehu danced his passengers through on thorough-braces. His land-going craft dived at the mountains like a clipper upon high-piled ocean swells. Millionaire and muck shoveler, prima donna for Piper's Opera House and Chinese cook for Mrs. Moch's boarding house rode uncomplainingly, jubilantly, on those heaving strap-springs. Armed messengers rode beside the driver as the years wore on, or inside or concealed for battle in the baggage boot. Road-knights with masks and shotguns waited behind the yard-thick stems of the yellow pines. On the Pioneer and its great rival the California coursed. Each vale and pasture was stocked with satiny horses. Each ten or a dozen miles offered smithy, wayside resort, and relay station. Behind Pioneer's steeds, fifteen hundred passengers a month went skimming. In '64 the line averaged sixty passengers daily between California and Nevada, whisking them through by daylight over a dust-quenched road— in certain seasons the smoothest highland turnpike in the nation.

But not always smooth. In winter it became half impassable. Fifteen hours could be consumed laboring the forty-eight miles to Strawberry fifty-five hundred feet up. The winter scenery was grand, almost terrific. Branches of pines drooped to the ground under loads of snow. Gorges were filled with drifts. Tempests howled through the evergreens. In gathering twilight under nature's Christmas trees the coaches would bring their passengers up to the great yellow doorway of Strawberry Tavern. When the stage thundered up with clatter and flourish, and innkeeper, hostler, and postmaster joined in greeting the commander of the equipage, travelers turned stamping to the big barroom, the roaring chimney, the board well laden for the hungry, and beds laid open for the wayworn; though if travel was unusually heavy, midnight arrivals might have to seek their rest on baggage, plank floors, and stacks of shining "Washoe bricks."

Hoofs stamping again at dawn, all were off and away: three miles farther to be transferred to trains of sleighs drawn by six tail-whisking horses, and to skim on knives through the sharp air, into tunnels of dark snow-supporting boughs and out again. Under clear light of morning the summit would be reached and the seventy square miles of sky-mirroring Lake Tahoe would be in view saucered by snow-capped crests. Then on for Lake Valley, over a road hacked out of the mountain side, and down the joyous sleighs would flow like the wind. A rushing ride of six miles along the valley floor would bring all to Mac's station, where buckwheat cakes, strong waters, and smoking dishes of big lake trout awaited; to be followed by another dash, this time in a Concord mudwagon, up and over Daggett's Notch and down to Carson Valley, where snows soon vanished and all was sandy desert.

In 1864, thirty-three of the Pioneer Line's finest coaches voyaged around Cape Horn. Virginia City welcomed and renewed welcome of their clatter for a few ensuing years.

After that they fanned forth into service all over the West. They saw the outposts of Idaho, Montana, Wyoming, Oregon. They rattled in and out of Bannock and Deadwood. Toughnut Street in Tombstone heard their whipcrack and coach-horn. The handsome scenic effects painted on their panels gradually yielded to wind and weather. Their curtains and leather boots became riddled with arrows and bullets. Their ironwork turned rustily red under rain and blizzard. Yet on they fought, land-sailing clippers, frigates of defiance, bold galleons of commerce, to course the West until the last oxhide thorough-brace parted; and then pass over the rim of some arroyo and into legend. When they arrived, there were only five years left before the steam locomotive would replace both ox and horse on the trail across the continent; but there were many more years of usefulness and excitement awaiting those coaches on the byways of the coastal, mountain and intermountain country.

A feature of its Comstock service, as elsewhere, was the Wells Fargo fast freight, which moved up and down the Sierra roads in high-wheeled, canvas-covered wagons attached to six big horses. Machinery, fruits, vegetables, poultry, fresh fish and assorted merchandise took this conveyance, which galloped through almost as fast as the express stages. On the box beside the driver a "swamper" sat with five-foot horn, tootling blasts far and wide to clear mule-trains and buckboards out of the way for the Fast Freight's coming. Passengers at low fare rode inside with the merchandise on such seats as they could manage.

On a wintry morn of the mid-sixties two live articles,

an Irish miner and circular negress, left Virginia City under the Fast Freight's canvas top. In company with them journeyed caskets containing a miner late of Austin, Nevada, and a departed lady of the Washoe hills.

Friday's station near the summit was passed; night settled down. The great vehicle creaked and plunged. Wind moaned in the pines. Human and all other freight, living and departed, bounced and jounced. The driver's swamper just about that time got an idea. He parted the curtains behind his seat and pushed through his mega-phone-like horn until its mouth rested between the pair of coffins.

"Isn't it awful to be dead?" a voice murmured beneath the legs of the living passengers.

White traveler and black turned startled faces toward each other.

"It is that, and mighty disrespectful to us dead to be tumbled about."

"There's an Irishman," complained the first corpse, "sitting on my neck."

"I've got a fat cook on my chest," contributed the other, "and she weighs about two hundred and fifty pounds."

The freight wagon pulled up at Yank's station. With a yell that reëchoed among the pinnacles, Afric's buxom daughter burst out over the top of the tailgate, closely followed by her Gaelic companion.

Pat, after a drink, consented to climb back. But Auntie resolutely affirmed she'd wait for the morning stagecoach.

XII

THE HOLD–UP AT BULLION BEND

TOM POOLE, an undersheriff at Monterey, had a prisoner whom the courts directed him to hang. As his hour drew near, the prisoner got a reprieve. But Tom Poole hanged him anyway. He explained that the document misspelled the prisoner's name, which surely nullified it; and that he had no doubt of the fellow's guilt in any event.

Tom Poole was a man of action.

He was also a man of business. When a poor laborer's assets were attached in satisfaction of $53.25, the undersheriff sequestered his mare, stallion, work horse, two wagons, and thirty-seven hens and, according to the contemporary chronicle, charged him for "use of Poole's corral $32, hire of man $42, barley and hay to 3 horses, 7 days, $21, taking care of hens $12," and other fees, in all $168, to the utter ruin of that father of many children.

All of which matters were several years dispatched when, with a bright June dawn of 1864, two of a long string of coaches rolled up to Wells Fargo's Virginia City office from the Pioneer-Overland stables over by Boot Hill. The Queen of Camps was in general a single men's paradise, but among the California-bound twenty-eight passengers were four in basques, berthas, paletots, waterfalls, and handkerchief bonnets: cone-shaped beings fourteen yards around the hem. Driver Ned Blair, a personage in a magnificent waistcoat, white hat, and perfect gloves, disposed of two women and twelve men about his coach with practiced skill—"Gentlemen back in the inside corners and ladies' hoops to the middle"—and received from Agent Valentine several sacks of treasure. Driver Charley Watson also stowed away fourteen, seven inside and seven on top, with a sixteen-year-old miss in Garibaldi jacket and big jet buttons on the seat of honor beside him. "Watch out, Ned, you don't get bushed!" "Better get down, Charley, and have a look behind each tree!" So the crowd in front of the stage station bantered. "All abo-o-ard!" responded the king-whips, and away those eager tally-hos leaped, up C Street hill and over Mount Davidson's shoulder, for coaches that load in Virginia City by morning must discharge in Placerville by night. Peter Headley, express and stage agent in Gold Hill, had more treasure waiting on the porch of his new two-story brick building. Adown vertical Main Street and through Gold Canyon, brakes locked hard and all wheels sliding—west for Carson town and up the sky-propping Sierras. . . . Kingsbury's Station. . . . Friday's Station. . . . Mac's beside the blue mile-and-a-quarter-high Lake Tahoe, then called "Bigler." . . . Up from Lake Valley for Johnson's Pass, where late rains have made bogholes and the wheels suck deep—and Ned Blair gathers his ribbons, turns his head, and roars firmly: "All out"—saving the ladies, of course, God bless them—"and push!"

Gores, berthas, basques, paletots, gimps, handkerchief

bonnets, and fourteen-yard hems do not push stagecoaches. But there is no such luck for wide-awake or stovepipe hats and cashmere breeches. Thus over the crest, and all aboard again; through sugar-pine lanes and aisles of majestic red fir; at full spin around curves so sharp that the leaders vanish. But on Ned Blair guides his craft, and directly in his tracks comes Charley Watson, cigar uptilted, loquacity unending, foot resting lightly on footboard and brake. Afternoon glides into evening. Red dusk fills the canyon mouths and colors the tops of the yellow pines. Up from the Sacramento Valley rises a billow of midsummer heat.

It is ten o'clock. The Gothic crags and gables have given place to rounded lowland domes. Firs and pines have yielded to scrub oak and manzanita. Fourteen miles, and the lights of Placerville will twinkle. Ned Blair, never talkative, sits his Concord now in perfect silence. Charley Watson, teller of tall yarns, is tongue-weary at last on the coach barging along behind; the sixteen-year-old who sat all day beside him has crawled down inside and gone to sleep. Only an hour and a quarter to go. "Up now, Beauty. Step out, Prince!" Coach-curtains rustle, well-greased axles churn, yellow wheels skim briskly around a wide bend . . .

"Pull up, or we'll fire!"

Blair's coach slides to a halt. Passengers lurch and pile. An ex-policeman inside is jolted awake, and with large confusion hides his revolver between his legs under the cushion.

Ned Blair sits imperturbable. A ruffian on the bank at his left holds a heavy pistol directly on him. By the

James B. Hume, for long the Chief Special Agent, Wells, Fargo & Co., and nemesis of hundreds of stagecoach brigands.

candles of his coach lamps Blair studies this fellow: hooded, menacing, a second pistol thrust in his belt beside an ugly blade. In the corner of his eye Blair sees other hooded persons. The woods are full of them.

"We'll detain you but a moment. All we want is Wells Fargo's treasure." A figure climbs up, fumbles under Blair's feet, and four heavy sacks clank to the ground. More coachwheels, more hoofs approach. "Drive on a hundred yards, then stop again," directs the genteel drawl.

As Blair's stage draws off, the ex-police officer pulls out his revolver and fires point-blank through a rear window. There is a startled shout. The ball has smacked full on the pistol-handle of the robber who held the horses.

The desperadoes buzz like hornets. "We oughta line up and shoot the whole bunch. That's the way guerrillas handle them, don't they, cap'n?" By now the second stage has come into view. Charley Watson speaks up quickly. He pledges that no shooting will come from the vehicle under his command. He also urgently addresses his passengers. His team, they will remark, is on a grade; one jerk and the whole turnout might go down the bank.

The outlaw-chief approaches respectfully. He is tall, slim, urbane. "Gentlemen and ladies—for I see some of the sympathetic sex among you—I will tell you who we are. We are not ordinary robbers, but a company of Confederate soldiers. We do not prey on private citizens. Please do nothing foolish. All we want is Wells Fargo's bullion, to help us recruit for our army."

Watson throws out two sacks of silver. They ring expensively in the dust. One of the men suspects Charley of holding out something. He climbs to inspect behind the footboard, and two more treasure bags sail out, followed by a box of assorted express.

While search and confiscation are in progress, the miss of sixteen from her coach window braves the chieftain's revolver and engages him in repartee. It draws in two or three of his mates. With impudent curiosity she quizzes the freebooters about their calling. How are they going to carry off the heavy bullion? Where will they dispose of it? How do they live, and what do they do for their washing and mending? As she chats, the long-barreled .44 navy revolver occasionally brushes past her audacious nose. She requests the chief to lower it. Fra Diavolo acquiesces, assuring her that Southerners are dedicated to protecting, not frightening ladies. The conversation provoked by the juvenile is listened to attentively by her fellow travelers. It may aid later in voice identification.

A hat is passed for the bleeding Confederacy, and the leader hands Watson a prepared receipt signed by "Captain Ingram." With mutual farewells the stages and robbers part, the former burning the road to get to the telegraph office at Thirteen Mile House. With the adieus our narrative passes from the elegant to the terrific.

While babble and excitement were at crescendo in Thirteen Mile House, two men strolled in. Their masks were off and they kept apart from the travelers two-deep at the tavern bar. But their voices seemed to have familiar timbre. When the two coaches reached Placerville, the sheriff was organizing a pursuit party and Wells Fargo was already out with rewards of $1,000 for its treasure and $300 for each marauder.

Six hundred dollars' worth of the latter was promptly hauled out of bed at Thirteen Mile House by Sheriff Rogers' deputies. Among the weapons found in their clothing was one of peculiar ornament which Blair thought he remembered, except that the muzzle, when it had yawned on him from the roadbank, had looked about as big as a mine mouth.

Study of tracks indicated that several of the band had fled for the north fork of the Cosumnes River. This was rugged country. Deputy Staples and Constable Ranney, sending a third man back for aid, plunged ahead.

A crossroads tavern known as Somerset House stood on an oak-studded hillside twelve miles distant. It was a two-story frame hostelry of the coastal type with all public rooms and guest rooms opening on a narrow veranda. Staples approached cautiously and managed to catch sight of Mrs. Maria Reynolds, the taverness, getting breakfast in her kitchen.

"Hist!" the deputy signaled. She came out to him. "There's been a big robbery on the Placerville road—"

She nodded, and jerked her head toward the first room opening on the veranda. Farther along a shotgun leaned against the outside wall. This Staples snatched.

Ranney meanwhile marched boldly into Room No. 1. Six men were sprawled on bed and couch. They looked up startled. Ranney courteously beamed, "Good morning." He added:

"Can you gentlemen tell me the way to Grizzly Flat?"

"Ask the landlady."

The chorus was surly. Ranney delicately retired.

As he stepped out the door, which was kicked shut in his face, he met Joe Staples approaching. The deputy was grimly cocking the appropriated shotgun. Ranney seized his shoulder, whispered: "Hold on! We're right on top of them." But Staples had recently been in a brush with the Ike McCollum gang, stage robbers who had shot up a fellow deputy, and had heard rumors that his courage had been questioned. These half-dozen outlaws would make a tasty gag to stuff down the throats of his maligners. He lifted a heavy bootsole and kicked open the door.

"You are my prisoners!" he shouted.

Gunpowder belched. Staples reeled and fell. As the rush of buckshot entered his body his own charge tore across the room, brushing one of the occupants.

The discharge that slew Staples also ripped into George Ranney. By this time the room of "cultured" secessionists had become a den of wild animals.

With odds of five to a riddled one, Ranney tried to flee. He bounded for a tree, then for a big boulder fifty yards up the road. Another missile caught him in the side.

"Any more of you blood-money men around here?" The robbers were about him in a menacing circle.

"No," gasped Ranney.

"Did you think two damned Yankees could capture six Confederate soldiers?"

"Sixty!"

"Put some more lead into him!" A gun-muzzle was pressed to his head.

"Aren't you ashamed! Shooting a dead man!"

It was Mrs. Reynolds, fresh from her hotcake griddle. Vigorously she pushed the bravos aside and knelt to the stricken constable. "For shame! You pack of cowards!"

Sheepishly the "Confederates" lowered their weapons, sidled off to the barn, and fetched their horses. One dashed into the inn and stripped the dead deputy of sixty-five dollars and his pistols. Shouting that they were staunch Jeff Davis men and non-surrenderers, the quintet made off.

Mrs. Reynolds and a woman guest bore the half-dead Ranney into the house and managed to pull him back from the shadows.

Staples had been a popular officer. Fifty men were out before next daylight. While the victim was being buried with a full turnout of the militia and fire department at Placerville, the man he had wounded was brought in. This rogue announced through his bandages that he was Tom Poole, former undersheriff of Monterey County; that he knew nothing about any robbery, but had fallen in with the gang at the tavern only that morning. Charley Watson, listening to his voice, opined otherwise.

Searchers meanwhile ransacked the surroundings at Somerset House. Under the sill of the barn they found a bar of Comstock silver. In the woods they found a fine horse, saddled and bridled and equipped with blanket-roll, powder, bullets, and provisions for a long ride. The fugitives were trailed up a ten-mile gulch, past a ranch where they had stopped to buy bread and hay, and were seen to be making for the Big Tree trans-Sierra road.

Then set in as furious a chase as ever thrilled the Mother Lode. Down dark canyons, up rugged mountain sides, through thorny chamisal the posses raced. The desperadoes, strongly mounted, kept ever ahead. In Calaveras County to southward the trail became lost. The fugitives ascended a mountain where the summit view was wide, picketed their worn horses and rolled up for a good night's rest. Toward midnight the sentinel, peering down from his eyrie, saw the silhouettes of armed men pass from black shadow into brilliant moonlight. He kicked up his companions; they were out of blankets with a bound. Some were for fighting it out. They were overruled. As the mounting figures approached, moving in and out of the shadows of trees with obvious efforts at concealment, Jeff Davis' irregulars with a yell broke and fled down the other side, leaving horses, saddles, blankets and another bar of bullion.

Their commotion and flight completely disorganized the ascending party. For the visitors were not manhunters, but late associates of Ike McCollum—independent fugitives. They had just made a clutch for the Georgetown stage and were now pushing hell-for-leather for the same hideaway that nested "Captain Ingram's" band. Close on their heels was pounding Undersheriff James B. Hume, who later became an illustrious chief of Wells Fargo's detective forces. Hume's astonishment at the uproar on the mountain top, whence two detachments of stage-robbers were fleeing from each other in opposite directions, was not cleared up until a day later when he learned of the coach robbery above Thirteen Mile House and its Somerset sequel.

From the Mother Lode country the fleeing road agents made their way on foot down into San Joaquin Valley, crossed the state, and reorganized near San José.

South of that town lay the rich New Almaden quicksilver mine. Individuals lurking in the vicinity, known to residents as Wallace Clendenning, John C. Bulwer, and Al Glassby, ascertained that a pay roll was going to the mine on a night of mid-July.

The trio knocked up the ranch house of one Hill on the New Almaden road, demanding refreshment and lodging. Drawing Hill aside, they told him that the mine agent would soon be along with $10,000; that a hundred soldiers of Jeff Davis were at their backs; that he could throw in with them and share riches, or prove unaccommodating and be killed. The badly rattled rancher accepted the secessionist view of the matter, changed his mind, dressed in his Sunday best—a man always likes to make a neat corpse—told the robbers he was going out to pump water for his stock, crept into the tall wheat, and made the mile and a half to San José on his hands and knees in record time.

Midsummer's sun was just sinking beyond the Coast Range in a Gettysburg of crimson when Sheriff Adams finished throwing his cordon around the Hill ranchhouse and boldly stepped up. A pistol ball spat from the doorway and struck the officer's breast with what amounted to a clang. It had met his huge silver watch and caromed off. The farthest-west battle of the Great Rebellion was on.

Guns popping, the guerrillas sprang from the trap. Deputy Brownlee went down with two shots in the leg. Bulwer, leading the sally, flung his arms skyward, spun and dropped. Glassby, a youth of nineteen, was over-hauled and captured. Examined later, his clothing was found well sieved and the handle of his pistol shattered, its ramrod bent like a hairpin. It was the weapon Police-man McDougall had smashed with his point-blank shot from the coach at Bullion Bend.

The third desperado, Clendenning, was heavily salted in the back by buckshot, but with jackrabbit leaps made off into the thicket. Subsequently two civilians heard his groans, investigated, and pulled him out half paralyzed. Two hours later in San José jail he turned his face to the wall. Somewhere two others were fleeing—last remnants of Captain Ingram's "Rangers."

Glassby, flanked by officers and express agents, repaired to a spring in the hills near Bullion Bend and extracted all but $3,000 of the plunder of the Washoe Express. The rest had been recovered.

Fourteen months later, with the Rebellion past its Appomattox and all arms grounded, the prisoner calling himself Thomas B. Poole and undersheriff of Monterey, ascended the scaffold in Placerville's courthouse yard, conversed pleasantly with his custodians, and shook each by the hand. The prisoner made no public address, which was satisfactory to Sheriff Rogers; that officer of the law had been criticized considerably about the distraction of his district and was glad to get on with the business.

XIII

THE STAGECOACH CHIVALROUS

DISTANCE, in his day as now in retrospect, lent glamor to the stagecoach picaroon. But there had to be distance. Close inspection generally proved him to be an uncouth tramp, at his best an unmitigated nuisance, at less than his best a vicious fellow whose very inexpertness might cost the life of a stage horse or a passenger.

But the fable of picturesqueness did have help. Tom Bell, kneeling to dress the leg wound of a victim he had just pistoled; Dick Fellows, who couldn't take a purse without exchanging a bit of banter; Black Bart, single-handedly stopping twenty-eight coaches and lifting polite hat to the ladies—these were craftsmen with an air.

So, by a few artists here and there, was molded the legendary character of the road agent. A courteous rogue, whose style of joking just happened to be too far on the practical side. A hard-working operator who, buffeted by fate, was just trying to get even by dueling with the overgrown express company. A debonair adventurer who wanted nothing from private travelers if the treasure box was lined, and who was on excellent—almost too excellent—terms with the driver. Pillage and rough handling and disruption of the transport medium itself, leaving

passengers to walk where miles were long, did not ex-
tinguish the tradition. Robin Hood lived on. There
were just enough reincarnations of him to give the head-
line "Another Stage Robbery" a romantic thrill for all
who weren't present.

When the two Grass Valley to Colfax stages were
stopped one morning, the pair of waylayers shook the
express box of the first coach, decided that it was too light
to be worth smashing, and returned it with a smile and
a pleasantry. They did the same for the second stage, and
took both drivers' words for it that they didn't have the
keys to the built-in safes inside. Nick Dodsworth and
his son, of Sacramento, were the travelers on the outside
front seat of the first stage. When it came passenger
Dodsworth's turn to be rummaged for valuables, he held
both hands very high; and a sympathetic robber noticed
that a thumb had recently been amputated.

"Are you a working man?" inquired the robber, as he
removed twenty or thirty dollars from Dodsworth's person.

"I am," conceded the sky-reaching victim.

"Well, it's tough enough for a working man to cripple
his hand without losing anything else"—and the rascal
returned Dodsworth's money and watch. During this
dialogue the passenger, while thankful to get back his
property, perceived out of the corner of an eye that the
other rogue was exceedingly nervous. At the earnest request of the man whose hands were up, and of driver
Bob Scott who still sat his perch, the footpad lowered his
fowling piece. But as its muzzle went down, both barrels

let loose. Dodsworth narrowly escaped being amputated of considerably more than his thumb. The robbers felt so bad about this bit of technical awkwardness that they gave back a dollar each to all concerned, asking that drinks on them be bought as soon as the stages got to Colfax.

The spirit of chivalry could be inside the coach as well as out. A fine degree of it, combined with a nice display of personal valor, was produced by a certain Colonel A. W. Von Schmidt one summer day in 1875. The colonel and friends were returning from a pleasure trip in the rugged volcanic highlands and forestlands of Plumas County. The down-bound Quincy coach was approaching Oroville, with seventeen miles to go. Its passenger list was composed of four men, two women and a boy—the women and two of the males being inside, and the rest distributed beside the driver and on the roof. As the vehicle moved slowly up hill, with a bank on one side and a declivity on the other, the rude order came: "Throw up your hands." Inside the coach there was the usual consternation. A voice spoke sharply: "Don't fire!"

One of the inside passengers was the doughty colonel. A glance through the window showed him a masked robber on shoeless feet. He thought he also saw others, but could not be sure. Confiding briefly to his companions that he felt a fight coming on, the colonel sprang out the opposite coach door, drawing his revolver. With a swift stride he was out in the open, where any fire leveled on him would not impinge on the coach. Sensing his strategy, and braving the risk of a buckshot salvo, the driver whipped up his team. That left the colonel alone. "Drop that gun!" yelled the military man, and charged.

This was no way for a passenger to act. The surprised robber obeyed. His twelve-gauge clattered in the dust as its owner fled, picking his stockinged feet painfully as he stepped among the manzanita brambles. The colonel did not pursue, his physical condition being no match for his fighting heart, but he soon came puffing up to the stage, bearing all the honors of the war and the enemy's armament likewise. The coach rolled on with $9,000 in dust and other express matter intact. Wells Fargo hastened to bestow on passenger and driver a pair of stem-winding, repeating, hunting-case gold watches from its inexhaustible store, and general superintendent Valentine was moved to admire the chivalry of a man who chose to fight without protection rather than endanger his companions. "The distinction between courage and bravery, and valor and gallantry," he commented in presenting the colonel's watch, "is a delicate one, but the latter are rarer and more highly prized qualities, and we hold that your action stamps you as a man both valorous and gallant."

With endless actors, illimitable scenery and uncountable exits and entrances, the express box melodrama was bound, some time or other, to reach the true climax of chivalry, and so one night in 1866 it befell.

Two coaches swing out of Reno and cross the long sagebrush flats to southward. It is close to midnight. A late October moon hangs over the distant Sierra Nevada, plating it with silver. Steamboat Springs out on Washoe plain dances in the moonlight like a geyser of opals. Fourteen passengers and much baggage occupy the two coaches. Driver John Burnett of the advance coach has also in his charge a big express chest, made of boiler iron, bolted fast to the bed of his stage. The vehicles move up the tortuous Geiger grade, scaling the forbidding rampart that guards and contains Virginia City. Three miles short of the Queen of Camps, at the top of the grade and before the twelve horses can collect for the downhill scamper, five shadows detach from the boulders and artemisia.

Burnett's foot goes hard on the brake; his hands go up. The shotgun pointed at his breast wavers with excitement.

"Better turn that aside, young feller," advises Burnett with the coolness of long stage-going. "It might go off, and the verdict would be death at the hands of person or persons unknown, but considerably suspected!"

The robber complies, admitting he doesn't want to shoot anyone, but might.

"You will all immediately descend." The voice of the leader strives to be gruff, but finds difficulty in keeping out the note mellifluous. "You will kindly be seated in a row while we transact business with the express company."

The fourteen stage-farers file down. One, J. F. Calderwood, finds opportunity to toss his wallet with $400 to the top of his vehicle. The hundred dollars remaining in his pockets is presently appropriated, together with Judge Baldwin's sixty dollars and various contributions from others. Nothing is taken from the drivers. "You fellows work hard for what you get, and probably haven't got much, anyhow." A Miss Crowell, only feminine passenger, is also gallantly exempted. She is just returning from a shopping fray in Paul Verdier's exciting Parisian *magasin* at San Francisco, and her hooped-out skirt-hem avoids the ground by three audacious inches. She is led to a rock and there she sits, in tight-sleeved basque, blue skirt, petticoats broidered with flowers and wheat-ears, and soft blue hood and cape framing throat, eyes, ringlets. The robber repairs to the coach, returns with robes and cushions. From Empire waist to big-buckled shoes he tucks her snugly. There is about him, thinks Miss Crowell with a flutter, rather an air of the military.

Horses have meanwhile been unhitched and led aside. Two Dick Turpins set about chiseling the big hasp from the iron express box.

It is nearing two A.M. Rummaging in the coaches, the robbers bring forth overcoats and more robes, and toss them to the passengers. There is discovered, with gaiety, a consignment of champagne in a rear boot. While two of the quintet toil with chisels, and one stands sentry, two others busy themselves popping corks for the pre-dawn Hallowe'en party. There are toasts to Miss Crowell, to Wells Fargo, to the Comstock; to the late Abe Lincoln, who two years ago this day signed Nevada's statehood. Then a toast to Miss Crowell again. It is all very sociable.

The hasp is off. A pound and a half of black powder, the content of two cans, is pushed in and around the lock and a four-foot fuse ignited. While Miss Crowell holds fingers to her ears, and a solicitous rogue stands by, the spark burns along the string, is swallowed within the coach, travels unseen toward its awaiting terminus.

"The artemisia," says Miss Crowell in a strained voice that she strives to keep casual, "is pretty by moonlight, don't you think?"

"Beautiful," answers the robber—he *is* of military bearing. "Simply beautiful—and so brave."

"I mean the artemisia—the sagebrush," corrects Miss Crowell, whose hood has tumbled back, revealing chignon disturbingly frizzled, a bobbing pair of big steel earrings, and the long ends of a blue velvet throat-ribbon hanging down her back like reins.

There is an earth-shaking blast. The lid of the coffer leaps up and an iron end blows out. The enclasping coach lurches in convulsion on its thorough-braces; its leather curtains fly out as though on the wings of a "Washoe zephyr." The defile is full of din and soaring fragments. Miss Crowell's scream and the startled jump of chignon, earrings, throat ribbons, and jet is smothered in a military investment. Like a tired old lady who has lapsed in her chaperonage, the Concord slumps amid its dishonored leather petticoats.

Miss Crowell takes her fingers from her ears and her nose from strange men's shoulders. The bandits take $4,150 from the coffer. John Burnett takes his horses from the bandits. The rear coach takes his passengers from John Burnett. The robbers take their departure from Geiger Pass. The moon takes a last look, disappears behind the Washoes. Away move eight wheels behind twelve sets of hoofs. Into the gaslight of never-sleeping Virginia City the two coaches clatter—the one in advance listing drunkenly like a little old lady who has been out very,

very late and has managed to make herself very, very disreputable. Back at the top of Geiger grade there remain only a scattering of stagecoach fragments, champagne corks and bottles, and the artemisia nodding knowingly.

"Again we are called upon to chronicle one of those daring highway robberies peculiar to the land of sagebrush," ply the bored fingers of a compositor in the office of the Virginia *Union*.

The searching sun comes up over Carson Sink, coloring the tip of Mount Davidson and the façades of the brawling town. Before it's an hour high, Wells Fargo will be out with a reward of $4,000 for its treasure and $1,000 for each of the bandits; the Bank of California with $2,500 and the governor of Nevada with $2,500 more. Before it sets, Miss Crowell in her new walking costume of looped-up poplin, and bonnet with small elegant swallow perched atop, will have scanned and avoided direct glance of every male she meets on A or B Street—wondering if handkerchief mask would make him look military; and Calderwood, Judge Baldwin, and the other passengers will have recounted their adventure in each bar from the International to the top of C Street hill.

To whom none will have listened with more sympathetic tongue-clucking than mellow-voiced "Big Jack" Davis.

XIV

AFFAIRS ON THE ALKALI TRAIL

MAILS from the East still lagged. Rails across Panama fitted the mule tracks, but there were still two weeks between packets and the steamship owners on both seas were insufferably arrogant. The impatience of the West with this roundabout arrangement was never quite comprehended along the Potomac. Weren't letters getting through from New York to San Francisco in three and a half weeks?

Ah, Mr. Postmaster-General and members of Congress, but the routes are alien and the rates extortionate. Transport on wheels across all-American territory, across mountains, plains and deserts with daily frequency, will make this a Union in very fact. The iron horse can do the pulling as soon as may be; meanwhile give us horses of hair, hide, hoofs—but give us an overland post. In 1856 there arrived at Washington seventy-five thousand names in urgent petition.

It produced results. There had been private efforts to create an overland post before. But the federal government now found $600,000 a year for a thrice-a-week mail. The six-year contract was won by John Butterfield, William G. Fargo and a group of other New York expressmen in hot competition with pioneering mail-stage operators of the west coast.

It took nearly a year to get ready, for the designated route dipped far to the south—a southern postmaster-general saw to that—and invaded an arid and inhospitable land. Wells were sunk into sands and gravels fifty, a hundred feet. Stations were built at twenty-mile intervals, strong enough to withstand Comanches and Apaches. Hay and provisions were brought into position by the high-piled ton; horses, mules, anvils, coaches and wagons innumerable. Drivers skilled at keeping spirited mustangs from stampeding into the wide mesquite, and station-tenders versed in shoeing mules to the whirr and plunk of occasional arrow, were marshaled and distributed. The one thing imperative to modern notions, a bit of genuine roadwork, was bothered with least of all. Let the mail and express bounce! The coaches rode on multiple straps, and if passengers rattled a trifle, there were arm straps for their steadying also. Army engineers graded down the "natural" highway as well as means permitted.

The selected route moved from forked starts at St. Louis and Memphis to a junction in the Ozarks and thence southwest to El Paso, west to Tucson and Yuma, and up the interior coastal valley to the Golden Gate. Though it was a thousand miles longer than the familiar Salt Lake or central pathway, the official explanation given for its nine-degree curve was avoidance of the Rocky Mountain and Sierra Nevada snows.

On September 15, 1858, the first two coaches of the Great Southern Overland Mail left their termini in the Mississippi Valley and on the edge of the Pacific Ocean

and set out on the magnificent 2730-mile swing to greet
and pass each other. Others followed at scheduled intervals. At seven o'clock on October 9, which was a Sabbath morning, San Francisco's late revelers on their way
to bed were regaled by the "taranta" of the transcontinental coach horn. Horses at gallop, wheels flinging
sand, twenty-four days out from St. Louis, the bright red
diligence tore into town with OVERLAND MAIL dancing on its head-rail. Near St. Louis the first eastbound
also stormed home amid wild applause. The longest continuous stage line in history was an operating fact.

By beating its schedule and arriving at such a distress-
ing hour, the first coach into its western halting place
cheated itself out of an appropriate welcome; but the second got in the next day, bearing one battered passenger
and an express, and met with enthusiasm stirring enough
for both. Pat Hunt, Wells Fargo messenger, intercepted
it south of town and took off its eastern newspapers.
Thrown from his horse, Pat rose, dusted himself, disre-
garded his anatomical derangements, commandeered another steed, and spurred on, leading the van of carriages
and buggies, while "men threw their hats under the horses'
heels, cheers vociferous and prolonged rent the air," and
the Monumental Fire Company touched off a salute of
gunpowder in the Plaza. The steamship from Panama
entered the Golden Gate a few hours later, bringing the
same budget of Atlantic coast dispatches. But the triumph
of land transportation was complete. The news borne by
the *John L. Stephens* had already arrived by stagecoach
and was leaping from the presses.

For the next two years, right powerfully Butterfield's

Great Southern Overland served the West, though howls never ceased over its wasteful and exasperating length. Troy and Concord stage wagons for five passengers were used at the start. Soon larger Concords went on the run, capacity six to nine inside. Baggage, mail and express went into the boot at the rear. If there were too many mail sacks, the excess went in with the human cargo, who fought with it, reclined on it or ignored it as best they could. Passengers paid $200 for the trip, a sum later reduced; ate catch-as-catch-can; got what sleep they could in the stage as it bucked and swayed, and gained in hardening what they missed in comfort.

The stages averaged five miles an hour day and night, making up at a gallop, where conditions favored, what they lost in fords, sand-holes, steeps, and detours. An armed guard or "conductor" rode beside the driver. Coaches were provided with three lights, but hostile demonstrations soon prompted their extinguishment and night driving was done in the dark, which didn't help the internal delight any. Mexican drivers and desert bronchos or strong, tough mules were used across the heat belt of the lower Colorado and the valley of the Gila.

Indians took pot shot at them. Washouts and upsets lurked in the bends. Southwestern temperatures dragged the grease from the axle-boxes. One stage was enveloped for hours by a whirling sandstorm. Yet the land-ferries rolled on. By the spring of 1860 the Overland was bearing a postal cargo exceeding that of the ocean carriers.

Cochise the Apache declared war and raged like a

red tornado through the Arizona mountains. His braves fell on ranches, mines, emigrant wagons, wreaking massacre and havoc, and rode their little bronchos into foam to catch the galloping Butterfield coaches. Driver James F. Wallace and three passengers in '61 were seized in Apache Pass and bloodily lanced to death. Two weeks later the west-bound arrived at Tucson with its conductor at the reins and its driver inside on the cushions, shot through back and breast. These were incidents of travel. Nothing, it would seem, could halt the Southern Overland.

Yet less than three years after Butterfield's bumbling wagons first set out east and west over the wishbone trail, Apaches peered down from the grim Dragoons to behold those big leather carryalls for the last time change horses and drive away.

Freight wagons followed, gathering up supplies. Two thousand horses and mules were called in from corrals and pastures. Stations grew silent. Doors creaked on idle hinges. Windows stared vacantly at the hard blue sky. As the dust of the last coach and four settled over that horseshoe route, and drifting sand filled its tracks, the watching Indians may be forgiven for exulting that the white man had left their land forever.

What had struck the Butterfield Great Southern Overland? Two smashing blows, one of them overwhelming —the Pony Express, and Civil War.

Through early 1860, strange stir might have been noticed at widely scattered points along the central overland trail. Horses were being posted at 190 stations improvised along a 2,000-mile front. Pintos, calicos, buckskins, slant-eared cayuses and Missouri thoroughbreds, they were being cantered into position by a far-strewn army of youths lithe as whiplashes and leathery as their own flat saddles. Before going to their posts the hardy

riders, as tough and capable a batch of youngsters as ever forked horse, had taken the following unusual oath:

"I do hereby swear, before the Great and Living God, that during my engagement, while I am employe of Russell, Majors & Waddell, I will under no circumstances use profane language; that I will drink no intoxicating liquors; that I will not quarrel or fight with any employe of the firm; and that in every respect I will conduct myself honestly, be faithful to my duties, and so direct all my acts as to win the confidence of my employers. So help me God."

What was preparing?

Surely the most vigorous, dramatic episode in a hundred years of history. It was the challenge of the short central pathway to the interminable roundaboutness of the Southern Overland. Plans were sweeping. Russell, Majors & Waddell, a great firm of Kansas freight-masters, had come into possession of stage and mail lines running

PASSING AN EMIGRANT TRAIN ON THE PLAINS

from Leavenworth to Denver and Salt Lake. With a mail contract like Butterfield's they could extend to the Pacific and knock days from Butterfield's time. Argument over the merits of the two pathways had lasted long enough. The hour for showdown had come—for an all-seasons relay horse-race against Butterfield, Indians, snow, heat, politics, and time. San Francisco to Missouri in ten days! Congress and the nation properly convinced, lucrative mail contracts would follow. The Central Overland· California & Pike's Peak Express, a large name for large purposing, would hitch a surcingle half around the continent.

The pledge was nervy. The promised schedule would slash nearly in half the best transcontinental mail time ever made—the 17 days 12 hours by a one-trip saddle-horse relay that was tried in '58—and would beat both the Panama steamships and the Southern Overland by two weeks. An incessant steeplechase at headlong gait with the whole width of the West for racecourse. An astonishing, valorous, galloping, bright mad dream. Could it be realized? Veteran horsemen wondered.

First eastbound rider out of Sacramento, where the steamboat from San Francisco docked on the morning of April 4, was Harry Roff—mounted on a milk-white broncho that did not long stay white. Twenty miles in fifty-nine minutes, and to horse again. Fifty-five miles in 2 hours 59 minutes, with one more change between. At Placerville he flung the letter packet to "Boston," who streamed with it for the summit of the Sierra Nevada. Sam Hamilton was waiting at Friday's station. Fifteen hours and 20 minutes out from the river-landing and the express was at Fort Churchill, 285 miles from the Golden Gate. On, Haslam! On, Kelley! Four days out from San Francisco and the mail-express was pitched into Salt Lake City. It used to take stage wagons thirty days to make that trek. On, on for the Missouri River!

As the hard-pounding pintos, calicos and buckskins flashed east, they passed Billy Richardson, Alex Carlisle, Johnny Frey and other Reveres on their frothy mounts lashing west. That first westbound-horse, out of St. Joe with twilight of April 3rd, had become Number Seventy-

one when the letter-express stormed into Placerville at
2:30 P.M. of April 13th. A cavalcade of enraptured citizens escorted Sam Hamilton and his roan down the last
few miles from Mud Springs, throwing such dust that
horse and rider could scarcely breathe; but in they came.
Guns boomed and speeches spouted, but succeeding mount
and rider had no time to hear.

Sacramento was won at 5:30. Flags, bunting and hats

SWIMMING THE STORM–SWOLLEN STREAM

waved for the mustang who passed, mane and tail astream,
for the river-landing. "Morning readers scarcely believed their eyes when they read 'news' from the great
Pike county nation and other civilized countries east, that
was news only nine days old," admired the *Union*.

Ten and a half days from the banks of the Missouri,
the seventy-fifth four-footed bearer of the mails sprang
ashore at his destination from the tooting *Antelope*. His
midnight arrival was unexpected, but San Francisco was

never a town to stay abed. Bonfires blazed on the Plaza. Engine companies and the band turned out. Inhabitants cheered until their throats hurt. The particular horse whom destiny had chosen to travel from one hay barn at Sacramento to another at San Francisco may have wondered what the racket was about; but "He was the veritable Hippagriff who shoved a continent behind his hoofs so easily; who snuffed up sandy plains, sent lakes and mountains, prairies and forests whizzing behind him like one great river rushing eastward," and "The greatest excitement prevailed . . . after which the various parties who participated in the celebration adjourned pleased with themselves and the rest of mankind, and the Pony Express in particular. All took a drink at their own expense." So exulted the press.

On April 29th the pony which had started the initial dash eastward came pounding into Sacramento at the conclusion of the first roundtrip, bringing word that the eastbound express had indeed reached St. Joe: bringing reports of the immense excitement at that terminus—public meeting, speeches, banners, flags, music and a grand parade. The pony also brought: "The [New York] *Herald's* Washington correspondent says that the Butterfield Overland Mail Company is now under the control of Wells, Fargo & Company. Mr. Butterfield has been deposed from the presidency and superseded by William B. Dinsmore, of Adams Express Co. . . . Probably one cause of difference between the retiring president and his co-laborers was the Pony Express. It has been understood for a long time that Mr. Butterfield wished to start a horse express for the conveyance of valuable packages, but was opposed by others of the company."

For several uninterrupted trips the pony plied the staccato of his hurrying hoofs, while the nation cheered him on and the West eagerly absorbed his weekly budget of news—taking more momentary interest, it must be admitted, in John C. Heenan's 42-round victory in England over Tom Sayers for the heavyweight championship than in the very imminence of Rebellion.

Then the pony's furious pace slowed down. On May 30th his echoing hoofbeats clattered to abrupt stop. "The Pony Express has not yet been heard from, and it is much feared that this little animal has been captured by Indians." Not quite; route agent Ruffin reported in next day from east of Carson: "I have just returned from Cold Springs—was driven away by the Indians who attacked us night before last. Three men at Dry Creek station have been killed, and it is thought the Roberts Creek station has been destroyed. The Express"—westbound from St. Joe—"turned back after hearing the news from Dry Creek." Three days later Sam Hamilton arrived at Carson from Sand Springs, sixty miles out, bringing stock and men. East of Sand Springs silence reigned; all was cut off. The stations straddled the only waterholes available to wandering bunches of Utes, Shoshones and Bannocks, and each was guarded by only two or three white men.

Efforts were made to turn out the military. There was considerable creaking of governmental machinery, finally effective. Ben Ficklin, the manager of the swift express.

grimly affirmed that henceforth "the more the Indians interfere, the faster the Pony will travel." Resumption came in time to bring news of Douglas' nomination against Lincoln.

Thereafter to the finish of his days, eighteen months in all, the pony continued to play the telegraph key of his pounding hoofs. The average stretch to a rider was fifty, afterwards a hundred miles a day, with fresh mounts at each ten or a dozen miles and only seconds allotted to shift saddle. At any moment day or night thirty or forty horsemen were reeling off the vivid cyclorama where the covered wagons of emigrants still wandered. In buckskin shirt, light trousers, jockey cap or slouch hat, and very occasionally girt with a brace of pistols but almost always with a heavy bowie knife, through rain and sleet and sunbeam and starlight they pounded. The *mochila* or leather skirt of four letter-pouches that rested over their saddles contained at most twenty pounds of dispatches, at $5 the half ounce.

Adventure along the way? Galore. Bill Cates, dashing westward with President Buchanan's last message, was scarcely in saddle across the Missouri before bidding his cayuse to lay back its ears and outrun whooping Arapahoes and Kiowas. "Pony Bob" Haslam west of Salt Lake found a whole tribal league assembled for his personal and private massacre, and dashed through with a yell. Reese Hawley, wondering why a relay station in eastern Nevada was so dark, entered and stumbled over the keeper's murdered form; darted out to hear the hoofbeats of his stolen horse grow fainter. He picked up his pouch

and carried it afoot. Station keepers in Egan Canyon
near the Nevada-Utah border were captured and compelled to cook bread before taking the tomahawk special
for the happy hunting grounds; but they cooked it so
tastily that the braves gorged themselves into stupor and
permitted United States cavalry to ride up in the nick

CROSSING THE SIERRAS IN A SNOWSTORM

of time. Jay Kelley entered a quaking asp forest where
the last man ahead had been shot; hurtled through with
lines thrown over the neck of his horse, rifle at full cock
and spurs driven deep. Howard Egan charged full tilt
into a hostile Nevada Indian camp, filled the night air
with shouts and pistol shots and sent the warriors scurrying while he galloped through—later to learn that the
encampment was there for the precise purpose of stopping
an express rider to see what he was carrying in such a
hurry.

Fortitude? Plenty. Egan again, riding out from Salt Lake City, added his brother's stretch to his own as a special favor; returned from this double tour to find his successor missing, so on with the mail again—total, when he finally spilled from saddle, 330 continuous miles. Fourteen-year-old Will Cody, not yet at the stature he would some day attain as Buffalo Bill, turned in 320 miles in 21 hours, 40 minutes. Young Will again, finding his relief slain, spurring on for a record total of 384 miles. Jim Moore, after 140 miles, clattering up to Old Julesburg near the Nebraska-Colorado corner, finding his relief ill, and within ten minutes heading back again for the whole almighty stretch. Bob Haslam ripping across western Nevada, finding the station a torch and his relief a cinder, and indomitably coursing on—total, over 300 miles.

Speed? Bill James, 18-year-old Virginian, reeled off 120 miles of intermountain sagebrush in 12 hours, including all stops. Jack Keetley, another of the hard-to-stop breed, did 300 miles in a few minutes under 24 hours. Seventeen-year-old Don Rising in southern Nebraska gave them all something to shoot at with a continuous gait of 20 miles an hour, twice established. The over-all record,—turned in by the whole westbound 75 with the news of Lincoln's election—was 6 days, 17 hours from St. Joe to the telegraph station at the eastern foot of the Sierras.

So through the vales of adventure coursed the Pony Express, racing out the bet with bankruptcy made by its promoters—that a string of streaking saddlehorses could run away with a million-dollar-a-year daily stagecoach mail. And run away with it the pony could, so far as speed was concerned; but only at fearful cost of operation. His charges had to be proportionately high, and in consequence the Butterfield coaches on the long, slow rival route continued to bring in a mail that grew ever more mountainous.

South Carolina seceded, followed by six sister states. Shots were heaved at a federal ship in Charleston harbor. Now ride, ride, you pony expressmen!

The next few weeks saw unusual bustle along the line. Barns and granaries rising at Fort Kearney on the Platte. Hammering and heavy freight arrivals at Julesburg. Stir at Forts Laramie and Bridger east and west of the continental divide. At Major Egan's Deep Creek Ranch on the Utah-Nevada border new stables of adobe were going up, ox teams were breaking up new pastures for grain; there were new corrals, new kitchen, and a new smithy. So at Ruby Valley out in the heart of the sagebrush basin. So at Fort Churchill off toward the base of the Sierra Nevada.

A springtime storm swept down. Snowslides in the Sierras obliterated all semblance of a trail. The Express was three days crossing from Carson to Sacramento. Its rider was compelled to abandon horse high at Yank's station and foot the thirteen miles to Strawberry. Being more at home in stirrups than on snowshoes, he was presently down on his hands and knees. Frostbitten he made his way over drifts and down and up gullies, bearing on his back dispatches that included: "Reports favoring the evacuation of Fort Sumter still prevail," and that a contract, signed in Washington, directed "the removal of the Butterfield Company to the Central route."

Sumter fell. Lincoln called for volunteers. Now the reason for those new stations on the pony's route became manifest. Before the alarums of war there went streaming northward the whole Southern Overland equipment of neighing, braying livestock, bounding Concords, and freight wagons piled high with supplies, smithy outfits. and station tenders' families—everything removable; though the loss in immovables was huge.

Into the section between Virginia City and Salt Lake City was fitted what Confederates and Apaches did not intercept of the great Overland Mail. Transport from California up over the Sierras to Virginia City was entrusted to the dashing Pioneer Stage Line. Both sections of the overland coach mail were now Wells Fargo subsidiaries.

The Central Overland California & Pike's Peak Express got the section of the new Million Dollar Mail between the Missouri River and Salt Lake. But its sponsors were not to enjoy their victory. Three-quarters of a million dollars had gone into the saddlebag express and considerably less had come out. The promoters were writing checks for the difference, and the difference was making end of the promoters.

On April 16th, President Russell of the Pony Express transferred everything connected with the western two-thirds of that gallant enterprise to Wells, Fargo & Company, who reduced rates, put more letters on the pony's back and set him going thrice weekly. For the final six months of his career, the pony carried the express mochilas of that concern from San Francisco to the Rockies.

By July the galloping equine understood those new granaries, so far beyond his dainty personal capacity, and those redly-glowing smithies. On the first of that month the new Central Route stagecoaches started out east and

west from Placerville and St. Joseph on their daily schedule. Somewhere in the vicinity of South Pass they met, to repass daily thereafter for eight tremendous years. As the burly Concords rose and fell over the grades of the mid-continent, the pony for four more months continued to whiz past both.

But only for months. On July 4th sixty men and thirty wagons started from Fort Churchill, seventeen miles east of Carson, and entered the desert. Their wagons were

162 *Treasure Express*

laden with poles, twenty-five to the mile; with reels of wire; with presents for the Indians. At the same time other crews and pole-piled wagons started out from Salt Lake City.

The express horse kicked his heels as he capered by. What were wagons with poles and wire doing out on his expanse? By October his story was over. What he had borne in days the telegraph now handled in seconds.

As the pony slowed to a final halt, winter of unexampled fury rolled down on the trans-Missouri country. Snows swirled high on the path of the Central Overland. Concords sank into bogs. Many a mudhole was filled with sacked mail to give coachwheels traction. Nothing so terrific had been planned for. Costs of operation went to the skies. These titanic stormblasts spelled the finish of the C. O. C. & P. P. E., still laboring with the daily mail coaches in the section over the Rocky Mountains. Early in the new year the struggles of Russell, Majors & Waddell were over, and one Ben Holladay, who was to be both colleague and obstreperous rival of Wells Fargo, took possession by foreclosure between Salt Lake City and the Missouri River.

A character of power was Ben Holladay, Kentucky farm boy, military courier at seventeen, tavern-keeper at twenty-two, who now at thirty-eight was about to be over-lord of half the stage routes of western America. Organizer, visualizer, chance-taker, he was a born Prince of Push, a King of Get. Had there been one or two others of his kind to help him, he would have put through the Pacific Railroad; the astonishing thing is that he did not try. Already proprietor of sixteen steamships plying between the Pacific Coast, the Orient and Panama, he was casting about for new transportation worlds to conquer when the mail-coach opportunity came, and he found the acquisition of the eastward portion of the Central Overland Daily Mail a subject that was right up his private leafy lane.

Holladay thoroughly valued the word "Overland." It was popular next to "gold" in the western lexicon. As soon as he got the C. O. C. & P. P. E. he changed all lettering on its coaches to "The Overland Stage Line." As division superintendents he installed a number of little Ben Holladays to bully and bluff and jam the mail-express through. These included the remarkable Jack Slade, who, with not more than one authentic murder to his record, by notching his guns and carrying human ears in his pocket ballooned himself into the supreme bad man of the prairies. To Holladay's drivers' seats climbed commanders who had no fear of God or man; of Indian, road agent, prairie fire or cyclone; of any force or calamity save the disintegrating ire of tall, bearded, bald Ben Holladay or the little Holladays who helped extend his shadow. Holladay was boss. He was king. He was Jove and all his thunderbolts. In the end, after swinging stage lines, ship lines, rail lines, legislators and senators around him like a cowboy with a reata or a sun with planets, all smashed; but the smash was in another decade and no longer mattered.

The career of the King of the Overland presents a jumpy picture in these early '60's. He is in and out of his castle on the Hudson, his brownstone on Fifth Avenue and his mansion full of books—Ben rarely read books—at Washington; he is no sooner cornered in Lincoln's study, wheedling concessions from that diverted man, than he is half across the Far West in a bounding Concord. He is at San Francisco, announcing himself potentate of all the line; he is up and down the Platte, reviewing hames, cruppers, oat bins; he is diving down the Sierras; he is roaring like a tornado over South Pass. In July of '62 the Pacific Mailer *Golden Gate* takes fire at sea. The flaming hulk speeds for Manzanillo harbor; a hundred and ninety-two passengers die in flames or throw themselves into the sea; there are unpleasant glimpses of a woman offering to a tall bald man her babe to save, and he declining the tender; of a bearded man lifting a ladder from the hold, regardless of whom he entraps in the belly of the fire-ship, and pitching it overboard for life-raft into the sea. The bearded one lowers himself by the forward chains, is swept beneath a paddlewheel, emerges to be bludgeoned by the rudder, finally grabs the floating ladder; is picked up by an overcrowded skiff whose leaking seams are calked with petticoats . . . Ben Holladay, bound from Panama for San Francisco, was on board the *Golden Gate*.

The man was everywhere, on two halves of a continent and on two oceans.

Under its million-dollar subsidy and its three-part management, much was expected of the Central Overland, and much it delivered. From Atchison on the Missouri to Placerville on the west foot of the Sierra there were

153 relay posts, every third or fourth of which was a "home station" with storm-tight and arrow-tight sleeping and dining rooms, telegraph office and shops; with women and children in residence, and rifles in the racks. Every morning at eight o'clock a coach or stage wagon left at each end, with passengers armed and a thousand pounds of mail tossed in. Monday's was a "messenger coach"— no mail, few passengers, much treasure, and a heavy Wells Fargo miscellaneous express. The bulk of the treasure rode in a built-in safe that was anchored to the bed of the coach. Other expressage rode in the foreward boot in a box that, for safety, required two men to lift. Over it, next to the driver, perched one or more guards or "conductors." Drivers might change every fifty miles, but the armed messengers clung to their outdoor perches day and night in all weather for a week, ready for battle with anything that wore hair or feathers. Between the two major mountain ranges most of the Concords were of the low-slung, canvas-covered variety known as "mud wagons." What they gave up in splendor they gained in sand-worthiness and hill-worthiness, and their pilots took them through in style. Holladay's horses and mules brought the Overland up the Platte and across the Rockies at four to five miles an hour. Beyond Salt Lake, wheels moved rather faster—575 miles in 72 hours, or eight miles an hour. Speediest of all went the Pioneer's coach wheels, from the silver-stuffed Washoes up and over the Sierra, past blue lakes and through down-swooping forest lands, around brinks of cliffs and through almost citified traffic— harness jingling, coach horn tooting, passengers wrapped

in armstraps, ten to a dozen miles an hour—there goes your hat!

Ben Holladay on one of his rifle-bullet trips was whirled through from Atchison to Placerville in time that made the record. The coach was his and the horses were largely his, and at no point was the mighty man kept waiting. Nevertheless, when Ben emerged from the stomach of the leather land-leviathan after twelve continuous days and nights over roads that were mainly "natural," he knew, like Jonah, that he had been traveling.

The ordinary passenger also knew he had been traveling. Thumping and rattling by day and by night through the wilderness, seventeen days to the journey, twenty-four hours to each day, four to eight miles to the hour, 1,056 revolutions to the mile, 1,913 chuck-holed miles to go— yes, he knew.

But the stages, spaced at a little more than one hundred miles apart continuously in both directions, rose and fell over the bumps and the ranges with their mails, passengers, and express. The millions they bore in treasure eastward financed no small part of the Civil War. With all their discomforts and genuine perils they were the safest, quickest form of transport across half of America. To all practical intents the Overland functioned as one continuous line. Passengers were ticketed straight through, and straight through went the cargoes.

That is, all went straight through when Indians would permit.

It was in the second year of the Daily Overland that the red man struck hard.

When "Happy Harry" Harper approached a stage station, it was his habit to let kitchen, smithy, near pastures and farthermost crags know about it for certain. Traces tinkling, leaders prancing, he would flourish into view and announce himself with a yell that loosened the cones in the tops of piñon trees and rattled spare harness behind the coach-house door. The yell served a purpose. It told the world how Happy Harry felt, and it woke the station tender if the son-of-six-bits happened to be napping.

On March 22, 1863, Happy Harper brought the east-bound into sight of Eight Mile Station in "Western Utah." He had an elderly passenger, two small boys and a congressman-elect down inside. Behind lay the long road from the Sierras; an hour farther on lay the meadows and farmstead of Deep Creek Station at the present Utah-Nevada line.

Eight Mile Station's one-story adobes were built with their backs to a creek-hollow and the messhouse, stable and granary facing three sides of a square. The kitchen was in charge of a cook who always got furiously busy with pots and griddle when he heard Happy's huge wah-hoo-oo-oo. Stable and teams were in charge of a dependable young man named Wood, who always made a flattering audience for Happy's yarns.

But this day, as he was about to let loose the grandfather of all yells, Happy's opened jaws—went shut. He eyed the station more closely. There was a white man —it looked like the cook—outside the messhouse door. Indians stood near in a group. The white man was lying in the dust and wasn't moving.

Harper abruptly drew the line up on his off leader, touched brake to help swing the coach, and let off his fourteen-foot buckskin whip with a cannonlike bang in instinctive attempt to swing clear of the station. But he had shot up too close. Bowstrings and rifles went to shoulder. Harper's elderly passenger pitched into the boot. Another shot pierced Happy Harper through the body. He slumped from the box, kept grip on the lines.

"Come out!" he shouted to Judge Gordon Mott on the inside cushions. "You've got to take this team."

Never to have clear recollection of how he scrambled out of the coach door and up to the swaying seat, the congressman nevertheless found himself up there. "I've got 'em, Harry—but I can't drive!"

"I'll tell you how!" The desert was taking on a red tinge, a misty red that wouldn't brush away, however Harry wiped his eyes. He pushed his whip-handle into his successor's fingers. "Handle 'em, Judge—we'll be followed sure!"

So with the dying reinsman giving instructions by signal of his fingers, Mott rose to the occasion. With two men shot, two frightened boys hanging tight and horses plunging, he brought the Overland Mail to Deep Creek Station.

Back at Eight Mile the cook lay with scalp and tongue removed. The Utes had superstitiously covered his face with flour to make him a white man again. Wood the hostler was lying stripped and slain fifty yards behind the houses. He had raced for the brush with his body a quiver for arrows, and had been felled by an ounce ball from a buffalo gun.

Though he had lost a trickle of brains, John Liverton, the father of the two boys, made one of those remarkable wilderness recoveries and eventually continued eastward with his little family. Happy Harry Harper, forever silenced, was laid away near Deep Creek ranch beside the transcontinental highway.

The Overland War of '63 had begun.

Six weeks later the Mail was moving westward by night from Salt Lake toward Austin. It was May; the desert was in flower and soft with aroma. Even the creosote bushes, in bridal mood, had put forth little yellow petals. The stars burned big. The moon was just rising. Except for the long-drawn howl of a distant coyote, all seemed placid in this empty land. Two women were inside the coach. They felt unusually snug and safe; for the rest of the passenger load included five soldiers, saber-belted, rifle-armed, and irresistible. The coach lumbered down into Schell Creek, lurched across, mounted the farther bank. From behind the pretty creosote bushes a shot rang out. A coach horse reared, fell in a crash of traces and lay thrashing. Out swarmed the soldiers. Night was filled with popping carbines. It was enough; the hostiles galloped off. The stricken horse was cut away. The soldiery re-entered the coach. Again the padding of hoofs in never-ending sand, the slap of well-oiled harness, the distant howl of a moonstruck coyote. The gentle passengers, pillowed on mail sacks, rifle barrels, and military shoulders, went back to contemplation of the stars.

Two weeks after, with soldiers inside and Major Howard Egan, the section superintendent, sitting beside

Driver Riley Simpson, the Mail passed under a rocky cliff near Canyon Station. There was a blast from above. Riley Simpson crumpled. Egan snatched the lines, pulled the dying man into the boot. The soldiers poured out. After a short skirmish the coach went on. Superintendent Egan brought in his driver dead and one member of the escort, swearing frightfully, shot between the toes.

On June 10th the eastbound was beset, approaching Salt Lake City. The driver and one other employee lost their lives and their hair, the Overland Mail its horses and coach, and Wells Fargo its express.

Canyon Station was a "swing," or intermediate relay point, east of Deep Creek. Having neither stream nor spring, it had to haul its water eight miles from Deep Creek slough. Water was life at Canyon Station. When Waterman "Deaf Bill" Riley went to fetch it, his cart moved in state, guarded by four outriding carbineers from Fort Douglas. Toward June's end Bill hitched up as usual, gathered his escort, and set forth. He was halfway to Deep Creek when a shot from a clump of sagebrush announced that the journey was not to be without incident. Though he did not hear the shot, Deaf Bill understood its message; one of his thumbs went with it. Bill forgot all 〈 it water, laid to his team with whip and lines. In the running retreat two soldiers were slain. Bill's water cart, bumping dizzily, made a record trip homeward and Canyon Station for a while wet its thirst and washed with whisky.

Chief White Horse of the Gosh-Utes was among the least belligerent of the desert folk. Chief White Horse was inclined to like white people. They gave him cast-off pants, broken pots to cook with, occasionally a handful of flour, and once or twice a broken bag of beans. His people asked but little: the right to live in their isolated canyons off behind Simpson's Spring, where papooses rolled in the sun and squaws caught and dried grasshoppers and gathered acorns and piñon nuts. But when Chief White Horse came home to his village and found every basket of winter stores upset and demolished, every old man, woman, and child shot or bayoneted, and his wife and papooses among the dead, he sadly revised his conceptions and hunted up his kinsmen.

The resulting blow fell on luckless Canyon Station. This oft-attacked outpost consisted of a canvas-roofed adobe stable and a rude dugout. Spies watched for some days. There were five men at the station. They slept in the barn to guard the horses and ate in the dugout. When at meals their arms were stacked just outside.

At daybreak of July 8th, barefooted warriors stole up. Arrows dipped in pitch had been prepared for the stable roof. When the whites went to breakfast, and four of the five had descended into the cave, there was a volley of flaming feathers, a yell and a rush. Deaf Bill Riley was currying a horse outside the stable. But the tidings of war this time reached him in the shape of a bullet through his ankle. Hopping and staggering, he made for the dry gulch back of the buildings. He ran tragically into the waiting foe.

The other whites, dashing from their dugout, were dropped one by one. A single figure gained the open.

He ran up the gully after Riley and into the same fate.

The station woodpile aflame, Riley's body was tossed atop. The soldier who had run up the swale was the only one of the late five over whom the Utes made delay about scalping. He presented a problem, for he was bald. But a brave solved even that. The white man had a set of brown whiskers. Chief White Horse's band took these and rode away.

Peace of a sort came to alkali land. Another flare-up took two more lives in '69 at Dry Creek, two other tenders barely escaping in a whirlwind ride of thirty miles.

Sixteen men killed, seven stations put to the torch, stages demolished, and stock run off was the price of Indian turmoil in the Nevada-Utah basin. But the mail and express went through. Coaches left on schedule and, if they arrived at their destinations at all—which they seldom failed to do—they arrived on time.

The red man had watched the march of the Forty-niners with amaze. Succeeding events had charged him with dismay. Horses that raced the lightning. Singing wires. White men that filled canyons with tented towns, sawmills, uproar—schemes to scare game. These things were undesirable; he would abolish them. White men bringing food, thunder-guns, straw-haired women. These objects were desirable; he would possess them.

So Holladay, the stagecoach king from Salt Lake eastward, had also been having troubles. The war had opened in his territory in '62.

Two westbound stages were dry-gulched near the

Sweetwater in Wyoming, in April. A fusillade of arrows sent the mule teams into frenzy, pierced four passengers. Mail bags and vehicles were turned into a fortification. Three times the Sioux charged. Three times the defenders behind their breastwork of coaches and sacked letters and newspapers turned the foe back. In the end, victorious, the whites staggered with their wounded to a station.

Other relay posts saw their stock go galloping off. There was widespread destruction of life, settlements, fortunes. The prairies went under martial law. The revolt crossed to the western, or Wells Fargo, side of the Rockies. But in '64 it broke out in Ben Holladay's territory anew, with a fury of massacres, scalping, and burnings. From Atchison far out into Nebraska the Overland was forced to suspend. Nothing moved for six weeks. Military measures helped some, but the war on a wagon road continued. Charred timbers, raped and murdered forms recorded its progress. Holladay watched his $125-a-cord woodpiles and his $150-a-ton haystacks go up in smoke. Repeatedly he pleaded with the government that there could be no Overland without cavalry regiments. But the national government just then was busy with its own Battle of the Wilderness, and was putting the torch to haystacks and granaries between Atlanta and the sea. It would do what it could for the West when the South was pacified.

Wells Fargo through these troublous times, despite the desert wars of '63, had been prospering. It was expressman, postman, and banker from the Mexican west coast clear up to Fraser River. From the Pacific to Salt Lake it was stage driver as well, and looked covetously across Holladay's frontier.

It was Idaho, Montana, and Colorado gold that kept Ben Holladay going. With his investment on the Plains ablaze, his stations in ruin, and his livestock whirling away before the Indian cyclone, mineral discoveries on both sides of the Bitter Roots created for him new treasure express, new freight, postal, and passenger traffic. The Pike's Peak region went increasingly quick-rich mad. Each mountain camp back of Denver found the bald, bluff king of the Overland swiftly astride its roads. His main line might be suffering heavily, but his spurs were grand payers.

The million-dollar mail subsidy arrangement had to be renewed with altered terms, disturbing to the three-part management, in the middle of 1864. In the new bidding it was Holladay, with a somewhat whittled fee, who emerged clutching the whole Missouri River to California contract. Neatly forked, Wells Fargo hastened to negotiate with its old associate and successful rival. It took the subcontract to carry Ben's mail from Salt Lake westward.

The king of the Overland agreed. He now held sway over more than four thousand miles of stagedom. A thousand coaches and wagons, five thousand horses and mules, and an army of whips and hostlers kept his wheels of empire spinning. His feed bill exceeded a million a year; his passengers paid him $150,000 to $200,000 a month and got little comfort for their money.

"Fine! Pack 'em in like cods!" exhorted Ben.

When suddenly, at the pinnacle of his career, the king

stepped down. Late in 1866, for cash and some Wells Fargo shares, he surrendered all his Concords, wagons, mules, stations, personnel and general stagecoaching ambitions.

Wells Fargo's coaching domain at a bound extended from the old Salt Lake City frontier clear to the banks of the Big Muddy. Under this spirit of expansion it also engineered a great consolidation of other stage lines all over its territory.

On October 8, 1867, the order clerk of the Abbot, Downing Company at Concord must have driven his quill with a good deal of pleasure, for he had just received from the western express concern the largest single order ever booked by the proud New Hampshire plant. The order called for—

Thirty-nine passenger coaches, inside three seats, bag footboard, leather sides, back boot, bodies roomy inside, candle lamps extra large size, weight 2,225 pounds. Paint bodies red, running gear straw. Letter "Wells, Fargo & Co., U. S. Mail."

Ben Holladay withdrew to Oregon, to dream of a north-and-south coastal railroad. To Wells Fargo the worry and the glory of the Overland; its old king had the cash. Perhaps his reason for selling lay in a new sound he had heard on the prairies, more fateful than whoop of Sioux or Cheyenne—the whistle of the westbound locomotive that had got itself as far as Junction City, Kansas.

XV

MERCHANDISE—LEAKY

CAPTAIN COX, dock superintendent at San Francisco for the Pacific Mail Steamship Company, eyed with disapproval a box just tossed from the hold of the Panama steamship *Sacramento*. Captain Cox was tidy of mind. And the box was sticky.

"Like maple syrup," grumbled the port skipper, "except in color. And," he said, after experiment, "except in taste. This here bites the tongue worse 'n green bananas. Canned banana juice—what'll they be shipping next? Carelessly packed, whatever it is, or stowed too loosely. John, you'd better tell the express people about it."

John the pick-up man pitched the parcel into his wagon with other goods and rattled it over the cobblestones to the Montgomery Street express office. The box had arrived on Friday, the 13th of April, 1866. It was now the 16th. John the wagonman stacked the damaged package in a courtyard at the rear of Wells Fargo's office and notified Freight Clerk F. E. Webster.

Webster examined the offending shipment. It was a wooden case about two feet long, a foot wide, and a foot high. "That's steamship handling," he told Express Superintendent Samuel Knight, and sent for Pacific Mail

Freight Clerk William H. Haven to come and altercate.

Claims and counterclaims were all in a lifetime for both clerkly gentlemen. It was nearing noon. There would be plenty of opportunity after lunch to dicker about damages. They ascended an external iron stair that led from the express courtyard to the Union Club's café, bar, and billiard room over G. W. Bell's Assay Office, where a genial meal was had. Mr. Webster and Mr. Haven then attempted to overcome each other at pool. With one o'clock whistles the two put their cues back in the rack and descended to the courtyard and to business.

The sticky area on the outside of the case had increased. It was a pale oily yellow. The consignment, according to waybill, had journeyed across the Atlantic from Europe, down the Caribbean from New York, over the Isthmus by Panama Railroad, and up the west coast to San Francisco; its ultimate destination was Los Angeles. The case was noncommittally marked "Merchandise" and bore the name of its consignee. Those facts were all the two clerks or anybody else could say about it.

"We'd better open it up," decided Mr. Webster.

Hammer and chisel were fetched by William Jester, the porter. Superintendent Knight came out into the court-yard to supervise.

Within the company offices a considerable throng was gathered as usual in the letter delivery department. The express office was still, as it had been for fifteen years, the unofficial but actual post office of the metropolis: eight or ten mails arriving daily from all points by stagecoach and steamship, three or four letter clerks standing in continual attendance, ten or twelve hundred pieces of mail an hour being handed over the long counters which occupied one complete side of the room.

William Jester placed his chisel under the lid of the box and brought down the hammer.

On the instant, a customer who had been working up to the head of the letter delivery line inside the office, and had just reached the counter, was conscious of a rush as of an immense rocket, followed by a thunderclap that rent his universe, and found himself, dumfoundedly dazed and shaken, in the middle of Montgomery Street. Simultaneously a glazier who had been working under the skylight found himself flung up through parting glass and onto the roof—a vertical irruption of about fifteen feet; where a cut and bruised fellow workman sprawled beside him stripped to his shoes and underwear. Gentlemen at luncheon in the Union Club found themselves torn from chairs that were no longer chairs, cast under tables that were no longer tables. The end of the building with its kitchen had disappeared outward. The external stairway and other ironwork had rolled up like wallpaper. The club clerk, who had been sitting behind his desk in the front office, lay between two pool tables which, a moment ago in perfect condition, were now crushed and jumbled under a torrent of brickbats and mortar. Bell's Assay Office under the clubrooms was a strawstack; the new two-and-a-half-story brick building of the water company adjoining had moved two inches on its foundations.

These points were perceived afterward. Just now a rain of window glass, bricks, woodwork, and indescribable fragments was descending. Into Cobb & Stinton's auction room across Montgomery Street plunged a human brain. Into Leidesdorff Street half a block east, with a row of buildings between, a shattered spine. From a third-story Leidesdorff Street window sill bounced a human arm, which rose again in short parabola, fell to the pavement. Silver half-dollars, bent double, landed in Bush Street. Everywhere people were pouring out of window-shattered buildings. From the crater that had been the courtyard of the express company rose a light yellowish vapor, gaseous and smelly, to a great height.

Clerks Webster and Haven and Porter Jester had completely vanished. The form of Superintendent Knight lay as if sleeping. It bore no visible scratch. The interior of the bastille-like building was a shambles. Toll: ten dead, eleven badly hurt, three waiters of the Union Club missing, lesser injuries uncountable.

In the vertigo of excitement that followed, Captain Cox remembered that sticky-stained parcel. Someone else recalled that a new invention called "blasting oil" or "nitroglycerine" had recently gone off with similar effect in Sweden, killing every man in the factory, including experimenter Nobel's brother.

The wreckage was still being cleared from San Francisco's streets when an overland coach came in, bearing news of a strange disaster on the Isthmus of Panama. The news came via New York.

Thirteen days prior to the explosion in the Wells Fargo courtyard, at seven o'clock in the morning, loiterers on the dock at Aspinwall had beheld an incredible thing.

The Liverpool steamer *European* was discharging. Her cargo was being hoisted overboard to the Panama Railroad's big stone freight house. The train from Panama should have been on the siding, but was a trifle late.

At this moment the afterdecks of the *European* bent apart. Into the sky flew hundreds of boxes, bales, spars, and splinters of wood. The iron roof of the 275-foot freight house rose from its walls, then dropped with a crash on goods and laborers within. An adjoining steamship was half wrecked, her smoke-stacks tossed drunkenly over her gunwales. When the train from Panama pulled in, the *European* was a sheet of flame. With grim courage a couple of British vessels in the harbor got lines to her and hauled her a mile to sea, when a second explosion tore apart what was left of the blazing vessel, threw her masts and remaining cargo high into the air and sent her to the bottom.

The toll from this display of the powers of the mother of dynamite exceeded sixty dead, including all officers of the *European,* and every house in Aspinwall was damaged.

New York then remembered that it had been puzzling for a half year over another mysterious catastrophe. The affair had destroyed a Greenwich Street hotel. Now it was discovered that the guests had included the promoters of a company importing Sweden's "blasting oil" for California's gold mines. The prophetic name of one of the promoters was "Bustinbinder." To him and his colleagues were traced these other fatal shipments.

Wells Fargo, which had heretofore accepted parcels

hard and soft, large and small, marked and unmarked, and even fire engines and human beings as express consignments, wrote into its agents' instruction manual:

Camphene, nitroglycerine, naptha, benzine, petroleum or other explosive burning fluids; gunpowder, giant powder, oil of vitriol, nitric or other chemical acids; turpentine, matches, phosphorus or loaded firearms, Must Not be received for transportation.

High on the west face of the Sierra, where laborers with picks and wheelbarrows were trying to hand-carve a railroad bed through solid granite, a construction foreman stared at the indurate summits and gave himself up to wonder at the ways of Providence. His prayer was answered for a tool that would drive the greatest and last tunnel through those massive mountains.

XVI

THE BIGGEST HOLD-UP OF ALL

To the stageman's eye the middle sixties were years of opulent promise. New ore was uncovered weekly in Idaho, Montana, Colorado, the firry Northwest, and down across the Southwest of mirage and cactus. New mines, new camps, new clamor for four-wheeled service. Rails might encroach on the stage-miles west of the Sierras and might nibble at eastern Nebraska and Kansas, but in the illimitable spaces between, coach-routes were thrusting in all directions.

Even the Southern Overland in effect had been revived. With the end of civil war, express, mails, and passengers by coach and buckboard were moving from Los Angeles out across the Mojave and Colorado deserts via San Bernardino to Prescott, onward to Santa Fé and up old caravan ruts to Kansas City. All over the farther West, towns that had once been coaching stops were now bustling coach centers. When Wells Fargo made its heavy consolidations of Holladay, Overland, Pioneer, and California Stage Company mileage and equipment, it looked forward to at least another decade of main-route staging. It had joined with Pacific Mail Steamship Company and California Stage Company in fighting the pro-

posed new railroad at every turn. The bluster that could
jostle aside bullwhacker and mule skinner, the skill that
could weave a ton and a quarter of Concord ash and leather
through close-packed wagon-freighting, the strong man-
agerial wrists that could send coaches and sixes careening
up and down mountain grades and along brinks of torrents, felt little concern for the rail-bound iron horse that
pawed and neighed two thousand miles away. Anything
up to fifty years was the popularly voiced estimate of the
time it would take to lay rails across plains, deserts and
two mountain systems.

But in this estimate the public and the express magnates
were bad guessers. It did not take fifty years nor ten
years to bring Union Pacific west and Central Pacific east
to their meeting-point out in the Salt Lake desert. Once
started, it took exactly three years, six months, and ten
days.

Progress in the initial stages was not alarming. Two
years after the Union Pacific was chartered it had pushed
out from Omaha but forty miles of rail. Hundreds of
miles of prairie stretched away toward rock-bastioned
mountains: prairies that were the breeding ground of
hostile redskins and savage blizzards, and that offered
scarcely a tree for ties or bridges. Central Pacific, pushing
from the west, had achieved even less. A year of construction, and four miles out of Sacramento. Chimerical!
Of course the Pacific Railroad was chimerical. Wells
Fargo felt secure.

On April 15, 1868, the Concord *Daily Monitor* announced to its New Hampshire readers:

A novel sight was presented in the Concord railroad yard, at noon Wednesday, in the shape of a special train of fifteen long platform cars, containing thirty elegant coaches from the world-renowned carriage manufactory of Messrs. Abbot, Downing & Company, and four long box cars, containing 60 four-horse sets of harnesses from James R. Hill & Co.'s celebrated harness manufactory, and spare work for repairing the coaches, such as bolts, hubs, spokes, thorough-braces, etc., all consigned to Wells, Fargo & Co., Omaha and Salt Lake City, the whole valued at $45,000 perhaps. It is the largest lot of coaches ever sent from one manufactory at one time, probably.

The coaches are finished in a superior manner, the bodies red, the running parts yellow. Each door has a handsome picture, and no two of the sixty are alike. They are gems of beauty, and would afford study for hours. They were painted by Mr. J. Borglum.

A few minutes after one P.M. the locomotive *Pembroke* gave a "premonitory puff," there were cheers from the throng of citizens, and the solid train of coach cars and harness cars moved off.

Alas for glory! The vistas so bravely painted by landscapist Borglum were soon to be targets for buckshot, fire arrows, and rifle bullets. The red bodies and yellow running parts were to wallow deep in redder road-clay and bleach yellower under sun, gale, sleet. But for all their years of usefulness ahead, those splendid coaches might well have deemed the *Pembroke*'s "premonitory puff" a snort of derision.

For the chimerical railroad was pressing on. The Union Pacific had crawled westward to Fort Kearney. The old stage road across the Platte could now grow weedy with disuse; in the previous summer its great coaches had been taken off forever. Though Indians and tornadoes cut across the iron trail with sharp-edged fury; though million-bisoned herds rolled down and disputed its incomprehensible progress; though the haulage of supplies through immense distances brought the cost of timber, cut in Michigan and Pennsylvania, to $2.50 a crosstie— still the rails writhed westward. Winter found them over the Wyoming border, with the gravest of the Indian troubles at last behind. Though now, in front, rose the sullen vast bulk of the Rockies.

The Central Pacific, working eastward, had been from the first against the high, steep Sierra Nevadas; against drifts of winter snow that filled canyons forty feet deep; against granite cliffs where picks and shovels and black powder thudded dully; against tunnels without end, precipices without balcony, gorges that tossed eternal snow avalanches down on man-made bridges with the humor of Titans playing ninepins. At this end, progress was measurable not in miles forward but in feet upward. Sixteen months after starting, ascent had been made of only a thousand feet. The next twelve miles, with eight hundred vertical feet, brought increasing difficulty. There remained more than five thousand feet to scale, and those the steepest, most remote, most difficult that iron track had ever set out to conquer.

But with Crocker, former blacksmith and former hardware merchant, driving and exhorting; with Huntington, prince of lobbyists, prying loose subsidies at Washington; with Stanford, overlord of legislators, levying on the

California counties, the most impudent of railroads was crawling up, up, up.

The last contract for mails by overland stage, after delay and contest, was awarded to Wells, Fargo & Company in October, 1868, for $1,750,000 a year, with deductions as distances should shorten between the approaching railheads. The Union Pacific had not yet tackled the continental divide, and the Central was still struggling at Cisco, a toehold on the Sierra cliff-side only ninety-one miles from its starting-point.

But the express company discounted the stimulation of a bonus of $32,000 a mile, and the energy of the four Sacramento tradesmen who were sharpening their tools of understanding as they went along on the grindstone of the Sierras. With summit tunnels still to be bored, advance gangs of the Central Pacific were already over the cordillera. High above Donner Lake they swarmed like ants, clinging to cliff-sides. Rearing $170,000-a-mile snowsheds as matchwood shields against the onslaughts of new winter. Chipping shelves and galleries in the sky for rails yet to come. Chipping a foot a day.

Three locomotives, twenty flat cars, and forty miles of rail iron appeared as by magic on the east side of the "insurmountable" Sierra. Had the summit tunnel been bored? Not yet; those materials had been dragged across crests on big sleds by preposterous mules.

And now, with Chinese gangs furiously hacking at each end of the longest, highest tunnel, nitroglycerine—tested in anguish in Wells Fargo's courtyard and now mastered at last—swept asunder the intervening granite. Mountain winds, ripping through the gap above Donner Lake, flattened out against the sky a triumphant American bunting. It was November 30, 1867.

Twenty-five thousand woodchoppers, graders, overseers, teamsters, tracklayers poured over the conquered height. Twenty-five sawmills whirred grand trees into ties, bridges, and fodder for the noisy locomotives. Thirty ships at once were out at sea, racing around the Horn with rails, plates, bolts, locomotives, flat cars. And off beyond deserts and divide the Union Pacific's insatiable sledges were ringing out three taps to a spike, ten spikes to a rail, four hundred thousand rails still left to go. The rivals were racing for a juncture. The Chinese versus the Irish.

The pace increased. Central Pacific was out of the Sierras, Union Pacific up and over the Rockies. Day by day the gap narrowed, the mileage of new iron grew. Two miles in a day. Three. Four. Triumphantly, five. By the end of the new year, not long after Wells Fargo had emerged, out of a struggle, with its final coach-mail contracts, the gap between railheads had narrowed to four hundred miles.

Wells Fargo clung as long as possible to the old Overland string of stage stations south of Great Salt Lake. The sledges of the tracklayers were ringing far to northward.

It is a daybreak in April, '69. Out on the bed of what was once a vast sea, whose ancient rims still curve in beach and terrace on the bare shore-mountains, a jaunty Chinese army under peaked woolen caps marches forward to a final battle with Space. It marches in chattering route-step by squads; by companies. Its tented camp has disgorged a thousand pigtailed warriors. Squads of white men are advancing, too. All in sight are picked toilers. They are setting out to accomplish the unheard-of: to lay ten miles of continuous railroad in a day. A train stands on yesterday's track, holding two miles of iron. It is unloaded in fifteen minutes.

Now they are at work, deployed by their overseers; the sky is still slate-pearly. Up the track comes a flat car loaded with rails. A team of horses, hitched tandem, gallops it onward. It meets another car, returning empty save for its crew, who swarm off, tip their vehicle on its side, cheer the loaded car on, right their own to the rails again. The laden flat reaches the end of construction. Waiting hands heave a beam beneath its wheels. Horses are detached, whisked rearward. From each side its cargo of rails is seized, rushed forward by muscular yellow arms, deposited where spikers and bolters can play their merry music. Fast as they ring and clink, other specialists advance with pick and shovel. The twin metal serpents creep forward.

The sky is not yet pink. But all are in stride now, a clanking symphony. Two hundred and forty feet of rail in one minute and twenty seconds. Two hundred and forty feet in one minute and fifteen seconds. Men do not walk unburdened across the sage lands faster than this. Ox-drawn emigrant wagons did not move across the sands much faster than this in the rush for El Dorado. And the wrinkles left by their wheels soon blew away, whereas these men leave iron creases.

Mr. Crocker, the Number One Man, dashes by in his carriage, with his first general, Mr. Strowbridge, beside him. They've a bet on with the Union Pacific crowd about this day's record. The Union Pacific recently laid, between dawn and dark, seven and one-half miles of rail and foolishly crowed about it.

The sky is past ruddy. It is six in the morning. Sand and sagebrush, wind and vacancy—the land of alkali and the roving Indian—have been two miles conquered since daybreak. A train chugs up over the new track with two more miles of iron lances: it puffs up to the very last spike and tie, hissing with impatience. Two hundred tons of iron, two tons of spikes. All off by hand in ten minutes. Wooden ties are meanwhile dashing past in wagons on the right-hand side of the tracklayers; water carts and tool wagons move in steady procession on the left.

Space is being gulped now at the rate of 144 feet a minute. Far at the rear an entire one-street village is in lively motion. Dining rooms, kitchens, tonight's sleeping quarters, are moving up. Soon they arrive; white workmen make for the tables, where they are fed like fighting cocks. The thrifty Chinese have brought their food with them, and squat for lunch along the line of work.

Night nears. The desert mountains turn chocolate, purple, ochre. The red sun is not yet down below the far Sierra pinelands. Dinner is snatched; then an hour spent bending the rails for the great curve which completes this day's work. Ten miles two hundred feet of track—a thousand tons of rails—have been spiked down, gauged, and bolted where yesterday and for a million years before were only gravel and greasewood. Superintendent Campbell runs a locomotive back and forth at fifteen miles an hour. Let Union Pacific contemplate *that*.

Union Pacific does contemplate it, and with awe. Likewise Wells Fargo. A month later the Pacific Railroad is an operating reality.

Before all this, with sadness and reluctance, Wells Fargo had realized that its Overland Mail Line was doomed. And so, with the unrailed gap remorselessly narrowing, interest in stagecoaching evaporated; in its dying days the Overland Mail became a sorry affair. Complaints were printed in the newspapers that mail pouches were often tied about the axle-trees, where the driver could not see them when they fell off.

Wells, Fargo & Co. were ten days in bringing the mail from Salt Lake City to the eastern terminus of the Central Pacific Railroad—a delay entirely inexcusable. In the slow days of the stages we invariably received our mails from Salt Lake—a distance of over 700 miles—in six days.

Such scolding was echoed in the press of every community. A traveler arrived on the Comstock reporting he had seen four hundred mail bags at Schell Creek Station, on the east side of Steptoe Slough, two hundred and thirty miles west of Salt Lake. The weight of this mail was twenty tons, and there seemed little probability of its removal for the next three months. The slough was three miles wide, a bog of soft, tough clay, covered with six inches of water.

"Happy Harry" Harper would have known how to manage through. But now in these faltering days passengers were compelled to hire Indians to pack their baggage over, and to either wade across or be carried— which latter style was especially favored by feminine travelers. The operation required four Indians, who had poles rigged with gunny sacks whereon the passenger was seated, and the impromptu sedan chair was then slung over the shoulders of the porters, who waded and floundered. It cost forty dollars to be packed across, with every instant precarious.

In such slough of despond and disinterest wallowed the grand old Overland, with Wells Fargo feebly yelling "Git eoup!" from the driver's seat. It was a curious glimpse of the drooping morale of the mighty express concern whose name for two decades had been synonymous with enterprise.

Fortunately for western heroics, Abbot, Downing & Company's proud old thorough-braced products, with their yellow wheels, red bodies, leather curtains, and door-panel landscapes, were not to sink wholly out of sight in Steptoe Slough. Before the bubbles of that doleful quag could rise over their tops completely, or the last silken tip of fourteen-foot whiplash disappear forever in the oblivion of Schell Creek ooze, rescuing hands of independent stagemen plucked them forth, separated them from their adhering mud and mail, and dispatched them for doughty service on the Deadwood road, the Tucson trail, the Oregon–California, Salt Lake to Montana and a hundred other paths that were still unrailed.

Wells Fargo watched them go, waved them onward perhaps, with the knockdown purchase money in its fingers. Its career as a central overland stagemaster had been brief, but had been tremendous.

Then, like the intrepid expressman it after all was, it turned to seeing what best might be done on this new cross-continent carrier which moved, not one coach behind many horses, but many coaches behind one horse noisy of bell and whistle.

Shock and surprise again were waiting.

There had sprung into being, during this track-laying frenzy, a competitor to the old treasure and express carrier known as the Pacific Union Express Company. Lloyd Tevis and D. O. Mills, hard-bitten buccaneers of business, were among the figures wearing the mask of the Pacific Union Express. Wells Fargo, which had beaten down all opposition so many times in the past, seems to have eyed this one good-naturedly. Possibly the eyesight of Louis and Charles McLane, heads of the established concern, were so filled with the dust of their many stage lines that they did not see the portentous trap that was being prepared. While Mills and Tevis were putting their new concern into the desirable western towns and mining camps, hiring the most efficient local men as agents, Wells Fargo with easy complacency ordered its whole general quarters moved from San Francisco to New York. When the railroad builders topped the Sierra, and the Pacific Union announced a daily connecting pony to cover the twenty-two miles from Reno to Virginia City, Wells Fargo countered enthusiastically by fetching the old Pony Express rider Bob Haslam from his Carson run and putting him astride its relays up and over the Geiger grade. Important business opposition the Wells Fargo management had forgotten how to meet; but a daily horse race—that was another matter.

And right joyfully the men along the Comstock entered into the carnival. It became the prime news of the Lode. "Wells, Fargo & Co.'s Pony Express made the run from Reno tonight in fifty-nine minutes and twenty-three seconds. Twelve horses were used." "An exciting race between the Express Companies came off tonight. Wells, Fargo & Co. ran a buggy and the Pacific Union a pony. The latter was barely ahead here and the former was ahead at Gold Hill." "The Wells Fargo messenger reached Virginia 6 minutes before the Pacific Union express yesterday. Time one hour and 4 minutes." "The rider for Wells, Fargo & Co. was 'Bob' Haslam, an old time Pony Express rider . . . Frank Henderson rode for the Pacific Union Express . . . Both riders were waiting for the mail at Reno. Each rider had 5 changes for horses about four miles apart, and both received their packages before the cars were stopped. The Pacific Express rider got about 10 rods start (Bob delayed until his bag was firmly fastened to his back), but Bob soon overhauled and passed him (in one mile) and kept ahead of him for the rest of the distance . . . Bennett, the driver of the Wells Fargo lightning express wagon, a light buckboard, came near beating both ponies but having worn out horses could not keep up." "The Pacific Union Pony was ahead tonight." Over the flats from Reno, up the long Geiger grade, around the flank of Mount Davidson they came neck and neck, nose and nose, the old carrier and the new. It was a repetition of fifteen years before—the brushes between Wells Fargo and Adams, Reynolds, Wines and Gregory. Thousands of dollars and half a thousand drinks rested on the first velvet nose, hung on the first jingling bridle to pass up C Street hill.

But the unglimpsed promoters behind the Pacific Union, and behind them four other shaggy Kings of Get—Stanford, Crocker, Huntington, Hopkins, the railroad builders —weren't worrying about twenty-two-mile horse races. Their ambush was now nearly arranged. No champagne party, no affable affair of receipt and seizure this. It would be an ambush that would blast the old driver completely off his perch; that would leave him sprawled in the dust while they lashed away with coach itself, all horses, and all treasure.

During the spring of final rail-laying the shares of Wells Fargo underwent inexplicable pounding on the stock boards of New York and San Francisco. From $100 a share they dropped to $13. At a satisfactory figure the conspirators quietly loaded up.

Wells Fargo continued cheering its ponies up the Comstock hill and boxing its headquarters files for transfer to New York. Somebody was playing with its stock, but its earnings were secure. Too much was being made in the public mind of this Pacific Union upstart. The veteran had been challenged before. The end was always the same. Let this new rival acquire a business and enjoy a few rousing losses, and the old expressman would move majestically in and take him over.

With Louis McLane still making private investments in far western stage lines, genial brother Charles running the express, and brother Allan president of the coöperating ocean monopolist, the Pacific Mail, the Wells Fargo management which had fought and outlived Haskell, Woods, Ben Holladay, and a thousand circumstances of banditry, Indians, and high water had no tremors for the future.

On a Monday in May, 1,086 miles from Omaha and 689 from Sacramento, locomotives from east and west at last met, touched noses and bleated their whistles out in the Salt Lake desert. There it was, the chimerical railroad— completed with a speed that paled even the stirring achievements of the Pony Express. With sawmill engineers at the throttles and stage tenders at the brakes, those trains had brought Pacific Ocean and Missouri River within five days of each other.

Wells Fargo had written off its overland coaches, and moved now to put its overland express on the new steam carrier. It was at this point that Tevis, Mills, and their associates stepped from ambush.

They stepped with one barrel of their shotgun loaded with something more than buckshot. They presented a contract, executed between the Central Pacific Railroad and the Pacific Union Express twenty months before, for the exclusive transport of the new company's express matter on the transcontinental line. The contract was dated September 23, 1867, for a life of ten years.

The effect was cataclysmic. William G. Fargo, Charles Fargo, and A. H. Barney—the latter, president of the old house,—were tumbled hurriedly out of New York and dispatched for Omaha, whither Mills, Tevis, and confederates moved to meet them. And when the western delegation arrived, they arrived with the other barrel of their shotgun also loaded. They had not only that exclusive rail contract, but practical control of Wells Fargo's stock as well.

For emphasis, they also presented a pistol: the fact that an additional express company had been organized by the Union Pacific Railroad to operate between Ogden and Omaha, precluding through shipments by the express contractor on the west except by swap arrangements. And the only man who could negotiate such swap appeared to be Charley Crocker of the Tevis-Mills combination.

The hold-up was complete. From the closed room where these doings were in progress there emanated an agreement to increase Wells Fargo's stock by a third and make the additional issue over to Pacific Union Express as the price of its absorption. Tom Bell, Captain Ingram, Jack Davis and Tom Poole had been but timid road-agents. These bolder practitioners, with mere paper weapons, in one swift assault had relieved the grand old fighting corporation of a third of its $10,000,000 assets.

The headquarters of Wells Fargo were ordered back to the Golden Gate almost before the filing boxes at New York had been unpacked. One by one new, western names appeared on the directorate. Old passengers, with New York addresses, got out of the coach. The ambushers climbed aboard and took the reins, with the result there was no more financial ambushing.

In 1872 Lloyd Tevis of San Francisco ascended to the Wells Fargo presidency, a driver's seat which he occupied for the next twenty years.

XVII

THE ARIZONA APPASSIONATA

As Abilene, Dodge City, and the other cowboy capitals of the prairie country yielded to sweetness and culture and their bad men fled, Arizona threw her arms wide to all. And over her borders they tumbled: gamblers and murderers and barroom bravos and their old pursuers, the not less murderous professional marshals. To all these swaggerers and nuisances Arizona was a rainbow's end. Its mines belched gold, then silver, then copper, and anything that happened could always be attributed to lawless Sonorans or Apaches. Americans who wanted their hell served up in a hurry gathered joyfully in the one-stored adobe towns with their low-ceilinged saloons, monte and faro dens, and honky-tonks where mandolins tinkled, light heels twinkled, and the percentage girls swayed to castanets and Mexican guitars.

On November 26, 1879, three Sonorans dry-gulched the Prescott stage near Gillett, disarmed the driver, bayoneted to death William Thompson, a passenger; then robbed the stage. The incident was casual. Renegades and desperadoes were streaming in. It was the dawning era of Curly Bill and John Ringo, Zwing Hunt and Billy

Grounds, the Clanton gang and fast-shooting Buckskin Frank Leslie; of the gun-minded Earps—Wyatt, deputy United States marshal; Virgil, city marshal of Tombstone; Morgan, the younger brother who by turns served as shotgun messenger for Wells Fargo and Tombstone police officer; and their faithful and deadly ally, the morose, quick-fingered, consumptive dentist-gambler, John H. Holliday.

The stage was set. Actors were making resounding entrances and were about to make fast exits. Before it was over, the sands of Arizona would run thoroughly red; murders and outlawry would be the largest subject before the legislature; vigorous men would "dance on air" and look up the pitiless length of a vigilante rope; and the roar of lawless guns would reach clear to Presidential ears at Washington.

Luck, inscrutable lady, was with Bob Paul on the morning of March 15, 1881.

Bob Paul was shotgun guard for Wells Fargo, and he rode on the Sandy Bob coach as it pulled out from Tombstone on the Benson road.

Luck knew that a grim group awaited in the defile near Drew's ranch on the rude north road. Luck knew whether three local ne'er-do-wells, Crane, Head, and Lennord, were numbered among this dour quartet. Luck also knew whether "Doc" Holliday, the saturnine dentist, who so preferred filling his patients with lead to silver amalgam, was also lurking in the pass. Luck knew why "Doc" had hired a fast horse from a Tombstone stable just after the coach had left; knew what direction he had taken on a cross-country gallop. Luck knew that "Doc" had often been reminded by his cronies, the marshal and deputy marshal at Tombstone, that he was too trigger-hasty. Luck knew what was in the Wells Fargo box. Luck knew everything. So when Bud Philpot, the driver, said, "You take the lines awhile, Bob, and I'll hold your gun," Luck smiled on Bob Paul the Wells Fargo messenger, saving him for other uses, and sighed forlornly over poor Bud Philpot.

A few moments later a shot rang out, and the holder of the Wells Fargo shotgun pitched dead from the top of the stage. Another shot, almost an echo of the first, and a passenger lurched to the road beside him, pierced through the heart.

The sudden assault sent the team clattering in wild panic. Their headlong dash saved the bullion. Stocky Bob Paul of the toothbrush moustache, future sheriff of Pima County, clawed and dragged them to a halt. The robbers, frustrated by the stampede and general to-do, leaped to saddle and fled.

Shortly afterward "Doc" Holliday, on a badly blown mount, returned to Tombstone town; turned in his lathered steed at the livery stable, engaged a fresh animal, tied it ostentatiously in front of the Bob Hatch saloon, and disappeared within.

"Coming with us, Doc?" asked the Earps, marshal and deputy marshal, as they paused in Bob Hatch's barroom to pour libation to a successful man-hunt.

The hair-trigger operator rather thought he would.

A man feels the need of a good brisk ride after standing by a dentist's chair all day.

On January 6, 1882, the coach from Tombstone for Bisbee absorbed a fusillade of bullets from a band of robbers who, stationed about one hundred yards ahead, had emptied their rifles without warning. With one horse wounded, Driver W. S. Wait succeeded in turning his team and started back for Tombstone on the run. Charles A. Bartholomew, Wells Fargo messenger, defended the running fort with his Winchester for about four miles, when three of the robbers, who had galloped ahead by a short cut, again got in front of the vehicle.

But a headed stage is not a surrendered stage. The fight-minded messenger with his grown-up Henry rifle continued to make the vehicle more thorny than a many-fanged cholla bush.

The robbers, after circling vainly and wounding several passengers, fell back on strategy. They saw a Mexican approaching on a load of wood. Him they directed to go and relieve the stagecoach of its treasure-box on pain of instant extermination. With three rifles pointing at his back, the luckless Mexican approached the stage with huge sombrero politely lifted. A shot or two into the sand behind his heels sustained his purpose. Messenger Bartholomew in simple pity withheld his fire. The Mexican, in halting English, explained. If the Americans would leave their coach and retire some distance up the road, no one would be the loser but Wells Fargo, and he, the wood-hauler, would be permitted to proceed, with the mother of God's goodness, to his many waiting children. If the instruction were not obeyed, all, including wood-hauler, messenger, driver, and passengers would unquestionably be killed.

Messenger Bartholomew was still full of martial ardor. But the will of the wounded passengers prevailed. All retired from the vehicle and withdrew to a distance; the robbers secured the $6,500 pay roll of the Bisbee mine; then the coach, minus two horses and its chest and carrying its casualties, moved back to Tombstone.

C. B. Hawley was engaged in the wood and charcoal business at Globe, Arizona, where he "stood fair as a citizen," in the early eighties; removing therefrom with his family to Salt Lake City in search of a better living. Business at the city of saints languishing, it occurred to him that affairs could be made to thrive by a brisk stroke at his old home place. He returned to Globe, consulted with Lafayette B. Grimes, a young man who was said to have had past experience in the proposed line in northern California; and on August 20, 1882, the two went together four miles out of town to a summit position on the Pinal mountains and built a stone breastwork.

A string of mules slowly wound up the sun-baked Pinals. It was the Express, conveying, among other property, $5,000 in gold coin en route from San Francisco and in charge of capable Messenger Andy Hall.

Andy Hall was popular in Globe and one of Wells Fargo's most trusted couriers. His valor was not confined to gun toting. He had been with Major Powell's

party in its epic descent and exploration of the Colorado
River through the thunderous and perilous Grand Canyon. With Andy Hall on this mule-express journey was
a packer named Porter; and for a portion of the journey
they had ridden accompanied by Dr. W. F. Vail, who was
returning from an inspection of some mines.

As the string of mules, plodding sweatily behind its
jingling bell-mare, came within range of the breastwork,
Grimes and Hawley rose and released a volley of winged
lead. Chaos was immediate. But the mule carrying the
express box had not been hit. Porter leaped for his rear-
ing animals. Andy Hall in a flash had his revolver out
and was after the assailants, who sprang from their shelter,
lashed the express-mule before them, and fled. Porter,
wrestling with his plunging mules, saw Andy ride around
the shoulder of a gully and disappear. Shots reëchoed
among the tawny hills, followed by a vast silence.

Porter was unarmed. Tethering what was left of his
string, he clapped spurs to his horse and fairly flew down
the slopes of the Pinals, rounded up the first man he saw,
and returned with him. They rode hard in the direction
the assailants had taken with Andy Hall following. A
mile beyond, lying on his face with eight bullet holes
in his body—all in front—lay the late Grand Canyon
explorer and faithful messenger. All chambers of his
revolver had been emptied before he lost the battle. Riding farther, the two came to the abandoned camp of the
assailants. Dr. Vail lay outstretched in the hot sun,
breathing painfully. He too, hearing the banging, had
ridden after the bandits and been raked with lead. The

robbers had made off with the $5,000. Speaking with effort, Dr. Vail described them; then expired.

One tall and dark. One short and light. That would be Grimes and Hawley. On the evening of the fourth day following, the sheriff and posse brought in the two men from Bloody Tank. While they cowered in the Globe town jail, a mass meeting took place just outside, followed by a parley between officers and townsmen which the townsmen won. Then the prisoners were dragged forth tightly surrounded, and escorted to Stalla's Hall, where a citizens' court had been organized.

The prisoners asked for three hours' time, promising to reveal the hiding place of the money. This was granted. In company with thirty citizens they repaired to the foothills and pointed out the cache. Most of the loot still remained. Vosburgh, the express agent, took it tenderly in charge. The party then returned to the hall. Hawley asked to make a written confession, purged his soul by means of this document; and at 1:45 A.M. the church bells began to toll. A procession moved in the direction of a big sycamore on Main Street near Pinal Creek. Saloons had closed their doors. Not even a drunk was to be seen on the street. No word was uttered. It was all very genteel.

A few minutes later bells stopped tolling, saloon doors burst inward, and there sounded once more the clink of genial glassware, the merry click of roulette and castanet.

On August 10, 1883, the express, mail, and passenger stage pulled out of Florence in the Gila River valley for

Globe, forty-five miles northeastward. On the seat beside the driver sat Wells Fargo Messenger J. H. Collins, his double-barreled shotgun between his knees; beneath his feet was the treasure box, containing a substantial dispatch of silver bullion. On the roof of the coach sat "Red Jack" Almer, as light-hearted a young man as ever wore red flannel shirt, ornamented with gleaming white neckerchief, under the rose-tinted glow of an Arizona summer twilight. As the coach bowled along, darkness fell and the moon rose. Red Jack Almer felt his spirits mount. In view of so much scenery, such adequate moonlight and such all-round well-being, he broke forth in far-carrying song:

"I'm on my best horse and I'm lopin' at a run,
I'm the fastest-shootin' cowboy that ever pulled a gun,
Coma ti yi yoopy, yoopy yay, yoopy yay,
Coma ti yi yoopy, yoopy yay."

Sweeping along over the uneven road, the outfit dipped into a dry wash on the south side of the Gila. As the stage moved into this gully Jack Almer's song was slightly interrupted by the passing indisposition known as a frog-in-the-throat. However, he gulped this down and continued vocalizing lustily. The stage clambered up the other side. Once or twice Almer looked behind. Perhaps he saw something moving. Adjusting his white kerchief more prominently than ever—he had spent some care washing it out to such chaste snowiness—Red Jack held his red-flanneled arms high, stretched ostentatiously, and caroled as though his manly heart would burst.

The horses were changed at Evan's Station. At some distance from the road, moving parallel through the mesquite, two shadowy horsemen might have been seen cantering. Across the river at a point known as Riverside, beyond Putnam's ranch, there was a sudden crashing rattle from the creosote bushes. Messenger Collins straightened up as if to make a speech, turned it into a bow, and toppled off the box, his body riddled with eight bullets, his shotgun clattering with him beneath the horses' heels. "Red Jack" Almer slid off the stage. As he slid, his knife came to his hand from his leather belt-scabbard. He used it, however, not for fighting the highwaymen, but to slash the traces and further cripple the stage. One robber took the near-leader out of the slashed traces. Another laid to the Wells Fargo box with a hand axe.

The Gila River country had been preyed on for months by a well-organized bandit gang. Its rocky defiles and canyons offered perfect hiding-places. Isolated ranches, generally suspected of being outposts of the band, were stocked with provisions and fresh horses. One of these ranches was owned by Len G. Redfield, who had come to Arizona seven years before and prospered inexplicably. Another was A. S. Hartzel's ranch seventy-five miles to southward up San Pedro Valley. The syndicate, one of the best organized since Hell, Inc., had opened for business over the Spanish-American Southwest, operated over an area a hundred miles square.

Leaving the scene of robbery with $3,500 from the express box and the stolen coach horse on a lead-rope, the killers made for Redfield's ranch. Dawn was coming up over the Pinals. Joe Tuttle went into the kitchen and cooked a hearty breakfast. After this meal, feeling weary from the labors of the night, he and Redfield elected to remain. Red Jack and Charley Hensley preferred to keep moving. They pushed southward into the mountains and cached the stolen silver at a water hole.

It was while dawn was lighting Tuttle's endeavors over the breakfast stove that a posse out of Florence, including Agent Brickwood and Special Agent Casanega of Wells, Fargo & Company, paused at the scene of wanton slaying and studied its curious relics. For such practiced and expert freebooters the Hensley-Redfield band had laid preposterous clues. One was a hand axe, left on the ground near the splintered express box: it was from Smith & Murray's general store at Florence, and the merchants had no difficulty recalling that they had sold it to Len Redfield. Another was a pair of saddlebags, recognized as the property of Joe Tuttle. The third was Red Jack's knife. The pursuers divided; one division moving on a lope for the Redfield ranch, another turning sharply south and making for the Hartzel property.

The Redfield gallopers burst upon that too-prosperous ranchman and his killer-cook and dragged them to Florence, where Tuttle confessed; whereupon a lynching party escorted them to the corridor of the county jail and demonstrated a new use for Jailer Scanlan's rafters.

While Hartzel was being dragged out of his eyrie and shaken into confessing that Hensley and Almer had lately stopped there, Sheriff Bob Paul of Pima doggedly took up the trail; pursuit had moved into his county. It was a twisting trail and a wearisome, and at times all but vanished. But two weeks later he picked up tidings. Hensley had been seen in the Rincon Mountains near Tucson; he was encamped somewhere along the summits, and had found time to engage in a blood feud with a local miner, whom he had sworn to settle. On the night of August 27th the robbers indeed came down, and unknown to Paul's party, who were encamped on the mountain, spent the night on a ledge almost directly above their heads. With morning the vengeful Hensley crawled farther down the hill, waylaid his foeman on his way to the mine, and took the promised shot; failing, however, to hit. The assaulted miner sprinted for all he was worth, yelling bloody murder. So close did this secondary battle occur to the camping posse that Paul and Brickwood rushed to the encounter and even succeeded in getting in a shot at the departing Hensley. But it was a day of shots that missed. The pair of robbers dodged up the canyons and became lost in their mazes, leaving to the sheriff their horses, ammunition, and all provisions.

Again the trail vanished. Weeks passed. It became the conviction of the countryside that the fugitives had returned to the Gila, found friends and new horses, and dusted out completely. But Paul and Special Agent Casanega stuck to the trail. In October came authentic word that the wanted men had been seen at Perry Brothers' ranch thirty miles from Wilcox.

The trail-end was nearing. It was further learned that Hensley and Almer would appear on a certain night at the Perry ranch to receive provisions. The men were desperate; they had sworn to "go out smoking"; the badly needed food was to be placed for them on the tailboard of a big freight wagon in the ranch yard.

On a night of wild wind and rain, with possemen in wait under several wagons, the hunted men came to the bait. Paul rose in the blackness and yelled "Halt!"

The wanted pair ducked, dodged, ran, and began firing. The whole posse poured a volley into the dark. It lifted Hensley off his feet, catching him in breast and abdomen. But he came up fighting. The pursuers poured more fire in the direction of his gunflashes. One man-hunter went down with a bullet in his leg. Red Jack, the accomplished vocalist, who had fallen at first volley with a charge of buckshot in stomach and a rifle ball through his skull, lay thoroughly and admirably dead. Hensley's gun had flown out of its owner's hand. He crawled to Almer and felt for the latter's weapon. The piece had a shattered butt but was still shootin'-sound. Trailing this rifle, and holding his mangled middle together with one hand, Hensley crawled about four hundred yards through darkness and located his horse. An hour after the opening salvo, during which time the sheriff's party had been delicately trying to locate their man in darkness and rain, the clatter of hoofs told them that the robber chief had again escaped. More than clatter of hoofs announced it. As the wounded Hensley departed, he tossed three more shots at the sheriff, one of which took that official's horse out from under him.

Another daybreak. The trail was plainer now than it had been for weeks: it was a trail of crimson on leaves and rocks. Eight miles onward, in a little canyon, Paul dismounted and scouted ahead. A bullet-smack on the rocks behind told him that he had again found range of the bandit's sting. Hensley was down behind a little oak. His horse was standing beside him, plainly visible against a boulder. The desperado, grimly game, was lying on his stomach in a little gully and shooting uphill. Paul signaled his men to circle wide. While he drew the fire, Deputies Carillo, Casanega, and McClarty flanked the foe and sent ten bullets into their quarry.

When they turned the leader of the extirpated robber-gang over, they beheld with amazement a body virtually drained white after the savage wounding and desperate flight of the night just ended.

Pearl Hart was a lady who was no lady. She invaded Arizona in the late eighties as one of the Junos of a vivid blond sisterhood. Brown's "Congress Hall" at Tucson, the "Oriental" at Tombstone, and Gus Hirschfeldt's "Palace" at Phoenix knew Pearl extremely well—or a lot of girls confusingly like her. Amidst the tables Pearl moved with scarlet lips, dyed lashes, a handsome bust, large hips, inveigling ankles; while Mexicans over against the wall strummed "Cielito Lindo" and "La Golondrina" sleepily and the air grew smoky-blue. It may be presumed that many a pair of eyes were pulled up from blackjack stack or tumbler of coffin-varnish to stare into the orbs of imposing Pearl; and that Pearl, whatever her frailties, was quite able to stare back.

One of the customers of a Phoenix establishment, Mr.

Joe Boot, having essayed his evening's all on a cocked ace, sadly saw the box deliver a queen of hearts. Businesslike rattle of croupier's rake was supported by businesslike laughter from the watching Miss Hart, whose lips curved like a cupid's bow—or an Apache's—and whose breasts were sultry. Queens appearing to have it that evening, Mr. Boot arose from Gus Hirschfeldt's faro layout and sat down with this trouble-promiser at another table. They had a number of drinks, Mr. Boot consuming most, Miss Hart pocketing the commissions, and before the night was over they had become old chums. Such chums that the next time Mr. Boot entered the dive he handed glamorous Pearl the even half of a small fortune, having had some luck, he intimated, at highway-mining out Prescott way. Pearl pressed for particulars. Joe reluctantly advanced them. Divulging that her nature craved more adventure than "Palace" or "Congress Hall" provided, she proposed a partnership. Joe Boot accepted.

They adjourned, that 1889 October, to Cane Springs Canyon on the slope of Four Peaks and waited for the stage. When it arrived, Mr. Boot expertly rifled express box and passengers, while Miss Hart stood guard, first taking his gun away from the indignant driver.

The stage rolled on, and a posse came back, and a matter of high-heeled footprints landed Hart & Boot in jail. The liquidation of their affairs went hard on Mr. Boot, who got quite a stretch; but a jury of her peers just couldn't bear to be stern with queenly Pearl. They gallantly acquitted her of levying on passengers or express box.

But the law had resources. It picked Miss Hart up again and put her on trial for lifting that sixshooter from the stage driver. About this charge her peers were not so gallant; in some matters the masculine sex must stand together. Scarlet Pearl was sent to do her future trouble-making in Yuma penitentiary.

Down in Brown's "Congress Hall" at Tucson, the "Oriental" at Tombstone, and Hirschfeldt's "Palace" at Phoenix the Mexican orchestras continued to twank "Golondrina" and "Paloma." Smugglers, gamblers, marshals, rogues, and average citizens continued to push their way to the faro tables or to thump the bars for jolts of coffin varnish. Mirrors continued to glitter and the air to grow smoky blue. Vivid blond Junos and dusky Conchitas continued to move amidst the tables, swishing shoulders, hips, and ankles for what it got them. Memory grew dim of Joe Boot the easy loser and Pearl Hart the bounteous wife of half a camp.

And out on the desert the Spanish bayonet, mesquite, barrel cactus, and ocatilla bush grew and grew.

XVIII

THE TRAIN OF EVENTS

WE meet once more Jack Davis and his jolly brotherhood.

It is late autumn on the Great Basin borderline. To five men who lounge in a deserted mine tunnel on Ravine Mountain, three miles west of Reno, life is cozy. The cave is fitted with rugs, blankets, and a fireplace. A touch less domestic is provided by scattered cards, discarded bottles and an arsenal of shotguns and rifles. But it is a clubby spot, well concealed from winds and public eyesight, and the entrance to the hole affords sweeping view of the new Central Pacific Railroad as it winds down from the mountains.

If the group in this sequestered place were to follow those rails three hundred and eighty-five miles eastward —which they won't; they haven't traveled forty rods in days—they would be impressed by a coincidence. For they would come on a layout curiously like their own, even to the cards, bottles and rifles, in a hidden spot in Nevada-Utah's Pequop Mountains. Minds of a like sort, it seems, run in like channels. But the group under the Sierra Nevadas is not interested in affairs on that horizon.

A sentinel squats at the entrance on the heels of small

custom-shod feet. He stirs, cocks his rifle. A step has sounded.

"It's only me, boys. Telegram."

"I'll take it!" One of the cave's tenants, who looks like a minister, extends a lean white hand. Others crowd around. "*San Francisco, 4th November. Sol. Jones, Reno. Send sixty dollars today if possible. Joseph Enrique.*"

" 'Sixty.' " The mellifluous one translates. "That'll mean there's sixty thousand dollars aboard. '*Today.*' That means the train just started. The Yellow Jacket pay roll, if I know anything, and Yellow Jacket means honey. I guess we're moving, boys."

Central Pacific No. One, the eastbound express, didn't know when it pulled out of Oakland Mole on the morning of November 4, 1870, that it was a train of destiny. Overland rail travel after eighteen months of existence was still an adventure, but what was now impending had yet to be encountered by any train on the line. Nevertheless, No. One was about to be held up—not once, but twice.

Unaware, and therefore unconcernedly, No. One, consisting of a combination baggage and express car, a day coach, and a round-ended sleeper, thumped across California behind its shiny red wood-burning locomotive and labored up and over the Sierra Nevada. Near Truckee, just east of the summit, it was delayed for two hours by a freight collision ahead. Collisions were not unusual to the new art of mountain railroading. With monte games and two solid blocks of bar-rooms for their entertainment, passengers and train crew endured the layover in the Sierra village. Getting under steam again, shortly after midnight, the train dropped quickly and entered the desert at Verdi, a lumber siding.

Bright moon looked down on bare hills. Into its disc Crystal Peak thrust up a stony apex. From the black shadows of the lumber siding seven men, in masks and dusters, caught the train as it trundled by and swung swiftly aboard. Some hooked to the front of the baggage-express. Others sprang to its rear. Conductor Mitchell and a brakeman, coming out of the day coach just behind the express car, found themselves confronted by rough-looking passengers with hand guns instead of tickets. Conductor and brakeman ducked inside. Meanwhile other brigands, crawling over the tender, had leaped into the cab and enormously startled the engineer and fireman.

Conductor Mitchell, whose through clients were lustily snoring, meditated a moment under the swinging kerosene lamps. It did not occur to him that his new passengers wanted to steal a whole train. He thought they merely wanted to steal a ride. That meant trouble for himself with the General Auditor; and Conductor Mitchell, who had small fear of avalanches, blazing trestles, bridges out, snowsheds afire, Utes, Shoshones, hell, or high water, could find quavers in his soul when he thought of the General Auditor. Meanwhile his train was rocking along at reckless gait. The locomotive whistled for brakes. The brakeman darted for the rear platform. That left Conductor Mitchell alone. What he needed, to enforce the dignity of his railroad, was a weapon. His eye fell on a fire axe held to the wall by two hooks. Conductor

Mitchell detached that axe and advanced once more toward the front platform. It was empty.

With a gun in his ribs, Engineer Small had been ordered to stop. It was in response to this order that he had drawn on the whistle-cord. Fast-working hands unhooked the two passenger coaches from the engine and express. When Conductor Mitchell stepped down to the roadbed, gripping his axe, it was to see with amaze the business end of his train starting up again and moving off, with ever-increasing momentum, on the long downhill grade of western Nevada in the direction of Humboldt Sink. Laved in the light of a brilliant full moon and many desert stars, engine and express sped onward, till a curve caught them, and sight and sound of the runaway rolling-stock vanished. Conductor Mitchell went back to his passenger coaches. He wondered what the General Auditor would have to say about *that*.

Unscheduled halts in the mountains and desert were not disconcerting to Wells Fargo Messenger Marshall, who put down this stop beyond Verdi to general engine cussedness or one of the little games flagmen love to play, running up and down the tracks with signal flares and torpedoes. He was alone in his half of the partitioned baggage-express with a heavy shipment in gold coin and bar silver. The gold was to be put off at Reno. Messenger Marshall sat down on his locked express box and prepared to receive the agent at the door.

It was not Reno, this next stop, but an old trackside quarry; it was not Nels Hammond, the Wells Fargo Reno agent, who appeared at his car door, but a stranger, backed by other strangers, and also backed by the biggest shotgun Marshall had ever stared into. His own weapons were in a corner. The initiative was all with the callers.

Into the car with him were propelled the engineer and fireman. The three were commanded into a corner. The invitation, was gestured with the big fowling-piece, and was accepted. Into the car then mounted other brigands, who threw out the treasure box and some assorted matter, dismissed as unworthy of attention such silver coins as tumbled to the floor, and also ignored $8,000 worth of bar silver which they adjudged too weighty for carrying. All told they tossed out $41,600 in gold and specie. A pickaxe was produced from the quarry, the treasure box was beaten open, its contents were stuffed into some old boots as convenient gripsacks. And the seven dispersed.

Conductor Mitchell was a man of resource. When he saw the front end of his train go gliding off in silvery moonlight, to the hoots of a desert coyote and the snores of his passengers, he unclamped the brakes and set off in pursuit with the headless remainder. He had no engine, but he had downhill tracks. Just as Engineer Small and his fireman were about concluding that it would be all right to climb back on their engine and return for the coaches, around a curve and upon them came the day coach and round-end sleeper. No time was lost hooking up and speeding the remaining miles to Reno, where telegraph wires were set sputtering and the world was apprised that something very commotional had happened to western railroading.

Wells Fargo offered $10,000. The Central Pacific, the State of Nevada, and the violated county offered $20,000 more. Off into pearling dawn, with relief crew and new expressage, No. One moved to its second rendezvous with tribulation.

In no part of the world [assured a popular tourists' handbook of the decade] is travel made so easy and comfortable as on the Pacific Railroad. To travelers from the East it is a constant delight, and to ladies and families it is accompanied with absolutely no fatigue or discomfort. One lives at home in the Palace Car with as much true enjoyment as in the home drawing-room. . . . The slow rate of speed, which averages but twenty to thirty miles per hour day and night, produces a peculiarly smooth, gentle, and easy motion, most soothing and agreeable. The days of boisterous times, rough railroad men and bullies in the Far West, are gone.

Three hundred and eighty-five miles onward, at 11:15 P.M. of the same day, the Train of Events attained this rendezvous.

It pulled out of Independence, a station which is no metropolis now and in 1870 was less so. The moon which had beheld such bold doings in western Nevada was now overcast. From behind a vacant shed near the track four men slipped out. Two jumped the engine steps and the others each took an end of the baggage-express. They gripped two Henry rifles, two carbines, and a set of revolvers. While the new engineer was feeling and considering the cold muzzle of a rifle at the top of his spine and the short hairs at the fireman's neck were being similarly titillated, the raider at the rear of the express car cut its signal cord and unchained from the rest of the train. Carter, now conductor, was inside counting tickets when he felt his car losing momentum. He ran to the platform, saw black ground widening between himself and the accelerating express, and yelled to its messenger:

"Pull your signal cord! You're losing part of your train!"

The messenger heard him and yanked. But the engineer kept on. That rifle insisted on nuzzling the base of his skull. With vehemence he kept on.

The grade was steadily upward; in no time the severed cars were far behind, and stalled. Six miles beyond Independence, fireman, mail clerk, and messenger were thrust off the kidnaped head end, and the engineer told to keep going. The messenger before ejection managed to slip $10,000 into a hiding place in his car where it later went unnoticed. Near Pequop, another siding, the engine was stopped. Raiders rifled the express car, selected $1,400 in coin, $2,600 in gold dust, twenty-three packages of mail, and a bar of silver. The quartet then waved farewell and leaped to waiting horses.

Conductor Carter had been hearing all day about the robbery of the previous night. Each of his passengers had hinted, with varying emphasis, that the Verdi seven would have been completely routed if he, the speaking passenger, had only been awake. During this second seizure of the front end of the same train, Conductor Carter had been busy among his warlike overland passengers. When he told them they should now have their chance, and to please get out their weapons, several dropped revolvers behind cushions and out of windows;

others discovered their ammunition in bad order or chambers jammed; but a fair-sized armament was nevertheless assembled. The volunteer infantry hastily set off up the track at the heels of the conductor. Tripping over ties in the dark—where *was* that moon?—the small army nearly reached the spot where fireman, mail clerk, and express messenger had been thrust off to botanize amid the midnight sagebrush, when all were met by the engineer backing downhill with his engine and express. Return was made to Independence for the rest of the rolling stock, passengers there waiting promptly recovered their firearms and demanded to be shown something to shoot at, and the Train of Events rolled on.

Two attacks on the same train sent a shock of admiration through the road-agent profession and brought out posters announcing additional thousands in rewards. Pursuers were out in force on both borders of the Sagebrush State.

We follow, under November's moon, the first batch of brigands.

The Verdi hold-up occurred in the early hours of Saturday. That evening a lone traveler, followed at an interval by two others, appeared at N. Pearson's little alpine tavern in Sardine Valley northwest of Verdi and called for supper. After supper he called for a bed. His name was John Squires. Innkeeper Pearson, after seeing to the supper of the second arrivals, lighted him to a room upstairs. The two newcomers, Parsons and Gilchrist, also desired a bed. They were lodged together across the hall

from Squires. Business appeared to be booming in Sardine
Valley.

But for men who had seemed strangers at supper, some
quaint bond operated in the small hours of Sunday morning. Squires' pine-floored chamber was directly over that
of the proprietors. Mrs. Pearson heard her guest's
bed creak, heard him get up, heard him cross the hall
to the other bedroom and stay long in whispered conversation.

Mrs. Pearson was a woman of curiosity.

After breakfast Squires and Parsons, who had been
such strangers the night before, checked out together and
rode away northward, leaving Gilchrist behind.

Business indeed was brisk. No sooner did Squires and
Parsons pull out than Nels Hammond, the Wells Fargo
agent, and Deputy Sheriff Lamb arrived. They surveyed
Gilchrist casually; Gilchrist returned the stare.

"Any more guests here last night?" they asked Mrs.
Pearson.

"Two. They rode for Sierra Valley."

Sierra Valley led to Downieville and the California
plains. The man-trailers pushed on.

Immediately upon their departure, Gilchrist's manner
changed. He watched their backs vanish through the pine-
wood aisles. When express agent and deputy were thoroughly gone, but not until then, he stole away to an out-
building whose purpose in all rural climes is ever the
same. Such shyness and male modesty completely undid
the inquisitive Mrs. Pearson. By circuitous route through
the pinewoods she made her own way to the back of the

structure, and applied matronly and unabashed eye to a knothole.

Eleven thousand six hundred dollars in twenty-dollar gold pieces do flash cheerily, when unloaded from an old boot even in a darkened shack. Mrs. Pearson thought she was beholding enough money to buy all northern California and build a Grand Hotel in the middle of it. Gilchrist lowered his money into the vault and then made exit.

Mrs. Pearson returned to her tavern. On its veranda she passed Gilchrist. She eyed him with triumphant understanding and passed on to her husband in the bar. Gilchrist looked after his landlady with the disinterest of one who is not the least suspicious of knotholes. In due sequence, with Mrs. Pearson back in her kitchen, Innkeeper Pearson untied his bar apron, put on his coat, and moved with immense nonchalance down the path. Innkeeper Pearson was not a brave man. That slow stroll until out of sight was the most difficult piece of business he ever managed in his life. Wondering what a shot between the shoulder-blades might feel like, he found it hard to keep his back-muscles from twitching.

Gilchrist watched him going. A little later it occurred to the guest to look again to his cache.

It was gone.

Pearson, once out of sight of his own front porch and suspecting that Squires might be doing just what Squires in fact was doing, covered the dozen miles in search of a sheriff in jig time. Pearson could have struck out in any direction, and encountered sheriffs; the West's first train hold-up, followed in less than twelve hours by another, had set every town and hamlet within fifty miles of Truckee abuzz with man-chasers. Undersheriff James Kinkead of Washoe County, after throwing a cordon about all roads and trails, had gone to the stone quarry into which the Verdi robbers had pitched their loot. First examination had revealed the broken treasure coffer, the pickaxe which had burst it asunder, and a forgotten shotgun. Continuing search had produced the heelmark of a boot: a very small masculine heelmark, suggesting a very small heel, and by that sign indicating that most exquisite of dressers, the Mother Lode or Comstock professional gambler. There had been only one heelmark. Evidently its maker had taken to the wooden ties. Kinkead had followed the railroad tracks, and then observed where at last Smallheels had struck off into the mountains. It was while moving up this trail to Sardine Valley that the sheriff and a deputy met Innkeeper Pearson.

Considerably braver with a pair of officers beside him, Pearson turned around and the three hurried back for the hostel. Gilchrist was gone. But Kinkead read the new snow, saw no outgoing tracks, and investigated the barn. From its oaten loft he pulled the first of the robber band. Gilchrist, undone by a woman's curiosity, was turned over to the deputy and dispatched for the Truckee calaboose.

But it was not Gilchrist who had worn small-heeled gambler's boots. Gilchrist's foot was broad and heavy. The hour was now ten o'clock of a Sunday night, and a real snow falling. With a boy of the Pearson establishment for guide, Kinkead rode on.

At midnight he reached the hamlet of Loyalton, fifteen miles north. Landlord Boise admitted that he had a stranger in Room 14. A stranger with guns. The boniface regretted that the duties at his bar prevented his accompanying the sheriff thither. He thought, in recollection of those guns, that Kinkead might not care to go either. But Kinkead took a lamp, and with free hand gripping his rifle advanced down the draughty hallway.

Boise's tavern was of rough construction. The latch to Room 14 being broken, its place was taken by a chair pushed against the inside of the door. Kinkead reached in, moved the chair delicately aside. By the light of his lamp he spied a pair of gambler's small-heeled boots standing tidily under the pallet. Their owner, C. B. Parsons of Virginia City, snoozed peacefully above.

Jim Kinkead recognized those boots. He had helped to finance several such pairs in Virginia's resorts. Hitherto he had uniformly underestimated what cards Parsons might be holding. There would be no underestimating now. He set down his lamp with nicety. Then he slipped in. Parsons still slept, the supple hands dangling from the bedclothes.

Cautiously Kinkead drew a heavy Smith & Wesson from under the pillow. With his own royal flush, in the shape of a sixteen-loaded Henry rifle, the man of law then rumpled the slumberer, who woke with a glare, made a snatch under his pillow—to sink back, hands aloft. He was marched to a dependable saloon in the village for safe-keeping. Kinkead again mounted horse.

He pushed through darkness and a growing gale for

Sierraville a dozen miles farther. This tiny community harbored an honest farmer whose brother, John Squires, had been revealed to the officer as the man he wanted next. By this time snow was falling in big flakes. Kinkead located the Squires farmhouse and passed the rest of the night in a chilly clump of alders. He emerged and slipped into the house unseen when the farmer came out to milk.

For the second time he was tiptoing softly, trying various doors. A farther room contained the object of his search. He removed the sleeping man's firearms and routed him from slumber, again with the muzzle of the serviceable Henry.

It was an extralegal situation: Kinkead was a Nevada officer and his man was in California. However, two revolvers and a rifle can do a lot of extraditing. The astonished milker came in to find his brother dressed and ready to go with a sheriff, and was prevailed upon to hitch up and drive the two to Truckee.

It was easier now. Gilchrist at the Truckee jail was being mined like a bonanza for further information. First ore brought up out of his anguished interior was the name of A. J. Davis of Virginia City. Kinkead sighed at that— Big Jack had been such a pleasant companion around a green table. But for that matter, so had Parsons, and duty was duty. Captain Downey of the Virginia police, on telegraphed advices, captured and shook full confession from genial Big Jack Davis. The mellifluous one returned with his captor to the scene of the robbery, and from under a culvert drew forth $19,760.

Tilton Cockerill, a former army officer, was arrested in a public house on the Nevada border. Other man-hunters meanwhile pounded after Sol Jones, the bearer of the code telegram that had tripped the hold-up mechanism. Jones, riding a spirited horse, was not caught until three days later. Dragged back by ungentle hands, he revealed a spot where he and Cockerill had buried $7,345.

Other pursuers were hot after one J. E. Chapman, revealed as the spy who had sent the "Joseph Enrique" telegram. They searched for him in San Francisco. They searched for him in Oakland. Finally empty-handed they returned to Reno. Unknown to them, their man was a passenger on the same train. "Joseph Enrique" arrived in Reno with his pursuers on the fifth day after the hold-up and, being chilled and convivial, dropped into a place of alcoholic spirit and drew up to the stove. As he was about to toss off a drink, Officers Burke and Edwards kicked open the door and came in, also cold and convivial, pushing the just-captured Sol Jones before them. Jones saw his fellow-member of the brotherhood and exclaimed genially: "Hello, Chapman! What brings you here?"

Chapman sputtered and dropped his drink. The identifying greeting got him eighteen years from a judge, half of which he served.

The round-up solved many previous mysteries, including the champagne affair on Geiger grade. Gilchrist and one Roberts went free for state's evidence. Squires, Jones, Cockerill and Parsons drew twenty-one years each, took part in a murderous wholesale delivery out of Carson penitentiary, helped a pack of human tigers claw a trail of blood down the border which still leaves the name "Convict Lake" on the sageland map. Davis the limber-tongued talked his judge down to a ten year sentence, talked a governor into a pardon in three, and in his own immaculate pair of gambler's boots died by an error of judgment in '77. His error of judgment was in trying to stop a stage defended by Wells Fargo messengers Eugene Blair, who never lost a battle, and Jimmy Brown.

The law's fast pounce upon the Verdi robbers was duplicated across the sagebrush. The second band to descend on No. One Passenger Express had made a dozen blunders. Two had worn army uniforms. They were quickly identified as deserters from Fort Halleck; one had even left his glove by the scene of robbery, with the name Carr in it. A trail of new half-dollars, dated 1870, that were known to have been part of the stolen expressage, was strewn through various wayside refreshment places. Four posses with special engines, and a troop of Fort Halleck cavalrymen, followed the clumsy desperadoes. Eighty-five miles south of Great Salt Lake the band was sighted, throwing out of their saddlebags minted gold, minted silver, packages of gold dust and rolls of greenbacks as they galloped. Two were run into the arms of the Mormon authorities, and the other pair were taken on the open range.

There is dispute among antiquarians in sin as to just who invented train robbery. Jesse James, who pried up the bolts and pulled away a rail just as a Rock Island flyer came around a curve in '73, for a while held the popular nomination. But Jack Davis and his crew were three years ahead of that schedule. Four years before the Nevada experiments the Reno brothers of Indiana had tried it and ten members and friends of the errant family were swung from sycamore trees. As early as 1851 the town of Detroit was arresting forty suspects who had plotted to blow up some tracks and a train of cars with a torpedo for the purpose of big-scale robbery.

So just who started bedeviling American trains is an item of unimportant research that lies deep in the history of railroading. One thing is certain. Central Pacific No. One, which started eastward from Oakland that Monday morning in November, 1870, helped the new profession notably to launch itself in its own particular theatre—not once, but twice.

With characteristic vigor the Wide West let No. One have it, and while on the subject let her have it with both barrels.

XIX

THE STAGECOACH PERFIDIOUS

ONE day in the Ben Holladay railroad-building era on the Coast a man known as Dan Smith approached the superintendent of the California & Oregon Stage Line at Roseburg and asked him for a job.

The individual admitted that he knew something about horses. To prove it, he brought a coach and six into town on the dead run and twirled the outfit around before the stage office as if spinning on a two-bit piece. He was plainly one of the craftsmen who could get obedience from his horses with a whisper, and send that whisper to each in turn through a magic handful of loose reins. He got his job. Holladay's railroad by now had pushed down from Portland as far as Roseburg and another link was up from Sacramento as far as Redding. Between railheads lay the sprawling, knotted bulk of the Siskiyou Mountains, traversed only by horse-drawn vehicles. A section of this roadway the newcomer was assigned to drive.

In a few months Dan Smith proved himself the undisputed champion of the whole southern Oregon section of the express and mail route. No jehu between Mount Hood and Mount Shasta could compare with him. Where he came from, nobody knew. But when he cast leaders, swings and wheelers around the curves of the Umpqua, down the long flats of Camas Swale and over the flanks of Burg Mountain, it was with the consummate ease of a master, and his horses sprang, spun or halted as if worked on invisible wires.

Dan was good-looking, aware of his prowess, and aware of the interest both qualities could excite in feminine eyes. But under the latter influence Dan was himself inclined to spring, spin or halt at the scarce-spoken word of command. His route along under the timbered reaches of the Cascade Mountains led him past the cottage of one provocative person, who for one reason and another became a frequent passenger. The lady had a husband named Montgomery. He was Dan's close friend.

But an occasion came when Dan Smith, driving rapidly as usual, failed to telegraph quite the right whisper to his trotters and the stage overturned with a crash. This was inexplicable, but Dan's lack of proper chagrin when he reported the accident was even more inexplicable. For if he had any pride in his name, as a king whip should, his mortification should have been acute. Deeply puzzled, the superintendent went and looked at the spot where Dan had toppled. Here his wonder grew. The place was so broad that a boy could have guided the stagecoach past it. The superintendent concluded Dan was taking too many of his meals out of three-finger tumblers. Not even chagrined at being told he was fired, Dan Smith, the mighty reinsman, left the Oregon country.

Weeks before, a robbery had occurred on Dan's route.

A mail pouch containing gold dust, greenbacks and drafts of value had been dispatched from Portland for San Francisco, and nothing more had ever been heard of it. No amount of inquiry had uncovered any clue. But now that Dan was gone, and under curious circumstances, mail agents began to ponder. Suspicion deepened when it was discovered that Dan had made off with his friend Montgomery's wife. If the driver could listen to the serpent in this case, why not in the other? The most vigorous detectives could not equal in zeal the sleuthing that now was being done by the outraged husband. From information he furnished, the story was pieced out.

Dan had deliberately upset his coach in order to be fired. He had sought dismissal in order to disappear, as he thought, without comment. The missing mail pouch had been purloined by Dan to finance his honeymoon. He had pilfered the consignment from his stage and tucked it in his feed sack. For a week it had ridden there, while government officials looked high and low along a hundred miles of varied countryside.

Dan had no idea what his haul amounted to, passenger traffic being heavy for several days and no secure opportunity offering to take a look. But at length he had found himself with only one passenger, and that one asleep. The driver drew forth his loot from under his horses' nuzzling muzzles and opened it in a wayside barn. The $4,000 in yellow dust went into his shirt bosom. With lofty contempt for paper money, Dan shoved a roll of greenbacks back into the pouch, crowded several thousand dollars' worth of drafts after them, added a couple of big rocks for sinkers and heaved the whole into Umpqua River. There the authorities, aided by Montgomery, found it all months later. Dan and his Eve were traced to Salt Lake, to Philadelphia—where the dust had been sold at the mint—and finally to a little town in Texas, where the law caught up. "Smith" proved to be an alias. Dan's real name was Hamilton, and it was one of the thumping names in western whipcraft. What previous sin had sent him to the Umpqua country under an assumed name did not appear. But he was a knight of the lash of a competency so vast that the very silliness of his mishap convicted him.

The treasure coach, it seems, could be perfidious.

There were other examples. A traveler with $400 in his pocket boarded the stage across northern Nevada one fine May morning in 1874. Bull Run's two saloons and four shacks fell away behind, the white fenceless road to Winnemucca stretched on before. There was no other passenger. When the stage reached Winnemucca, there was not even one passenger and the driver, J. C. Clark, was all of five minutes getting rid of about $400 at the three-card monte tables which gamesters maintained beside the overland railroad tracks.

Assuming the worst, Wells Fargo had Clark arrested and examined the express box afterwards. Mystery deepened when it was found that express and mails were not disturbed. Driver Clark was taken to Elko and charged with various malfeasances against the Nevada code, but he protested volubly that the passenger had simply left his wallet behind on the stage and gone for a walk. As space for walking in that region was extraordinarily available, the court had to take his word for it.

Gifted, but a little less adroit, was the driver of another stage which moved in that year between rowdy Hamilton and still rowdier Pioche. When the night vehicle reached the latter town of many hard citizens its driver had a yarn to spin, but no mail or express to hand over.

Three grim men, he averred, had emerged out of nowhere. They had halted his horses, bound him to a tree and sacked his coach. He had struggled with his bonds for an hour before getting loose. The southeastern Nevadans who listened to his story could easily credit the three bad men. But none could visualize on that part of the route any kind of a tree. The more the driver descanted the louder they laughed, agreeing with him that "nowhere" was a good name for the place his brigands had come from. Finally they clapped him into jail. Two sympathizers who had the temerity to suggest that they, too, thought they remembered a tree in that world of rock and sagebrush were tossed into jail with him. But the hiding place of the treasure remained a secret of the sandwastes.

There was also the quaint case of a stage moving between Mohave and Panamint Junction on an October night two years later. This likewise was lonesome country. On the left the Sierra Nevadas rose abruptly to their loftiest pinnacles, ten thousand feet above the desert. On the right, rolling greasewood stretched away to the Panamints, guardian range of Death Valley. The stage was out in vacant space interrupted only by bare heights, lethal valleys, soda lakes, a couple of mining camps and a string of isolated relay stations. It was 7 P.M. and quite dark. Two passengers were sunk in the stupor of pained numbness inside the vehicle. They had been traveling more or less forever and the jogging journey would continue endlessly on.

Indian Wells was passed. Two miles beyond the stage came to a halt and remained stationary for a minute or two. Then its wheels grated on. Eventually one of the passengers roused himself sufficiently to ask what had caused the stop. The driver cheerfully replied that "a road agent had overhauled him." Both passengers then recalled that they had heard a soft thud, as of an express box dropping in sand. It was all done so silently and wordlessly that they doubted whether the hold-up man had bothered to be present. He could come that way next morning, they reasoned, and gather up the waiting box just as well.

Such falls from grace, however, were rare. The stagecoach and its lowly relations, the mud wagon, the jerkey and the buckboard, were faithful and indomitable performers. Riches and poverty, greed and generosity, beauty and uncouthness, godliness and sin jolted singly or close-commingled in their holds. The stages rolled on. Legroom might be lacking and there might be supperless nights, hurricane or ambush ahead, but a thing so foul as disloyalty seldom sat the box.

All the more paralyzing, therefore, was that most famous piece of treachery which befell a stage-load of

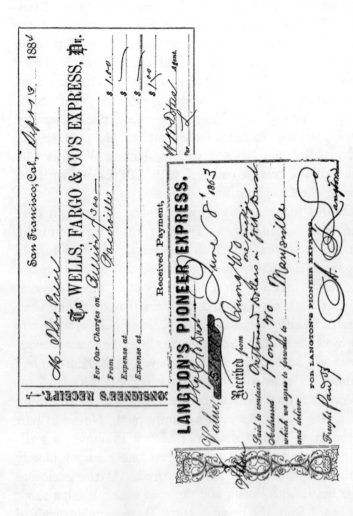

RECEIPTS FOR THE TREASURE EXPRESS

travelers out of Montana in the summer of 1866. Montana's Virginia City was one of the camps east of the Bitter Root Mountains created by the overflow from Orofino, Elk City, Florence and the general "inferno" north of Snake River in the early '60's. The entire region was called Idaho and a rough, ruthless, greedy arena it was where the goddess of Fortune played strange pranks, and the enameled ladies laughed, and men wrested and grubbed and lynched with heartiness. Virginia City and Bannack were connected with Salt Lake City by a spur of the Overland Stage Line.

On this July morning the southbound stage might have been seen loading up in front of the Virginia Hotel. "Frank Williams" sat with the reins. He was full of directions about the stowing of his passengers' baggage. The carpet gripsacks were heavy. So, too, was the assortment of buckskin bags and canisters that contained their metallic wealth. Gripsacks, at Williams' behest, went into the hind boot. Bags and canisters were concealed under the inside seats. "Robbers 'll never find them there," grinned the man with the whiplash.

Portneuf Canyon was reached, a place of narrowing walls. Its dark rocks held a grim repute. No small part of the many sinister doings of Henry Plummer, a well-hanged sheriff-bandit, and at least one piece of bloody public vengeance, had here occurred. As the enclosure grew heavy with brush, and the road took a bend, a shout was heard from the driver's seat. To those who survived the next few minutes it sounded like "Here they are, boys!" And at the signal, seven figures on horseback, their faces smeared with charcoal, pushed the thicket aside.

Someone in the stage let fly. There was an answering bellow from the horsemen's guns. Tally: four passengers dead, one coach riddled and abandoned, $70,000, seven highwaymen and stage driver gone in flight.

It was a clear piece of prearrangement. Though only one of the perpetrators was run down, poetic justice saw to it that he was the driver. The producer of that whoop of greeting, who had led his passengers into the trap, was trailed to Salt Lake and over the mountains to Denver.

There, still as "Frank Williams," Bob Martin, former Pony Express rider and one of the few stage drivers who ever betrayed his passengers, was hoisted kicking and dropped by the neck one sunny dawn on the bank of Cherry Creek.

XX

THE STAGECOACH UNPREDICTABLE

ANYTHING could happen in a stagecoach. Anything could happen in a rocking, lurching land-barge that contained passengers in odd assortment and much treasure, moving over roads of every kind behind horses of every temperament and through every circumstance of countryside and weather.

Anything could happen, and the explosions at Aspinwall and San Francisco made travelers aware that one more possibility had been injected into the general hilarity of stagecoach travel. The notion was not allayed by any effort of the newspapers. One particularly popular morsel dealt with an eastern coachman who oiled the wheel-hubs of his carriage with the article, supposing it to be common lubricating oil. The vehicle had been in motion only a few moments when a grand explosion occurred, demolishing everything, and the driver and passengers nor any part of them were ever seen again. Few editorial shears along the Pacific could resist that one.

"We are informed," supplemented the *Nevada County Gazette* in a spirit more enterprising than comforting, "that nitroglycerine, in small quantities, is occasionally smuggled into this county, to test its qualities for blasting in the mines. In the present excitement, and fear of its liability to explosion, teamsters will not haul it in their wagons, but parties manage to get up small quantities clandestinely. Not long ago, a man brought up a small can of the article, carrying it in his hands."

In view of the current apprehension of anything in small packages, there was more than passing excitement on the Mokelumne Hill stage one day when a parcel between a passenger's knees was seen to be giving vent to pale, curling smoke. Fellow-travelers screamed and left by both doors. The driver looked, whooped and abandoned his team. The horses took cue from their driver and bolted. Down the winding grade flew vehicle and team, its solitary passenger still clutching his parcel and ricocheting from side to side and seat to seat. At length all brought up with a smash against a bank. Far behind the passengers stood rooted, fingers to their ears. When nothing happened to the terrestrial ball they stood on, they advanced cautiously. They were scarcely able to believe their eyes upon beholding the coach intact. The innocent cause of all this diversion crawled out and quenched the fumes of his liquids. He was a photographer, and the chemicals of his trade had taken fire.

Anything could happen in a stagecoach. A fugitive from Montana justice, by name Hauschild, who got as far as Denver and still felt unsafe, boarded an overland coach one day in 1866 and set out for points east. With Hauschild rode six fellow-passengers, one a United States marshal named Barlow, and one a well-to-do ranchman of the Platte named Rice. In Hauschild's breast there evidently rode a most uneasy conscience, which the sight of Barlow's federal badge did not assuage.

The trip was long and the passengers were talkative. Discourse ranged all gamuts, including graphic narratives of frontier lynchings. Whenever one of these episodes was touched upon, Hauschild registered such distinct alarm that his condition called for jesting; and while he was riding inside, one passenger let down from the roof a looped and knotted rope. At this apparition outside his window, Hauschild paled and yelled, gripped his fellow-passengers, and begged to be taken into custody and not hanged. The gentlemen detached his gripping fingers from their persons and advised him to sit down, assuring him that they neither knew anything about him nor wanted to known anything. The conversation then turned, for Hauschild's greater peace of mind, upon Indians and Indian fighting. In the course of this the nervous man learned that but two of the passengers were armed.

The two were Marshal Barlow and Sheepman Rice. Early next morning when all were asleep in or on the coach, Hauschild set to work to make himself forever safe. First he stabbed one passenger, who awoke in horror and seized the frenzied man's knife. With his free hand the fugitive from lynch law then shot Rice, causing instant demise. The knife once more loose, he stabbed Barlow in the cheek. The driver became acutely aware of this furious commotion down inside as a shot ripped through the coach roof behind him, nibbling the skin of an outside traveler. Team was halted, driver and deck passengers pitched into the fray, Barlow was rescued just

"The Stagecoach Unpredictable."

in time, and the desperate man who had sought to slay all his fellow-passengers was hurried on to Fort Kearney and the justice he had little desired.

Anything could happen on a stagecoach. Off in Nevada, one spring day in '73, three men held up the Hamilton stage. Its driver put whip to his horses, and was shot from the box. The hold-up men then fled, and riding circuitously reached town and mingled with acquaintances. Loud was their expressed horror when the stage came in, driven by a passenger, with its driver a corpse on the cushions. Their vociferousness landed them on the coroner's jury. Duties of the office compelled them to sit in the presence of the remains. When somebody adjusted the victim's head, one eye flew open. Two of the three murderers promptly fled, and the third—a certain George Smith—gave a yell and confessed. His confederates were promptly corralled and brought back, and in the accusing glare of the dead man's eye were given expeditious punishment.

The middle Seventies, and middle Nevada, were unusually provocative of the weird and unpredictable in treasure-coach travel. There was the unique sight revealed to the driver of a stage out of Eureka, when he drove one night along the road approaching Garden Pass and heard cries for help coming from the roadside herbage. A man was sitting deep in sand, buried nearly to his neck. His rescue was effected with a shovel, and passengers and driver gave him rough and ready first aid. Then he divulged his tale. He was a coach washer for the stage company at the relay station at Alpha. On his recent night off he had proceeded to Eureka, bucked the tiger, deprived that animal of a handful or two of its hair, and started back for Alpha on horseback.

Two gamblers, he averred, had followed him. At a satisfactory spot they had pounced, taken his riches lately won on the whirr of the roulette wheel, and after detaining him in the sagebrush for twenty-four hours had produced shovels and planted him alive in his grave. The work was not quite finished and his head was still sticking up when a passing freight wagon caused them to leave hurriedly. Thereafter the bound and buried man had sat in his hole, baking throughout the shadeless day, and unrelieved by anybody until the night stage at last came along. It was a yarn that gave rise to prolonged barroom arguments, the conclusion finally being that victim and his assailants were all rival robbers who had collided in the dark while waiting for the stage at the top of the grade; that the buried man had merely been an unpopular minority, and his plight due to his unwillingness to let the majority have a clear field in that particular region.

Yes, anything could happen to or in a stagecoach. There was an incident of travel out Pioche way as unpredictable as any, though no doubt duplicated often enough where roads were rough and long.

From Hamilton to Pioche was 100 miles as the crow flew, but vehicles operated by Wes Travers' stage line did not travel as the crow made it. Setting forth from Hamilton and Treasure Hill, with the juniper-studded Pancake Range on the west, they creaked and grunted for two hundred miles through the nut-pine defiles of the

Egan and Ely ranges on their way to the temporary mining metropolis of southeastern Nevada.

Two hundred miles of sunbaked vacancy, where anything might happen and virtually nothing ever did. Wild
sheep might look down from the limestone, slate and
quartzite summits; rabbits might peer from wild rose and
willow thickets beside the few far-scattered springs; antelope and mule deer might take to their heels when the
stages lumbered up over the horizon; but in the main it
was a land given over to greasewood, sunblast and mo-
notony. Two hundred miles of such going were a lot of
miles, especially in warm weather. But when driver L. A.
Grange left Hamilton with sixteen passengers and turned
up at Pioche with seventeen, he had something new to report, and reported it.

"Who's the deadhead?" thundered stage agent W. B.
Daugherty, counting the fares. "Where did he get on?"

"He must have been with us from Treasure Hill,"
confessed the driver, "though I didn't know it. I got
sight of him later."

"Who let him on?"

"The passengers all sort o' took a hand, everybody
being more or less crowded-like."

"What were you doing?"

"Minding my horses."

A high wail came from behind the drawn canvas curtains of the dusty vehicle. And with it, Daugherty's brow
cleared.

"Drinks on the management, boys!" he invited the
assembled Piochers.

One hundred miles isn't much, the way a crow makes it. But two hundred miles is a strain for a stork, even with the assistance of sixteen assorted passengers.

Yes, anything could happen, as was discovered by a young woman who took the train from San Francisco Bay in '73, changing to a stagecoach at an appropriate point for the laudable purpose of advancing on the mines and getting herself a husband. On a summer Sabbath evening the eastbound overland train halted fussily at Colfax, discharged travelers and way baggage from its five trailing coaches, tooted its whistle, clanked its bell, tossed a geyser of sparks from its wood-stoked smokestack, and laid laboriously to the charge up the face of the Sierra.

In the wide station street of the mountain town a group of persons crossed with portmanteaus and carpetbags to the waiting stage, on which sat Bob Scott, silver-mounted whip in hand. The thirteen persons who climbed aboard included United States Senator Sargent, a railroad politician; E. Black Ryan, railroad paymaster; Judge McFarland, railroad attorney; Brigadier Charles C. Cadwalader, railroad engineer; and Miss Eleanor Berry, a Gilroy schoolmistress, twenty-two and marriageable. With the exception of Miss Berry the stage-load was believed to be escorting a considerable sum of railroad money to Nevada City, where court was to be held, and where railroad political fences were understood to be in need of fixing. While the express agent hustled packets—of railroad greenbacks, presumably—from his office to the vehicle's internals, Reinsman Bob Scott untangled from his

Jovian calm and helped Miss Berry to the place of honor beside him at the stagecoach heights. Her small Saratoga trunk was stowed on the roof behind.

She swept the scenery with appraising eye.

It was the hour of charm and meditation. The hills lay blue under evening haze. Below foamed Bear River. The coach rumbled down to the water's edge and lurched across. Above and behind Miss Berry sat Passenger Ryan, who saluted the gathering gloaming with a baritone solo. It was "The Low-Backed Car."

> *"When first I saw sweet Peggy,*
>   *'Twas on a market day.*
> *A low-backed car she drove, and sat*
>   *Upon a truss of hay."*

Through the ford they splashed, the great carriage heaving forward easily with its two-ton momentum; and so up the long grade northward, while the harness jingled to Passenger Ryan's increasing resonance.

> *"While she drove in a low-backed car,*
>   *To be married by Father Maher.*
> *Oh, my heart would beat high at her glance and sigh,*
>   *Though it beat in a low-backed car."*

Five miles short of Grass Valley the coachwheels came to a screeching stop and Paymaster Ryan's song broke off. An apparition familiar to travelers had stepped out from the Sheets Ranch gateway. It wore a black hood with eyeholes, the curtain falling to the shoulders. Behind this ominous figure ranged a second, a third, and a fourth. Miss Berry thought absurdly of harlequins. But the spirit of the masqueraders was not playful. They leveled on Scott and his passengers.

"No express box on this stage. It's coming up behind," said Driver Scott with guile. There were regularly two stages on the run; Sundays was the exception.

"In that case we'll just hold you here, and wait." The robber spokesman had plenty of time. Silence followed, while his chronometer ticked in the stage driver's vest. In the game of patience that ensued, honors went to the hold-up men. "Well," admitted Scott at last, "there's no use wasting more time. No other stage is following. I've got a young lady here who's due in Grass Valley to be married in about thirty minutes."

The coach was of the overland type, with a boiler-iron express box hidden under its inside cushions—forming, in fact, the rear seat of the vehicle—there being faith in the councils of the express company that highwaymen might not think of looking for it there, or know what to do with it if they found it. But these fellows seemed to know exactly where to look and what to do. Driver Scott's face grew dubious.

The passengers were ordered out. The horses were unhitched. The knights of the gloaming set rapidly and methodically to work. First they produced giant powder in cartridges. Then they produced blasting powder in flasks. Then caps and fuses. The passengers were herded into a nervous row. There they sat, ten paces distant, guarded by a man with a shotgun who whispered that he was by nature hair-triggered, and that his weapon was as high-strung as he.

"Always did jump at sudden noises, even as a boy. Hope nothing excites me now," he affirmed.

Senator Sargent sat still as a mouse, suppressing even a desire to cough lest it alarm this nervous warder who stood close over them. General Cadwalader, whose hands had been stealing slyly toward a derringer in his pocket, thrust them resolutely aloft and put all temptation behind him. Judge McFarland nudged Paymaster Ryan and asked him, for its soothing effect on the man with the gun, to repeat "The Low-Backed Car." Ryan whispered hoarsely that he'd clean forgotten the demnition words.

With the fuse about to be lighted, there was a scream that caused the shotgun sentinel to leap convulsively. "My trunk!" cried the bride-to-be. "Gentlemen, my trousseau is in that trunk. Won't you take it down before you blow up the coach?"

"With pleasure, miss." While one robber climbed to the deck and passed the Saratoga down, his chief caught it from below. The effort caused his coatsleeve to fall back, revealing an irregular scar.

With a roar deep in the coach the explosives went off, sundering the cushions and flinging the lid of the coffer straight up through the roof. The contents of the box, about $7,000, were rapidly scooped up. There was some chagrin among the road agents at the smallness of the haul, considering the weightiness of its escort. Scott was then permitted to take charge of what was left of his equipage. The running gear was about all. He rehitched, stowed his passengers and Miss Berry's trunk wherever he could, and sent his broken chariot slowly forward—a low-backed car indeed. The brigands remained standing like statues until swallowed by darkness.

At Grass Valley the young woman descended at a cottage gate. A motherly woman met her with embraces. It was the bridegroom's landlady. He was momentarily delayed by business; he was out of town so frequently; but he would soon return. The young lady retired to her room that was waiting, and changed her frock.

There was a footstep on the path outside. Miss Berry ran forth, a confection in lawn and ribbons.

"Miss Berry! Eleanor!"

"Mr. Dreibelbis! Louis!"

"You're twenty times prettier than your picture!"

It had been a correspondence romance, inspired by an advertisement in a San Francisco literary journal: "Lonesome miner wants wife to share stake and prospects." With satisfaction the mail-order lovers cemented their acquaintance, while the landlady and clergyman looked on benevolently from the cottage windows. Dramatically then Miss Berry told of her recent experience.

"A mere incident of the country," the bridegroom deprecated. He turned to the man of the cloth. "Let's get on with the hitching."

In the cottage parlor they were wedded; after which the groom advanced to the marble-topped walnut table to sign the papers. As he moved his pen, the light of the table lamp fell on his forearm. The bride gave utterance to a shriek. . . .

"Lay her here," indicated the motherly landlady, clearing a sofa. "Head down—so. Now sniff this, my dear. Weddings are such an ordeal. I've been through three of them myself. Heaven be praised for giving us women smelling salts."

On the following morning Bob Scott had a new stage, and the stage had a young woman passenger. All night long she had been heard alternately laughing and screaming. With dawn she had risen announcing that her memory was gone: that she could recall nothing save that dimly, as in a dream, she had been carried off by robbers. In vain landlady, parson, and witnesses labored with her. She could remember nothing of any marriage ceremony, and the very sight of the papers made her recoil in horror. She repacked her Saratoga, and from dawn onwards sat firmly on it in the cottage parlor. As she boarded Scott's downbound stage there was a set to her jaw which indicated that neither shotgun agent, giant powder, nor any other nonsense was going to stop her departure.

As for the bridegroom Dreibelbis, he too left town—in the other direction.

XXI

THE NON–SURRENDERING STAGECOACH

It is conventional to dismiss western stagecoaching with contempt or sorrow following that epochal ceremony at Promontory Point, Utah, on May 10, 1869; to put the stout old Concord universally, then and there, on a down-hill grade behind runaway horses with its driver aplunge through darkness and unable to get foot on the brake. Did not a new transportation era open with the strokes of sledge upon golden spike—strokes whose every impact thudded through the fiber of the nation and clanged by telegraph at San Francisco on the big brass city hall bell?

Yes, a new era opened; but the old by no means closed. The completed Pacific Railroad ended central overland staging. But that string of shanty stations, water tanks and sidings in the desert no more ended western staging as a whole than they ended western vacancy.

Where stages continued to go—and they went to many a town and townlet far indeed from screech of locomotive whistle—there went the expresses. And where the ex-presses went, there excitement frequently waited. The closing days of 1884, which were a decade and a half af-ter the date inaugurating Union Pacific and Central Pacific rail travel, and which looked back on the completion of many another railroad line as well, may have found General Superintendent John J. Valentine of Wells, Fargo & Company sitting back in his revolving chair at San Francisco scanning a document of interest. Covering fourteen years, it presented a vivid tabular picture of how express treasure had in part been traveling:

Number of stage robberies	313
Attempted stage robberies	34
Burglaries	23
Train robberies	4
Attempted train robberies	4
Number of Wells Fargo guards killed	2
Number of Wells Fargo guards wounded	6
Number of stage drivers killed	4
Number of stage drivers wounded	4
Number of stage robbers killed	16
Number of stage robbers hanged by citizens	7
Number of horses killed	7
Number of horses stolen from teams	14
Convictions	240
Treasure stolen (promptly made good to customers)	$415,312.55
Rewards paid	73,451.00
Prosecutions and incidental expenses	90,079.00
Salaries of guards and special officers	326,417.00
Total cost to Wells Fargo due to highwaymen operating against 8 trains and 347 stages, during 14 years	$917,726.55

" 'Pears like a small cloud off there, getting larger," said Passenger Fred Kruger to Passenger Fred Loring inside the westbound Prescott to San Bernardino coach. They were six miles out of Wickenburg in the Vulture Mountains.

"Oo-oo-ooh! Is a sandstorm coming?" Pretty Mollie Shepherd lifted herself between them to peep out the

Concord's window. "What will we do? Turn and run before it? Or just let it bury us in a dune, and there we'll be, traveling inside of it forever—a foot a day?"

Fred Loring didn't know. Fred Loring was fresh from Harvard, a rising young author who had come West to do descriptions—had surveyed a little with Lieutenant Wheeler's geologic expedition in the Colorado Desert—but had never fronted a desert sandstorm. And Fred Kruger didn't answer. Fred Kruger, a son of pioneer soil who knew its realities, usually fell tongue-tied before the imaginative queries of a blue-eyed lady.

They'd have to ask John Lance.

But "Dutch John" wasn't speaking either. He too was eyeing that puff of dust in this land where wells were fifty miles apart, their water two hundred feet down; where sandgales and red men alike come from nowhere out of dust stains no bigger than your handkerchief; and where "dry" arroyos, in November, could fill with water bank to bank, coach-high, in fifteen seconds. Though this was but his second run on the Wickenburg to La Paz stretch, "Dutch John" in coach or mud wagon, buckboard or jerky had amassed considerable experience of desert travel. Once he had lashed one hundred and thirty-eight miles in thirty-six hours, rested fifty minutes, and started right back again; and that through Apacheland, where a man, however weary, does well to keep his chin up off his vest.

The puff dissolved. Perhaps it had never been. These unclad mountains, these transfixed eruptions, were full of odd mirages and devil-queer tricks. Inside the coach

Kruger, Loring, and two other passengers went back to pointing out to Miss Shepherd the malignant cholla, that natural lizard's fortress whose fanglike thorns on contorted branches were fairly ready to spring at them as they passed—"a regular Apache bouquet," laughed Miss Mollie; at the great fluted sahuaro, or giant cactus, with its arms squared out like a prizefighter; at the armless barrel cactus, the desert drinking-fountain— "It has saved many a man," said Kruger; and they promised her, when darkness should fall, a glimpse of the creamy bell of the night-blooming cereus. Though it was far from the hour for night-blooming now: it was a clear Arizona Sunday morning of '71. As for Dutch John, up forward on the driver's seat with two passengers beside him, the Wells Fargo box underfoot, and the United States mail in the hind boot— now that the curious dust-puff was gone, he had never felt gayer, more full of reminiscence, or more like "putting 'er through" on time. Though occasionally his mind would stray back to that puff—devil take these mountains!

Down into an arroyo and toward a nose of stony erosion sped the stage. The leaders swung out of sight around the bluff where driver was never to follow. In the instant which it takes swing-span and wheelers to stride their own length, a blast of shots and arrows had wiped the deck of the coach clean of all life, halted and demoralized its horses, knocked young Loring's body asprawl on the inside cushions. Second volley felled another inside passenger who had leaped out the door and started sprinting up the gravel. Now he lay on his back, turning up to the Arizona sun forever sightless eyes. Almost as swiftly, a savage was bending over him, skillfully removing his hair.

And quite as swiftly, Kruger and Miss Shepherd had sprung from the coach and fled up a dry wash for the shielding high recesses of the Vulture Mountains. Kruger had been drilled through the shoulder at first fire, but was full of fight. His revolver was empty. It had served well, halting pursuers. He handed it hurriedly to his companion to recharge. But the girl too was shot. Through an arm, though he needn't mind her—it didn't hurt much, really—. Together they managed to reload, she holding the weapon with her serviceable hand, he fumblingly manipulating. . . .

Far down the slopes the six-horse team, in maddened stampede, brought up clattering in a snarl of traces when the coach banged into a bank. The off leader had crashed with a shot through his brown flanks. Indians raced to capture and drive off the remaining horses.

Two hours later, nine miles west, a buckboard bearing California's eastbound mail came upon two figures: a man and a woman. Each had one arm rudely bound; they were bloody and way-stained; one was hacking with his knife at a barrel cactus in fevered search for water.

Twenty-five men from the Vulture mine at Wickenburg, led by Superintendent Sexton, soon swarmed to the scene of the massacre. The riddled coach lay on its side. Mail was ripped and scattered. A roll of greenbacks lay untouched. The Wells Fargo box was unopened. The bodies of four passengers and Driver Lance lay where they had fallen at first assault; that of Passenger Adams, who had leaped out and started to run, lay fifty yards away. The trail of Indians and stolen horses lay in direction of Date Creek Reservation.

The coach was righted, new horses and driver found, and express and mail continued due west along the thirty-fourth parallel for the Colorado River and California.

Just under the crest line of the southern Sierras, one chilly pre-dawn of 1875, two men crouched in the sand beneath a grotesque Joshua tree. It was decidedly nippy up there, nearly a mile above the sea. Seventy-five miles away the sun was already beginning to glare down into Death Valley, and its red fingers were stealing along the ridge of the Sierras and making lighted torches of Mount Whitney, tallest summit in the United States, and its fourteen-thousand-foot companions. Lowest spot in the hemisphere and highest in the country—both were being warmed at the same instant, and in the same vicinity, by that rosy glow. But the dry hard cold of a night still gray was over Walker's Pass, that cleft in the mountains near whose summit the waiting figures knelt.

Down below on the bank of a creek the stone chimney of Canebrake Station was sending up a straight column of smoke. Breakfast was preparing—the two men could smell it and, in fancy, could fairly taste it. But they were not paying a call on Canebrake Station. They had other business in hand, requiring anonymity; though if the deal went through they promised themselves the biggest meal at the next station that had ever been served along the base of those sky-raking peaks.

Across the eastward-lying deserts the sun was finally

swinging up over the Panamints, the Argus Mountains and the Cosos, and the vastly higher Sierras were gold with it from top to toe, when the ears of the waiting men at length caught the pad-pad of approaching horses. The stage from Bakersfield and Havilah was coming. In an instant more it would have the ridgepole of the continent behind it and would be sloping down the long sandy valley that led to Lone Pine in the sunken sagelands. As the big vehicle loomed abreast, one of the men stepped out and covered Driver W. S. Ladd with a Remington six-gun.

Driver Ladd was an old, cool—very cool—hand. The six leather ribbons in his hands telegraphed not the least excitement to his horses. His jaws, moving serenely over a solacing quid, did not lose a single squidgy munch. "All right, hold your pistol," said Driver Ladd.

The man who had come out to greet him, this St. Patrick's morning, was standing on a bank about wheel-high above the road and two or three paces from the driver's face. Ladd's glance gathered in the portrait of a long-bearded, sandy-moustached figure. The fellow's lower face was somewhat concealed, and his collar was turned up against the wind. Without much doubt, there was an armed partner on the other side of the road; complete, paralyzed silence on the part of his six inside passengers convinced Ladd of that. His experienced ears also detected the slight jingle of falling purses and watches as the passengers thriftily shed what they could of their valuables in the direction of the coach floor. But their personal belongings were apparently unwanted. There was a thump

in the soft sand as Ladd dumped down the express box
and a jerk as the vehicle, still under orders, moved slowly
forward. After a hundred yards Ladd touched his team,
and the stage fairly flew down the long grade.

"That was pretty cool, but I think those fellows could
be caught," commented Passenger Mitchell, who was a
deputy sheriff from Los Angeles County. He was very
snug, however, on the middle back seat between a broad-
hipped woman passenger and a paunchy merchant, and did
not struggle to get out and try. Ladd drove smartly along
without remark. The white road flashed beneath his
wheels; the desert was beginning to rise and meet him.
Coyote Holes station was reached at a quarter to five, by
which time the passengers had become quite normal and,
in fact, gaily brave. At the Holes the westbound stage
for Bakersfield was waiting, with Driver Cline on the
box.

Ladd spoke to Cline. The latter nodded and agreed.
Arrangements were made with the men at the station to
handle the two teams for the continuance of their jour-
neys and the regular reinsmen went to the stable and
saddled a pair of mounts. After a brief breakfast they
were on their horses and cantering up the ten miles or so
of rude roadway toward the scene of the robbery. On
their way they passed two men afoot who nodded pleasantly. "A good St. Patrick's Day to you," said one.

"He's an Englishman, and doesn't mean a word of it,"
grunted Ladd to his companion.

They came to the top of the pass. The sandy terrain
was well tramped down. Ladd got down and studied

the ground. Somebody had been pacing back and forth there for some time. The restless party had been going through a regular drill—eight paces east, then eight paces west—until he had worn a regular track. Winter rains had not yet departed the land, and the ground furnished a good matrix for footprints. They were quite full of character: a circle of hobnails in each shoe, and a V of similar nails in each flat heel.

"Let's go back," said Ladd, "and see why that Englishman was up so early on St. Patrick's morning." They turned their horses.

Morning wind from the Inyo deserts was once more in Ladd's face as he fairly flew down the eastern grade. Cline pounding close behind, he reached and dismounted at the place where the two pedestrians had been encountered. Uneasy was the conscience that had tarried there. Coming down from the ridge, the footprints of one of the two contained a circle of nail marks and a V; but after meeting the horsemen the walkers had gone on single-file, quitting the road, with the footprints of one falling exactly into the tracks of the other.

Ladd and Cline returned to Coyote Holes. The work of the morning called for another breakfast, and they were having it when its altogether irresistible odor brought two pedestrians out of the brush and up to the door.

Ladd rose cordially. "I believe," he said, "we've met before. I handle horses and such for Bill Buckley's stage line. This here's Mr. Cline. He drives a bit, too."

"Howdy," said the older of the men, who had a beard and a sandy moustache. "I believe we did see you up the road a piece. I'm Castle, and this here's Wallack."

"Would you mind," said Ladd courteously, "lifting the sole of your foot? Don't stir otherwise—Mr. Cline has a gun on you and Mr. Cline is a dreadfully nervous man, whether with a gun or with horses. Thank you— that will do. Mr. Cline, while I hold your gun will you kindly do these gentlemen up in bale rope?"

"I don't like this here a bit," protested Castle. "We didn't hurt you none."

"Exactly," Ladd agreed. "Now that you are seated comfortably, and your hands are behind your back, Mr. Cline will feed you—won't you, Mr. Cline? These gentle- men have been up very early, and it's going to be a long ride to the Bakersfield jail. Fine St. Patrick's morning, isn't it?"

But Castle and Wallack, with sentences of fifteen years each ahead of them, could find nothing good to say about it.

Sixty miles below Los Angeles and three miles from the sea is San Juan Capistrano, a townlet about which the mantilla of colonial Spain still folds close. Its Francis- can mission, reared in 1797 and earthquake-battered in 1812, is a romantic huddle of vine-clad arches, ruddy clay roof tiles, padres' garden of very lovely roses, and *campanario* of soft-throated time-greened bells. The few marts serving the village are still *tiendas*, the numer- ous celebrations *fiestas*; it sleeps in the sun, and the coast- side four-horse stagecoach that lick-larruped past its plaza in '77 must have been fully the anachronism that the roaring motor car is today. "Your monstrous American *car-retas*, señor, they are of such a hurry and commotion."

A few miles north of San Juan Capistrano, on a murky March night, a figure lurked under roadside elders. It was the hour before midnight. The southbound Los Angeles to San Diego stage was due to pass any minute on its racketing charge toward the idyllic mission village. A gringo George H. Smith, master of spark-flinging horses, would come guiding a gringo Concord down a once-pastoral Spanish highway in a typical gringo hurry.

When the expected land-liner swept up, the man sprang out, threw rifle to shoulder, yelled to halt. He yelled, it must be admitted, with good, round gringo oathification. One passenger inside, and one on top, woke and looked with much disfavor on this interruption.

"Throw down the box!"

Instead, the inside passenger let fly with a load from his pistol. Smith gave sharp word to his leaders and the vehicle leaped forward. A crash from the highwayman's gun tore the ribbons bloodily out of his hands.

As in '63, when Major Howard Egan of the Overland caught the lines from stricken Riley Simpson and brought the Concord through to Deep Creek Station, so '77 provided a namesake of kindred spirit. He was Judge Richard Egan, Capistrano resident, whose province it was to keep the California peace if he had to hang somebody for it; and he now snatched the sagging reins from George Smith's hands. It was new to the judge to guide four tearing steeds by means of two big handfuls of leather, but he contrived it. He rocked through slithering mud and blackness for Capistrano. That hamlet, if given over to sleep by noonday, was the hall of death itself at midnight. But it woke when Judge Egan pulled in. With tumult and clatter that sent echoes flying through the ivied cloisters and jarred the four bronze bells in the mission's *campanario*, he fetched in his four-in-hand at a clean gallop, deposited his wounded driver at his own hacienda, looked about in vain for somebody to relieve him, and then gamely drove mails and express onward, through shore wind and rain, twenty-five miles to Las Flores.

The non-surrendering stagecoach, with new steeds and new jehu, continued for San Diego. George Smith recovered with hands too crippled for further coaching; but Billy Pridham, southern California express superintendent and former Pony Express rider, had a new job waiting for him as a Wells Fargo shotgun messenger.

"That's a mighty fine star," remarked Jimmy Brown, extra shotgun messenger, to Eugene Blair, regular shotgun messenger, as the stage plodded across Nevada bunchgrass between Eureka and Tybo. September dusk was merging into darkness. He pointed to a summit of the Pancake range overlooking Willow station.

"A red one, too," responded Blair.

The stage wagon creaked and slogged behind its four dusty horses, the pay roll of the Tybo mine clinking down inside. Blair was seated next to the driver; his assistant was perched on the dicky seat up behind.

"It looks now," said Jimmy, "as if that star was sort o' double."

"Let me know when you see four," said Blair good-naturedly. The evening air blew pleasantly on his face; night traveling across the desert was decidedly preferable to blinding day. Blair shifted the short shotgun to his left hand and gave a luxurious stretch.

Seven months before, in February of 1877, Blair had been called on for lively action. The daylight stage from Hamilton to Ward had reached a point two miles from its terminus, with substantial silver bullion on board, when two figures loomed out of a dry gully, waived formalities, and let fly. "Always fixed for company" was Blair's motto, and he promptly answered with a bucket or so of buckshot. Johnny Carlo, whose experience should have told him better than to tackle a stage defended by Blair, dropped with a well-filled arm. His partner, Jim Crawford, turned and fled. Blair brought the wounded man into Ward, where rough-and-ready surgery failed to save a worthless life. Then Blair returned to the scene of encounter—it was the following day.

Jim Crawford had sped up the barranca and onward in a general southerly direction. And up the barranca and onward in a general southerly direction followed Blair. Four days and nights the outward-bound steeplechase lasted, and six days and nights the return *jornada*. When the expressman showed up again at Ward he was not alone. Jim Crawford, sheepish and subdued, was marching in ahead of him. Since which affair, Blair's stages had fared well.

"How many stars is it now?" the veteran asked his comrade.

"Only one after all, but she's sure a beauty."

Willows station loomed ahead, usually attended by a solitary horse-wrangler.

"Wonder where that 'hustler' is," mused the driver.

"Back in a stall, taking a snooze most likely," considered Blair, "or thinking up a joke. He's the comicalest feller!"

Whereupon, as if to prove the Willows brand of waggishness, a shout came out of the dark. "Eugene Blair, surrender!"

"Didn't I tell you?" chuckled Blair to his companions.

The shout came again—a shrill yell. "Get down off there and surrender!"

Evidently this was no pleasantry after all. Blair's expression changed. Shifting the gun to his right hand, he jumped down. The barn door was black and cavernous. He started for it. Simultaneously two shots slammed at him, one from the side, one in front. The experienced messenger had instinctively crouched; the lead sailed over him, whiffing Jimmy Brown in the leg. Rising, Blair found twin muzzles against his chest.

Blair had never lost a fight and never intended to. He seized the barrels in his left hand and pushed them up. The two men clinched. The scuffle raged between stage wagon and stable. Two other foemen were also dancing in the darkness, trying for an opening. As the scufflers reeled about, each with a hand on the other's weapon, Blair spun his adversary squarely into the light of the wagon lamps. Jimmy Brown from the top of the stage turned loose his gun.

The other highwaymen fled. Two prisoners at the back of the barn, the hostler and an angry rancher who had stopped for a chat, were freed from their ropes. A. J. "Big Jack" Davis, erstwhile citizen of Virginia City, Geiger grade champagne host and Verdi train robber, was lifted from the dust where Brown's salute had felled him and placed in the stage, which turned about and put back at once for Eureka. But on its arrival the illustrious occupant was found to have turned it into a hearse.

The Hamilton brothers, who had danced about in darkness trying to get in a shot, and Tom Lauria, who had galloped out from Eureka to light the signal fires on Pancake Peak—two bonfires indicating two armed messengers—were duly rounded up. Tom Lauria had made one fatal mistake. The telegraphic bonfires, burning too close together, had merged at ten miles' distance into a single gleam. When the three highwaymen had converged on Blair, none had contemplated Brown.

"Queer, isn't it?" commented the driver of the up-bound Marysville to La Porte stage, whose route between the California plains and fir-tipped ridges was a succession of daily adventures and whose astonishment was not easily stirred.

"Mighty queer," agreed Wells Fargo Guard George M. Hackett.

The two men whom they had glimpsed continued to slink through the brush on a course that would bring them to the road in advance of the stage. But it was not this procedure which had the stagemen startled. Nor was it their sudden emergence with guns in their hands; Hackett was ready for that and his own artillery went to shoulder. The men ducked back.

"Sure was funny. A brand-new idea," mused the driver.

"I'm going after them." Hackett jumped down and darted into the manzanita thicket. The discomfited stage robbers were still going; he could hear them snapping boughs, pushing through with pain and effort and heartily swearing. This, in thornbush country, was understandable; for the pair had amazed the two stagemen by presenting themselves for the hold-up clad only in their underdrawers. It was a new conception of disguise in a stage-going region that had long grown weary of black masks and linen dusters.

After a chase of two hundred yards, Hackett lost his men, but fortune was with him. He stumbled upon their camp. In the camp was their clothing. The express messenger pounced upon the unoccupied garments and belongings; only yesterday, the 20th of June, 1879, the Forbestown–Oroville stage had been robbed of $620 in gold dust and some coin.

A valise contained the thirty-nine stolen ounces. The trousers of the wandering nudists contained the $256 in stolen coin. With his arms full of boots, shirts, pants and the gold-stuffed valise, Hackett returned to his stage.

"Drive on," he directed, "and pretend to keep going. But wait for me after half a mile."

The driver accommodated. His express treasure looked

to, Hackett returned to the woods and stole for the camp again. Its tenants had returned. In considerable bewilderment they were casting about for their habiliments.

"I'll give you a receipt for 'em," spoke Hackett from behind a thick madrone tree.

The robbers looked up dumfounded. One gave a yell and dashed into the underbrush. The other, after reading the message in a leveled pair of ten-gauge gun muzzles, put his hands to the sky.

"Do I get my pants?" plaintively asked "Liverpool Harry" Norton.

"I've sent 'em on to be pressed. They'll be waiting for you when you come out—in about fifteen years," appraised Shotgun Messenger Hackett.

His estimate of the judge's mind proved correct.

XXII

THE WAR ON MANY FRONTS

WITH unalloyed pleasure Big Whiskyjug, a Piute brave, was swinging in a swing on a back street of the sagebrush town of Belleville. Big Whiskyjug had long ago discovered this childish apparatus and investigation had proved to him that the Indian race had fallen heir to something good. When you start to swing it takes a little effort, but presently you are 'way up high where you can see things over the tops of cabins. Then you are rushing down backward, which is quite a sensation. In a jiffey you are up again where you can see all over Belleville and the California-Nevada border, and then you are rushing down once more with the wind in your back hair.

With his squaws making acorn-flour down by the creek, and a flask in the one remaining pocket of his pantaloons, Big Whiskyjug felt that the world was just about all right. It became still more all right when his calloused heels, sliding in the dust, plowed up the top of the leather handle of a sack of bullion.

There had been a daring robbery eight months before. In March of the year 1876 the Northern Stage Company's vehicle had been halted by three men between

Teel's Marsh and Aurora. The treasure box had contained nothing of value, but there had been on board a leathern bag containing eight thousand-dollar bars of fine bullion from the Northern Belle mine. A Mexican, a Peruvian and an American comprised the waylaying party. They snatched the bullion bag and two stage horses and made off over the treeless mountains. Wells Fargo posted a $500 reward for each thief and all three were bagged two weeks later at Old Coso in the vicinity of Death Valley. The robbery was cheerfully admitted and its perpetrators were cheerfully punished, but all information as to the location of the loot was sedulously concealed.

It was now November. Big Whiskyjug let his foot scuff the protruding handle while he pondered in two languages. The Indian knew what bullion satchels looked like. He also knew that they were dangerous things for Piute braves to be found carrying. But information can be swapped. Big Whiskyjug got out of his swing and made his way to a friendly emporium, where in exchange for what he knew he instantly got his bottle filled.

The proprietor of the establishment sold his information to Wells Fargo for a quarter of the prospective treasure. Messengers Mike Tovey and Hank Woodruff, digging all around the vicinity, uncovered more of the cache. Presently they had it all. The stolen bullion from the Northern Belle rolled on to Carson mint. The squaws down by the creek went on pounding their acorn-meal. Big Whiskyjug sat on his swing in the back street of Belleville, marveling at the perspiring energy of white

$750 REWARD!

Wells, Fargo & Co. will pay

$250 each for the arrest and conviction of the three men who robbed the Silver City bound stage, near Boise City, on the 10th inst.

AN ADDITIONAL

reward of ONE-FOURTH will be paid on all treasure recovered.

Wm. B. MORRIS,
Agent.

Boise City, Nov. 10th, 1875.

REWARD

WELLS. FARGO & CO.'S EXPRESS BOX

on COAST LINE STAGE CO'S ROUTE, from Soledad, was ROBBED this morning, by two men, about ten miles north of San Miguel.

$250 Each

will be paid for ARREST and CONVICTION of the Robbers.

JNO. J. VALENTINE, Gen. Supt.

San Francisco, July 15, 1875.

THE WAR ON MANY FRONTS

Circulars and reward posters

men, and convinced that life will treat you right if you just wait for its gifts and know where to exchange them.

When Virginia City was still unchristened, and its locators were making hullabaloo over the first surface color of the Comstock, one Waterman S. Body tramped over the looming heights above the Tuolumne country and down into the desert he found on the other side. Beyond that trough, whose chief feature was a big dead sea, rose other heights more barren than any the prospector had ever seen. But he set his feet upward, and half a mile above his dead sea came to some placer gold—and the result was Bodie, a camp that flared up for a moment even as Virginia, and then subsided into a two-decade sleep.

Waterman S. had become "Bill," and Body had become "Bodie" in local annals, and the founder of the camp had perished in a blizzard and been for more than twenty years a skull in a local saloon, when picks and shovels uncovered the ore mass of the Standard mine, and one of the great camps of history was on its joyful way. Bodie was twelve miles up-canyon and over the ridge from Aurora, a famous and splendiferous rival camp of the early Sixties; but these were now the late Seventies, and Bodie's great hour, with Aurora merely a halting place for coaches on their way with Bodie bullion for Carson mint. Down on the desert floor and to southward was Benton, another rowdy camp whose output passed that way.

"It looked like old times in Aurora at Wells, Fargo & Co.'s office last Thursday night," reported the Bodie

Standard in August of 1878. "There were ten leathern sacks—five from Bodie and five from Benton—lying on the floor, while three messengers armed with shot guns and self-cocking revolvers sat behind the counter. As the stage for Carson drove up everything was hurry and bustle. While the express agent was loading the passengers and their baggage in the stage, the messengers handled the precious metal and safely stowed it on board also. Two of the messengers got on the outside with the driver while the third occupied a seat inside. At the Five Mile House, where the Belleville intersects the Carson road, another messenger with four bars of bullion was added to the cargo. Armed and equipped as these four messengers were, it looked as though a company of soldiers could not capture the bullion and surely it would be a desperate gang of robbers that would make the attempt."

Yet attack they often did; the "bad man from Bodie" was very, very bad and very numerous. It took the superhuman efforts of a Martin "Mike" Tovey, shotgun messenger extraordinary, to keep the brotherhood out of the stages, and even indomitable Mike was not always successful.

Mike Tovey came to the western treasure fields from Canada, and in the hour of Bodie's greatness was about thirty years of age. He was a lonely character, who considered himself woman-shy, and though courtesy itself to female passengers was never known to presume upon or continue an acquaintance that began upon the deck of a stage. But Mike was not gun-shy or fight-shy. He was perpetually ready for battle, and on plenty of occasions got it; in which event his habit was to drop from the stage by the off hind wheel and do hearty hurt to the foe from between the spokes. Unless women were aboard. In which case all war moved into the open.

September 5, 1880, was a particularly busy day for the Bodie *Standard's* columns. The funeral of George Watkins, who had shot and killed an officer, took place in the morning. John Hackwell, a miner, was shot and killed by a Spaniard in front of a dance house. John Rann shot and killed a man named Costello in Wagner's saloon in a difficulty growing out of the arrest of the woman who was instrumental in the doing-in of Hackwell. And the Belleville stage was robbed by two highwaymen, who then went down the road to Dalzell's station and robbed another passing stage.

But the day was not yet complete; in fact it was still young. The two who held up the pair of stages found time to pay a call on the throbbing mountain town, discover that a Carson-bound express coach was to start in late afternoon, and go eight miles down the canyon to prepare for its coming. Even so, the day was not yet spent. The two bad men put in the interim erecting two little walls of stone, one on each side of the road.

As this was an important consignment, it moved heavily guarded. Mike Tovey rode on top and another shotgun defender, Tom Woodruff, was secreted within. Other passengers were discouraged from riding in the cushions, but were given seats in a buggy that followed at a discreet distance.

As the Concord neared the scene of one of the morn-

$600 REWARD!

WELLS, FARGO & CO.

Will pay for Arrest and Conviction of the three men, who attempted to rob the Express on MILTON AND COPPEROPOLIS ROUTE this morning.

$200 EACH.

JNO. J. VALENTINE,
GEN'L SUPT.

San Francisco, Oct. 12, 1875.

REWARD!

Wells, Fargo & Co.,

Will Pay a Reward of $250 each for the Arrest and Conviction of the San Juan Express Robbers.

JOHN J. VALENTINE,
General Superintendent,

San Francisco, December 17th, 1875.

THE WAR ON MANY FRONTS

Circulars and reward posters

ing's hold-ups, Mike Tovey climbed down. He preceded the stage on foot, advancing through deepening twilight with his shotgun on his arm. The two little forts melted into the dusk. He first became aware of their portent when a raking pistol fire lodged a slug in his arm and brought down a stage horse.

Tovey sprang into characteristic fighting position behind the coachwheels. The robbers made a rush, one on each side of the vehicle. He waited until one assailant was well within the light of the coach lamps, then cut loose. The forces arrayed against the express company promptly diminished by one decapitated half. Tom Woodruff, after fussing an unconscionably long time with the catch of his gun, managed to thrust its muzzle out the coach window and let go two barrels into the ether. The second robber gave a howl, ran off into the now black sagebrush and fell flat.

"They're both dead!" cried Woodruff exultantly. The buggy coming up, Tovey was lifted into it. He was removed to a ranch-house for treatment. Tom Woodruff, seeing him into friendly port, returned to guard the stage.

The driver of the frenzied team had been left to get his slain horse out of the traces as best he could. While struggling, he heard someone moving in the dark. It was the second robber, who evidently had been only playing 'possum to Woodruff's gun. "Partner, where are you?" the driver heard this robber calling. Apparently the fellow had yet to learn that his associate was no longer active in the firm.

The calls grew fainter as the desperado made off into

the distance. But he did not leave empty-handed. As subsequently discovered, he moved off with the treasure box in his arms.

Aaron Y. Ross, a most dependable messenger, later investigated Tom Woodruff's part in the affair and professed himself mightily puzzled that the latter's gun was so unready. Hints were voiced that the escape of the robber with the treasure was not without connivance.

A pass book on the defunct assailant showed a neat balance in a bank, and an address in San Francisco. Detectives waiting at the address collared Milton Sharp, the dead man's roommate, on the latter's return from Nevada, and sent him to Carson prison for a dozen years.

Mike Tovey, arm in a sling, went back on his messenger's perch.

John Shine was holding the reins over four fast-stepping horses as the Sonora–Milton stage swept around the curves of Funck Hill, a few counties to westward, on July 26, 1875. The lead horses shied and a passenger screamed. A grotesque figure in soiled linen duster, heavy socks pulled up over his shoes, and white flour sack over his head had sprung from behind a rock. His crouching movement took him close under the horses and he held a shotgun.

"Keep your eye on them, boys, and be ready with both barrels!" he cried to something or somebody that was presumed to be lurking in the thicket he had just quitted.

Out of the corner of his eye the driver saw several more gun barrels trained at his stage from the top of a boulder. "Take the box," he invited. And to his passengers: "Don't make trouble. We've run into a pretty big ambush, and they've got the drop on every one of us."

The wooden express box was tossed to the road. The animated scarecrow thanked Shine courteously, called, "All right, men, let them go," and waved the equipage onward. It was on his return trip up Funck Hill that the driver noticed, with considerable start, that row of gun muzzles still pointing from the boulder. He got down this time and looked. They were mere idle sticks.

"A lone robber," mused Shine, "and so polite. 'Kindly drive on,' he said to me, and 'All right, men, let them go.' Of all the colossal nerve!"

Yes, John. Stagedom and Wells Fargo were to have much occasion, over the next eight years, to remark on that quaint politeness and colossal nerve.

An affair took place five months later at Wells Fargo's expense on the down-bound stage from North San Juan for Marysville. This was some distance north of the Funck Hill robbery. Five more months, and a visitation from the same road agent befell the express stage moving south from Roseburg, Oregon. Stage hold-ups were so frequent that there was no particular disposition to attribute these to the Funck Hill robber.

Fourteen months later a stage was rattling eastward from Fort Ross on the California coast. It contained no passengers. At a bend, a man waited with duster, leg-wrappings, white hood and shotgun. It seemed to the driver that he saw other gun muzzles also protruding from the brush. He gave the benefit of the doubt to himself and the express box to the robber. Thanking him genially and taking also the United States mail bag, the highwayman sent him on. The sheriff who spurred to the scene found only a ripped mail sack and four lines of broad verse written on an old waybill and left in the smashed express box, together with the jeering if obscure salutation,

Driver, give my respects to our friend, the other driver; but I really had a notion to hang my old hat on his weather eye.

Respectfully,
B. B.

Whoever B. B. was, this was the first announcement to Wells Fargo that they had a poetaster to deal with. But the ensuing eleven months, though filled with the antics of other highwaymen, brought nothing further from B. B.

In July of 1878, at a point about a hundred miles northeast, a respectable-looking middle-aged pedestrian might have been seen seated beside the road. He was occupied with paper and pencil. Occasionally he stopped to admire the outflung landscape, mop brow with neatly laundered handkerchief, and wag his pencil like a musician considering the tempo of a theme. Valley quail whirred and pattered beside him. The mountain lilac, creeping down the hillsides, had shed its white bloom and now covered the folds with dusty green. The sky would shed no rain for months—most convenient for pedestrians and outdoor poets. At length the nature lover put away his pencil and withdrew into the lilac cover. The Quincy–Oroville stage was coming. Light blue eyes under heavy

eyebrows doubtless studied it carefully as it passed, noting
its rate of travel and its personnel. When the stage had
vanished in the dust the wayfarer came forth and resumed
his composing.

Next day at the same hour, when the stage approached,
the loiterer was waiting. He pounced out, crouched beneath the horses, presented his armament. Before departing with the contents of mail bag and box—the latter
affording $379 in cash, a silver watch and a diamond ring
—he affixed to a bending lilac bough a bit of doggerel.
This stanza, left fluttering like a ballad to Rosalind, was
a twelve-line reconstruction of the Fort Ross effort and
eight of its lines recited:

> *Here I lay me down to sleep*
> *To wait the coming morrow.*
> *Perhaps success, perhaps defeat,*
> *And everlasting sorrow.*
> *Yet come what will—I'll try it on,*
> *My condition can't be worse,*
> *And if there's money in that box*
> *'Tis munny for my purse.*

This time B. B. signed himself "Black Bart, the PO8,"
which presumably meant poet. For further information
about this shy genius the United States postal authorities
promptly put up $300, Wells Fargo $600—the total
more than any budding poet was usually worth but considerably less than Black Bart ultimately commanded.
For the time was to come when this industrious Orlando

Black Bart, who held up twenty-eight stagecoaches and never pulled a trigger.

George Hackett, a famous shotgun messenger, who had a brush with Black Bart.

would be priced at $18,000 dead or alive—a good round sum for any producing poet, and a world's record for a dead one.

Five days later the La Porte to Oroville stage was stopped. The fruits were but fifty dollars in gold and a silver watch. The great days of the bullion hauls were over. Two months after, on two successive days, Bart again assessed the express concern. For these transactions he selected the Ukiah stage not far from the scene of his fourth exploit. He proved himself the traditional gallant highwayman by handing back to a lady passenger her watch.

The nonchalance of Black Bart set a fad. While express people raged, half a dozen rogues set up in business with various waggish appropriations from his method. "Bill Smith" in the Sierras took to stopping stages and all other chancing vehicles, lining up their passengers in unhappy assembly, and holding them by the hour while he chaffingly relieved all. Dick Fellows was operating in the new intellectual manner on the Coast road south of San Francisco Bay. He was exasperatingly humorous. He was also hard to catch. The maneuvers of this imitator made Bart seem more ubiquitous than ever.

Only once did Bart the indefatigable run into gunfire, when he tangled with messenger George Hackett and felt the hat blown off his head. But Hackett had to stay with his coach and the lone bandit escaped. But even such sport as Bart's had to end. On his twenty-eighth sally the "PO8" was interrupted by a deer hunter, and fled—leaving behind a handkerchief. Its laundry mark traced him to lodgings in San Francisco. There one Charles E. Boles, a most respectable-looking fellow, was uncovered as the grotesque poet and put away for four years' duress. On his discharge he was paid $125 a month by Wells Fargo on his promise to rob no more stagecoaches.

At six on a May evening of 1892, the down-bound Shasta–Redding stage moved slowly up a grade five miles north of Redding. It approached Blue Cut, a cleft through a hillock on the left side of Middle Creek. The region was a choke of manzanita and chaparral, scrub pine and dwarf oak. It was known as a likely spot for highwaymen. The stage four days before had been held up in Blue Cut. Tonight John Boyce held the ribbons; his passenger was George Suhr; beneath his feet was a Wells Fargo box containing bullion from French Gulch.

As the coach entered Blue Cut, a man detached himself from a clump of manzanita. Red bandana mask, two-barreled shotgun, the top of the grade, the curt command, the swift compliance—all were there. And one other item. Buck Montgomery, Wells Fargo guard, was inside the coach and at this moment was softly pushing his sawed-off shotgun through the parting of the leather curtains.

Here was dangerous technique. It was unwritten law that a messenger never fired when his driver was covered. But as the express box hit the road, Buck Montgomery pulled trigger. His thundering crash knocked the highwayman to his knees.

Across the road and well concealed was a second individual, ready for just such exigency. When Bandit Charley Ruggles went to his knees, Bandit John D. Ruggles uprose and poured a demolishing charge into the other side of the coach.

It sprayed the whole vehicle, riddled seats and panels, filled the legs of driver and passenger. The team bolted. Suhr, in spite of a calf full of buckshot, made grab for the lines. Driver Boyce was down in the boot. The express box had no more defenders. The robbers, one badly done in, made off with it into the bush.

A Dr. Stevenson and wife, driving toward Shasta, chanced to pass the stage a few minutes later. Passenger Suhr was kneeling in the boot but still managing to guide the frantic team; Boyce, with his right knee nearly torn off, was grimly operating the brakes. Montgomery lay inside. The doctor gave first aid and helped the wounded men to Middle Creek Hotel. Montgomery died soon after.

The arrival of the bullet-torn stage at Redding caused a furor. Montgomery had been immensely popular. Members of Company E, California National Guard, turned out to a man. Though the hold-up had occurred in steep, wild country, tracks of the bandit pair were picked up and the treasure box, smashed, empty and blood-covered, was located in the darkness not far off.

The next day, Sunday, found every gulch and ravine being ransacked by the whole male population of Shasta County. At two o'clock some boys encountered one of the fugitives crouched in the brush. Charley Ruggles came of good family, and his unmasking was a sensation. Badly wounded, he had no fight to offer and was haled to Redding in a spring wagon.

A month later a brawny, sandy-haired, mustached, and bewhiskered man appeared at Woodland in the center of the state. The hardware clerk from whom he bought cartridges for a Smith & Wesson recognized John D. Ruggles from his posters. Before he could notify a sheriff, the man disappeared. Four days later he was seen again, entering the Opera Restaurant. This time deputy Sheriff Wykoff, Thacker of Wells Fargo, and other officers followed him in. The sandy-haired customer ordered beef heart Spanish and began on the bread. Deputy Wykoff sat down at the suspect's table and selected frijoles and ham. Some odor of the law manifested itself to Ruggles, who made shift to get his revolver into better position. As he reached, he saw himself reflected in the long blue barrel of Wykoff's Colt. Ruggles made a lunge, Wykoff fired; the ball met the bandit in the neck. Then followed a fearful hand-to-hand battle for the gun, with chairs, tables, dishes, entrées, gravy, hors d'œuvres, officers, and customers all involved in the mêlée. Stalwart and powerful, John Ruggles put up the fight of his life. He was finally brought crashing to the floor and handcuffed, and lifted into a baggage car for Redding.

The defense of the brothers lasted a month. Attorneys tried to make the dead Montgomery a party to the crime. Maudlin sympathy of Redding women—for the Ruggles pair were handsome—also reacted against the prisoners. At midnight on July 24th about forty masked men marched downhill toward Redding town and across the public square. They entered the courthouse. The jailer slept on the third floor. Watchers outside could see flare of torches through the windows. The jailer, shaken awake, protested that his keys were locked in a safe. With sledge, drills, and powder the mob set to getting them out of the safe. The falling blows of the sledge could be heard outside, and reverberated in the jail below. John and Charley Ruggles rose from their pallets and donned stockings, shirts, pants.

Presently the double doors of the jail creaked open. The brothers were waiting. Handcuffs were affixed, they were marched across the square, down an alley, a turn to the left, and halted by the tracks beneath a beam that lay in place between two pine trees.

John was asked where the treasure of the Blue Cut hold-up was cached.

"Spare Charley, and I'll tell you," he sought to bargain.

But the mob much preferred Charley's neck to Wells Fargo's treasure.

Charley Lambert, who drove stage up and down the long Donahue road in the coast redwood country, knew horses and he knew rifles. The Ballard rifle, for instance: it was a sporting arm of excellent balance and superior workmanship, with its bore deeply grooved for accuracy, and its hammer movement one of the fastest ever invented. For the hunter of small game this precise produce of Fall River, Massachusetts, had only one technical drawback. It was a single-shot weapon.

Judiciously Charley Lambert gazed adown the blue-black barrel of such a fast-working piece of ordnance. He looked with fascination from its fine front sight to its ingeniously elevated rear sight. He looked over its hammer, entirely too delicately poised, and along its walnut stock. Finally he stared into the blue eye that was squinting behind the hammer. The eye was surrounded by a mask of blue calico; nothing more of the wearer's face was visible.

Lambert's hands were up. "This is a joke!" he protested. It was a pleasant Sunday morning of 1891; in a little while the church bells would be sounding across the Sonoma Valley meadows; and up to this instant Charley, driving south, hadn't had a worry in the world.

"No, it isn't a joke. I mean business. Throw down that box."

His eye looking over the robber from head to foot, Charley complied.

"Now the mail bags."

"They're inside!"

"Climb down, then, and fork them out!"

A Ballard rifle, Charley Lambert reflected, is just too temperamental for argument. So he climbed down. He had no passengers. The horses had to be left to themselves. His head inside the hind boot, Charley caressed them by voice, "Whoa, Jeff. Steady, Dainty." As he rummaged for the mail sacks, he thought rapidly. That pretty rifle yonder: straight and hard-shooting it was; but still and all, with only one cartridge—. Well, he would risk one shot.

Charley spoke again to his horses, very quietly. And what he said wasn't "Whoa."

"They're backing down hill!" cried Charley Lambert a moment later, as if in great surprise. "You'll have to let me climb aboard and pull up to a level place!"

"All right! Get back on your seat and drive ahead a little way."

Lambert climbed up. This grade, nineteen miles north of Ukiah, was known as Robbers' Hill. Surrounding valleys, bordered with dense manzanita and madrone, had for years provided free lodgings for road agents. Some of the boldest pieces of highwaymanry in Pacific annals had occurred along this picturesque strip, now known as the Redwood Highway, and its stagecoaching laterals.

A few rods farther on and Charley and his team were at the hilltop. The instant he was over the rise, and his head somewhat protected by the top of the coach, Charley gave lusty bang to his whip and let out a large whooroop. The team leaped forward. Charley ducked and waited for his world to cleave. Not even the single cartridge spoke. The robber stood frozen in his tracks and watched his prey vanish, too surprised for action.

Into Ukiah the stagedriver lashed, considerably ahead of schedule. He located the sheriff. A tall, athletic fellow, Lambert described his assailant, clad in a drab duster and shod in hobnailed stogies. Sheriff J. M. Standley nodded and went back the nineteen miles to the scene of the hold-up. The express box lay smashed open. All that remained in it were a couple of waybills and a pair of baby's shoes.

To Willets, a nearby village, the sheriff then went to make inquiry. Farmer John Roop had been visited by a house-breaker two days before and robbed of a Ballard rifle, a blue calico dress and an old linen duster. Farmer Roop lamented that rifle. He had intended to fetch it down to Ukiah for the annual Thanksgiving turkey shoot and was sure it had been carried off by a jealous rival. The blue dress and duster—they were just a blind. With that Ballard rifle, now, he would knock you a head off a turkey with a bullet placed through either eye you liked.

The sheriff promised to get the weapon back in a hurry.

From Robber's Hill a set of hobnailed footprints led westward into a wilderness of thicket and down rocky gorges for nine miles to the ranch of one Thompson. The highwayman had stopped there the night before, leaving unceremoniously at midnight.

Circling widely, and scenting out every suggestion of a trail, a posse uncovered the culprit's tracks again at Clarke's logging camp five miles west. By now forty-eight hours had elapsed, and they missed their quarry. Evidently he had spent the previous day in the woods, coming out at evening to be fed by the Chinese cook. The trail pinched out.

But the man-hunters were of stubborn strain. They took counsel, then plunged south. This led into unique country. Stretches of almost impenetrable manzanita intervened between forests whose redwoods towered to immense heights, shutting off the sun. In the shadow-land between their great trunks there was no sound, no call or flutter of birds; scarcely an insect. All was thick-carpeted silence and the majesty of the ages. Out of these awesome virgin forests the trackers finally burst, coming upon the east-west stage route between Ukiah and the ocean.

At Low Gap a marauder had lately stolen a ham and an axe from a ranchman. Six miles farther on someone had made an overnight camp, now deserted.

The posse was warming to the chase. The stage route led them back to the Donahue highway, where at Hopland, south of Robber's Hill, they learned that a "Joe McKay" had been cutting wood for ranchman Henry Willard. The woodcutter was described as tall, athletic, blue-eyed, demi-blond. He had been in the habit of going to Hopland for his mail. On Wednesday evening, the eleventh of November, he had disappeared, and had reappeared without explanation on Thursday the nineteenth. Charley Lambert's stage had been held up on the fifteenth.

Back to the Willard woodpile, and there the legal guardians raked about and uncovered a crumpled envelope. Wet with dew and stained with leaves and sawdust, it still remarked its addressee as "Joseph McKay, Hopland, Cal." The letter was illuminating. It saluted "Dear Brother" and concluded "Your brother," with a signature that was not McKay. The letter was dated from the family seat of one of the West's rather renowned poets, who had himself served time in a Shasta jail for mule-stealing, and whose son the scapegrace "Joe McKay" evidently was.

The errant youth was found by Sheriff Standley sitting

in an armchair in Burns' Hotel at Santa Rosa farther down
the highway. He was reading about himself in a newspaper, and seemed to find it interesting. The man of
law and order, having chased far and strenuously, also
seated himself in an armchair. He puffed a cigar until
the reading was finished.

Then tapped his man.

XXIII

AARON ROSS'S FIGHTING BOOTS

From Helena to Pioche, and from Carson to Salt Lake City, the biggest feet attached to any express rider were those that formed the base of Aaron Y. Ross. They were well-known feet. When Ross drove buckboard stage in the Sixties between Helena and Fort Benton, a region infested with inquisitive Flatheads and Sioux, the mere sight of those feet on the dashboard, piling up their imposing silhouette against the sunset, quelled all aboriginal enthusiasm for a quarrel.

And the broad-rooted pine from Maine was proportioned to his feet. When he took them down from the dashboard and stood on them—preferably in his socks—he loomed up to an elevation of six feet four, presenting a bone and muscle massif of some two hundred and fifty pounds. This eighth of a ton of real man was efficiently distributed; there was nothing paunchy about Ross.

Ross's hair was black and his eyes were black, and his cheeks and chin were given over to a rugged stand of beard. Black beard. Add the fact that he was as brave as he was large, and put a shotgun in his hands, and you have a lot of express messenger. Like most big men, however, he was even-tempered. Beyond all challenges to strife he preferred riding comfortably in his socks with the wind blowing over his feet. "He is one of those peculiar men," said an admiring journal of his time, "who if struck in the back of the neck with a slungshot would turn upon the assailant and say 'fun's fun, boys, but don't you tickle me with that straw again. It puts my shirt collar out of kilter.' "

Ross first appeared on the Coast in 1857, digging for gold at Murphy's Camp in the Mother Lode placers. Four years of that, and he moved on to eastern Oregon. Then for a year or two Idaho's gold fields knew him; then Montana's. In 1867, when the wonderfully rich placers of Montana were beginning to fail, Ross the prospector turned Ross the stage driver. From the driver's seat he slid over, taking his feet with him, to become a Wells Fargo shotgun messenger between Helena, Montana, and Corinne, Utah. When Bodie shipments became heavy he was transferred to the bloody Bodie-Carson run, conveying raw silver up the California-Nevada border to the mint whose output was rocking the monetary balance of two hemispheres. He next carried the sawed-off shotgun for the express company between Pioche and Salt Lake, and on other runs where civil tranquillity was more a legal theory than a local practice.

Several times Ross had encounters and he bore the scars incident to a large target, but he had safely arrived within two months of his forty-seventh birthday and his record on this sharp January morning in 1882 was still one hundred per cent. He had never given up an express box or a box of bullion. It was as messenger in a

Wells Fargo express car that Ross was lying on his pallet in the crisp hours preceding sun-up, as No. One Central Pacific Eastbound moved across Nevada toward the Utah border.

Montello lay ahead, all but invisible in murky dawn under a powdering of snow; though even in brightest day it would have been barely visible. For Montello's improvements were but three: a rail siding, a water tank and a clapboard shack. At the moment, the first was empty; the second was full and frozen; and the third, being a stove-heated Chinese bunkhouse, was crammed full and very sultry.

As dawn came blearily up out of Great Salt Lake Desert, poppied dreams, paper-stuffed window and bolted door were shattered by a crash of rifle bullets. The salvo was augmented by heavily thrown stones, thump of gunstocks and white men's yells. The section hands waited not to stop, look, or listen. They sprang straight from tropic blankets into the midwinter outdoors, and kept going on bare toes over crusted snow for Toana, next stop west. Toano had a six-stall roundhouse, some coal sheds, and several shanties. More important, it had twenty-five miles' distance between it and Montello, and twenty-five miles' distance at the moment was just what the celestials craved.

With shots into the air to keep them going, the raiders took possession of the bunkhouse. The eastbound express would soon come puffing up the long straight grade, which reached its summit just west of Montello station. Meanwhile desert dawn was decidedly chill. The five white men stoked up the stove and sat down to review their plans.

Number One was faithfully approaching. Behind its bell-funneled locomotive lurched United States mail car, express car, baggage, and two or three passenger coaches. Three clerks were asleep in the mail car. They said later that they were unarmed, which was curious; they probably counted on attacks, if any, centering on the traditional express. In the baggage an attendant also slumbered. Wells Fargo's car, rolling along between, chanced to contain little specie or bullion. Ross had sorted his waybills at Toano, found everything in order, and was now likewise snatching an hour of sleep.

He was roused by a rap at his door. He assumed this to be the greeting of the station agent at Tecoma and rose from his pallet. Tecoma was a metropolis of three stores, five saloons, and a stockyard; it usually delivered to him a consignment of silver from the mines of Buel City, Lucin, Silver Islet, Deep Creek, and Delano. Ross moved in stockinged feet to the door, opened it slightly against its chain.

What he beheld was not teeming Tecoma but unimportant Montello, lately occupied by the eight Chinese track tampers and now by their five Caucasian successors, one of whom had jammed a rifle barrel through the crack. Its owner announced: "Hop out! We are going through you."

Fourteen years, by stagecoach and steam car, Aaron Ross had been escorting express matter. First and last, his orders had been to take this or that in charge and see that it reached, without deviation, a specific so-and-so.

The orders were succinct and had always proved sufficient. Eleven years before, the Montana stage he was defending had been stopped by armed men and contrary directions given. Ross had been at a slight disadvantage: his boots off and his stockinged feet on the dashboard; but when the shooting finished, several Montanans were discoverable on the ground and none was Ross. Those who got away felt that they owed it entirely to the shoeless state of the messenger. Men in that part of the country sometimes wondered what would happen if Ross got into a real battle with his boots on. Well, here they were again.

Ross leaped back, slammed his door, and shot its bolts and chain. Then he turned to his bunk for a few fast preparations.

More pounding, this time on the opposite door. The voices were irritated. "Open up and jump out! We are going to rob this train!"

There was momentary silence within, followed by a slowly drawled answer.

"Just wait till I get my boots on," the messenger requested.

"Never mind your boots! Hop right out here and we'll get through with you. Then you can pull your boots on."

Ross said no more. He continued drawing on his tremendous footgear. Socks were for comfort and informality, but this looked like official business. Then he drew his kit chest into position and threw his blankets over it. Following which, he caught up his Winchester, looked to its magazine, and waited for next remark from the opposition.

It came, yelled through whiskers that were stiff with frost and anger. "Open up or we will burn you out and murder you!"

Ross calculated the direction and answered with a lead slug through the side of his car. Silence ensued for a matter of minutes. Then a voice with a little more distance before it bore the pained appeal:

"Ain't you going to open the door and come out?"

Ross replaced the spent cartridge.

Footsteps crunched around his car in a wide circle. There was murmured colloquy. Then a last gruff order:

"Hop out!"

Ross chose instead to purse his lips in "Young Kate of Kilcummer," favorite and incessant air of Number One's brakeman.

Five shots, from five different angles, rang out in the cold air. They ripped five holes in Ross's citadel. They smashed the swinging lamp, which had been burning wanly; they ricocheted about on the car hardware; three struck the defender. Ross dropped behind his kit box with one wound in hip, another in his hand, a third just to the left of his watch pocket. The hip wound, caused by a spent ball, was more bruising than fateful. The breast shot had staggered him with the weight of its blow, but had been partially turned by a thick paper-crammed wallet.

Prolonged stillness followed. At length the robbers felt satisfied. Their man, it would seem, had been accounted for. They climbed to the rear of the car to cut the train. Ross was waiting for that maneuver. He pushed his rifle across the kit box and sent two shots through the wall in that direction. The climbers hastily got down.

There was another war council held in his hearing: "I thought there was only one in there." "Sure, there's only one!" "Not on your life! I distinctly saw two!"

Ross grinned. Seen hastily through a dark opening, he undoubtedly looked like two.

"Let's get coal and put a fire under them. That'll chase them out."

Ross took firmer grip of his rifle, and ceased grinning.

"No—we need the fuel for the engine. I've got a better idea."

A whistle was heard from the east. It was Number Two, the westbound overland. The raiders ordered Number One backed onto the Montello siding. When the two trains were abreast, westbound Conductor Clement shouted to eastbound Conductor Cassin: "What are you doing here? I want to talk to you." As he spoke, he became aware of the row of guns trained on his chest and forehead and heard peremptory orders to keep going. Westbound Number Two kept going. "That was the coldest shake I got," said Ross later, "hearing that train go by while the fusillade was on."

A few passengers had stepped down from their tarrying eastbound to observe the uncouth West in action. Probably seven out of ten had small pocket pistols, but these were of little avail against riding men's artillery. Show of the latter sent them hurriedly back for their cars. After all, human brotherhood might be human brotherhood, but this wasn't their fight.

The robbers went into another conference. One came out of it to make leap for the express car's front end. He sought to clamber to its roof. Ross heard his feet on the ladder. He knew the location of those rungs precisely. With his shot through the woodwork a man's body plumped hastily to the platform; the shot had gone between the knees.

More conferring outside. "I tell you I saw two men in there before we shot the light out." "Two or six, they're a plucky bunch of hombres."

The train crew had been impounded under guard of one highwayman up by the water tank. Robbers tramped thither and selected a brakeman. He was ordered, with some prompting from the hot end of a rifle, to uncouple Ross's car from the baggage car following. It was a ticklish assignment for the brakeman, who wanted to be friends with everybody. Ross might fire on him from within. To sustain his courage and prove his identity, he vigorously whistled. It took some doing to maintain the pucker, but he managed it.

> *As the rose to the bee,*
> *As the sunshine to summer,*
> *So welcome to me*
> *Is young Kate of Kilcummer—*

Ross recognized the whistler and withheld his fire. The wheels of his car began to roll. He wondered if he were to be kidnaped, and with mild interest considered whither. Then the brakes set hard. The defender heard the whistler swing off and run to the forward end, where again there was sound of uncoupling.

Ross's wounds hurt horribly. A crimson handkerchief was twisted around his damaged hand. The bullet had gouged the length of the index finger. For hip and breast he had nothing to staunch the flow, and no free hand with which to manage. Got to keep grip somehow on this rifle . . .

Again the engine labored forward, but this time Ross's car did not move. So that was it: they had cut his car out, and now it was standing alone.

One last offer to parley, and a banging of coal picks against his door. Was he coming out?

For answer the defender lifted the famous Aaron Ross bootsole and drove it resoundingly against his side of the door.

"Leapin' antelopes!" commented an awe-struck brigand. "What was that?"

"He musta slung the stove."

"Well, boys, I guess we'll throw something back. It'll be plenty."

The next move came fast. The engineer, nudged with a rifle, had pulled off. Now he launched locomotive, tender, and attendant mail car full at the obdurate express. The steam-driven missiles struck the stalled car with a titanic bang. At the impact, both express doors sprang open the length of their chain-fastenings. Ross saw daylight in sudden vertical rectangles. He made leap for one door, slammed it shut, then reached for the other—good thing now he had that six and a half feet of Herculean arm-reach—and readjusted their bolts. Then back to the rear end of his fort. There, using one hand, he struggled to pile up more boxes.

Engine and mail were drawn off, shot at him again. They sprang as from a catapult. Again the doors burst open. Laying down his rifle and working with his good hand, Ross closed and rechained one door before a firearm could poke through, then turned to the other. A man was at the orifice, swinging a gun on him. And this time the monumental boots, which had awed Flatheads and Sioux with their grandeur and made legend in the inter-mountain basin, went into action—or one of them did. Ross, minus his rifle, kicked. A body pitched through the air, fell heavily.

"Gawd," said an awe-struck voice again, as the messenger slammed and chained his door. "They heaved the safe."

Ross was bleeding ruinously and found it necessary to lean on his box parapet for a moment before regaining his rifle.

"Now we've *got* to build that fire. We'll holocaust the car."

Silence. The robbers swarmed for the tender. But the siege had lasted long; it was now past ten o'clock in the morning. And from the tender practically all fuel had been extracted to keep up steam. Ross grinned again when he heard a debate over this discovery. The raiders would find timber scarce in the intermountain country.

The familiar voice of the leader challenged him once more, this time a little more wheedingly.

"Ain't you ever going to hop out?"

No, Ross was never going to hop out.

One last slam from the catapulted mail car. But the blow was less stalwart. The up-grade was against it. The force was furnished by steam from a dying boiler.

Over the whited desert shut a more lasting silence. It endured some minutes: perhaps the robbers were plotting one last devilment. Then, faint at first and steadily nearing, another locomotive was discernible. Had Conductor Clement delivered his story at Toano? The robbers did not wait to learn. When the messenger applied eye to a bullet hole to review the field, he saw five defeated bandits posting swiftly for the horizon, one doubled over his saddle.

Three hours and twenty minutes had the siege endured when conductor, engineer, mail clerks, and brakeman opened to the one-man defender in his triumphant fort. Boots, pants, pockets and rifle magazine were full of valiant blood. The express money was secure. Loudly the mail clerks lamented that, had they been armed, they could have disposed of the highwaymen with ease. Ross shrugged. Forty bullets had entered his rolling fortress, including one that had pierced the double-walled wooden end, the zinc lining behind the stove, and the stovepipe, and finally had buried itself in the opposite wall.

Official business was over. Seating himself, Ross permitted his rescuers to take off his fighting boots.

The Wells Fargo car had contained but six hundred dollars. But it transpired that the mail car which had been used as a projectile had contained, all unsuspected, nearly half a million dollars in minted silver.

XXIV

THE CONCORD COACH ROLLS ON

ONE day in the great period of Consolidated Virginia and the other bonanza mines of the Comstock, a farmer from Truckee Valley drove into Virginia City. He brought to the Queen of Camps a load of chickens. The load was not unusual. But its mode of conveyance was a shock to the town which thought itself hardened to shocks.

For the vehicle was a once-proud Concord which had borne "Pioneer Stage Company" on its headrail in former days. The upper work had been cut out, leaving only the box in front, the boot behind, and the running gear below. This yawning cleft was filled up with noisy poultry coops, and the ranchman handled four shambling plugs from the throne once occupied by some Hank Monk, John Burnett, Baldy Green, or Charley Watson in the golden hours of the Overland Mail and its headlong Placerville run. Phantoms of six blooded horses swinging around mountain turns within an inch of precipices, never meeting with an accident and always getting the express through on time, stirred the breasts of old-timers who beheld this base end of the once-sumptuous conveyance. It may well be wondered whether the shades of Jack Davis and Captain Ingram stared with equal disapproval.

By this time more than the Concord coach had fallen on sad days. The very institution of stagecoach robbery was mouldering. With Black Bart safely behind bars and the use of money orders rapidly increasing, Wells Fargo's detective department in the year 1886 could find but fifteen successful stage hold-ups to report—two in Arizona, one each in Oregon, New Mexico, Montana and Nebraska, and in unregenerate California nine. Gold dust, gold and silver bullion and coin were traveling the roads in such diminished bulk that all fifteen robberies totaled but $2,600, most of which was recovered.

Yet were there stages in hundreds of places still pounding out their several total thousands of road-miles daily; and the road agent, if he no longer expected a rich haul, was no less abrupt when he struck, and no less sinister. Only the old-time suavity was fading.

"Right up here, miss!" said Driver Raggio at San Andreas to Miss Anna Rodersino, making place on the box for the small-waisted figure with the leg-of-mutton sleeves, prim high-necked collar, velvet chin strap, and long-handled parasol. Miss Rodersino was mistress at the Sheep Ranch school near the Calaveras Big Trees.

"Will there be room?" asked Miss Rodersino.

"Room and more room!" The stage driver chuckled to the male companion who was also preparing to mount the box. "Though I mind when there wasn't always so much space—not when gals did their travelin' in hoopskirts. Remember those days, Mike?"

"They called for careful packing-in," recollected Tovey.

"Were you ever held up, Mr. Raggio?"

"Sights o' times! Shouldn't wonder the shotgun messengers laid for me themselves! Feller gets used to it."

"I've heard about those days. Robbers used to joke with the passengers. Always polite to ladies, so I'm told."

"Generally were, miss. Most o' them must have been intended by nature for stage drivers. Courtly an' elegant instincts, that's what they had. But all that has changed. Highwaymen, like horses and coaches, aren't what they were."

"But highways at least are better. You forget this is 1892, Mr. Raggio."

"Degenerate days, miss."

In addition to Miss Rodersino and Messenger Tovey, the coach contained two women passengers inside. Its Wells Fargo box held the pay roll of the Sheep Ranch Mine. The coach moved steadily up the Calaveras grade.

The driver turned to Tovey. "Anything been heard of this fellow Sharp?"

"He's out again."

Milton Sharp was the bandit who had successfully looted the Bodie stage twelve years before, playing possum in the dark after his partner Jones was extinguished by Tovey's blast. Captured in San Francisco through the bank book found on his late associate, Sharp had been cast into Nevada State Prison and had twice escaped.

The stage rolled on.

From a tree at the left of the road a shotgun poked cautious muzzle. As the coach swept up, the gun spoke. Swift lead riddled the bow of the vehicle, miraculously missing the inside occupants; the fanlike wings of the buckshot charge caught Tovey in the arm, Raggio in chest and shoulder. The driver pitched forward. Tovey guided his stricken form safely into the boot. The veteran messenger then jumped down. The assailant, a heavy figure in black mask and brown overalls, had left. He could be heard crashing and crackling through dense brush in the direction of Stanislaus River. Climbing back, Tovey caught the lines, and with the wounded driver working the brake with his hands the stage moved on.

It was a situation that had happened on roads unnumbered, but this time with a signal difference. As he contemplated the fact, Tovey's eyes grew somber and his face looked old. Between him and Raggio, in her leg-of-mutton sleeves, prim high-necked collar and velvet chin strap, had been sitting Miss Rodersino. Gravely and gently at the nearest tavern she was lifted down. Life was extinct.

Yes, road agentry had changed.

It is five o'clock of a June afternoon, 1893. A man in blue jumper, carrying a Winchester rifle, stands under a buckeye bush beside a bare stretch of Sierra foothill roadway. Men at a distance are working in a hayfield. The air is sweetly pungent with drying grasses. The rifleman seats himself in the embrace of a low stone wall. He strikes a match, burns off a small patch of grass, rubs the black soot over his cheekbones like a mask, then nurses his rifle.

The distant thump is heard of the Ione–Jackson express. The waiting figure rises, draws farther into his leafy shelter, and cocks his weapon.

Seven persons ride in the oncoming Concord. Inside are two women, a boy, and a man; on the box is Clint Radcliffe, old-time jehu; beside him sits Mike Tovey, and behind and above them both sits one passenger.

East of this point three-quarters of a mile, the Ione–Jackson stage five months ago had an odd experience. Tovey was guard. Walking ahead in the dark of a midwinter night he encountered a strand of barbed wire stretched across the road. Evidently its purpose was to entangle the lead horses and entrap the stage. Tovey removed the barrier and there was no further molestation. Since the assault of the previous April and its slaughter of a young woman passenger, Tovey has been extraordinarily wary. Lately, moreover, he has received anonymous written warnings. The veteran has shrugged these off. Yet he has been dropping down behind the off hind wheel, fighting bandits, and defending Wells Fargo treasure, for half a lifetime. He bears scars, holes, and bullets in every part of his anatomy. Only yesterday he confided to Bill Scott at Ione that he rather expects to get knocked off sooner or later. He has journeyed long. Not that he is going to retire. The habits of a lifetime are too fixed for that. But when a man nears fifty, and has no family to miss him, and has spent three decades staring into gun barrels, he sometimes wonders if the moment isn't rather overdue . . .

But now Tovey is on duty, and the duty is guarding Wells Fargo treasure, and the highway over which $275,-

000,000 has rolled is no place for dreaming. So Tovey sits with well-polished shotgun on his knees. It is only because the countryside has become gentle and open that he has relaxed in the least—breaking his shotgun and extracting its shells, for his passengers' greater safety. A man who understands firearms thoroughly respects them thoroughly, and keeps them unloaded when possible.

A heavy shot booms just after the stage passes the buckeye bush. It cleaves Mike Tovey in the back, ranges upward and rips its .44-calibre way through his stout old heart and out at his left breast. He pitches forward. The empty shotgun with well-polished stock tumbles from his hands. Radcliffe and the passenger seize and lower him into the boot. The ambusher has now stepped out. He sends a second ball; it smashes the back of the driver's seat and sears Radcliffe's flesh. Travelers inside are shrieking. The horses are milling in terror. The assailant fires twice more. Each shot strikes a wheelhorse in the leg. Dragged and swept along by momentum, the coach travels two hundred yards, then stops in chaos. Radcliffe climbs down. Men come running from the hayfield. They lift Mike Tovey into the stage. The assassin picks up his empty shells and disappears along a division fence over the stubble field to southward. Radcliffe cuts the wounded horses out, hitches up the remaining four and drives for Jackson four miles distant.

The wing-weary petrel is dead.

And this, perhaps, is as good a place as another to wave farewell to the indomitable Concord. Clint Radcliffe and his kind drive it onward for a few more years, but they are a dying race; the Jingling Decades are over; drivers and their chariots have lasted out of their time.

Drive away, you knights of the lash, with hats aslant, reins lightly between fingers, treasure chests aclink and fortified messengers beside you with their short polished shotguns across their knees. Away with you up the trails of history, and for the high blue notch between the pines, with a ghostly Tom Poole or a Milt Sharp lurking at any bend. Your bourn is some far home-station. The others are there ahead of you. The end of it all is some back room in a quiet saloon in the azure, where old cronies sit and cackle and the stable odors blow pungently across Elysian fields. Bill Gristy is there, clinking beer mugs with Bill Dobson. Eugene Blair is showing Big Jack Davis just how he knocked up his gun-arm. Aaron Ross is resting his stockinged feet on the stove fender. Captain Ingram is writing a receipt and Black Bart is working on a poem. Gather up the loiterers by the way, you last jehu— friends and foemen, messengers and road agents, tumble them all in. Always room for one more in a stagecoach, boys, and this is her last trip forever!

And on for the Pass the dimming Concord rolls.

We look down from the clouds and this barroom in Elysium to the San Francisco of 1925. World-wide war has swept away the old express names save as they are preserved by banking houses, travel bureaus, and investment trusts. Wells Fargo Bank & Union Trust Company carries on the financial tradition in the old seaport of the Pacific, and Wells, Fargo & Company operates an express out of New York running to Mexico and Cuba; but the travel-weary errand man of El Dorado functions under that name no longer—he has withdrawn into history. John Parrott's Granite Block at California and Montgomery streets—archive of so much saga, scene of Adams & Company's historic failure, symbol of Wells Fargo's succession, scene of the revelation of the might of nitroglycerine and end of the Overland Trail—is in the hands of the wreckers.

As the massive walls come down and the great shutters are lifted from their frames, watchers haunt the scene.

"There is buried treasure, sure," runs the rumor through the crowd. "Mexican doubloons." "Stored and forgotten jewels." "Gold nuggets." "Rare whisky, too, and old liqueurs." One optimist, "only living heir to Donna Manuelita Brujas," whose family it seems once had a Spanish king's offhand gift of this ground, lays claim by right of heritage to the expected cache. As the walls go down, one treasure-seeker even appears with a mysterious parchment and a transit with which he tries to run confident sight-lines. But the last of the great stones from China are pulled apart, steam shovels enter, and soon there is nothing but the excavation for a fifteen-story office building. Of all the gold which once passed into those shielding vaults, and out again on twice-monthly steamer day, no crumb of dust, no grain or flake remains. The ledger is closed, the waybills filed, the receipts in good order, the glittering trust delivered.

Which just about sums up the Wells Fargo epic.

ACKNOWLEDGMENTS

Many an Old Timer has been drawn upon for his reminiscences and versions of the feats and incidents told in these pages. But the memories of Old Timers are tricky, and their versions are not always unvarnished. Nor is it the habit of eye-witnesses always to agree. Chief reliance has been, therefore, the contemporary printed or written record. Wells Fargo records largely went up in flames in the San Francisco Fire of 1906, but some remain. Old newspaper files have also been an important source of material. For the opportunity to review these, as well as certain pamphlets, private scrapbooks, old letters and written reminiscences, the author wishes to make grateful acknowledgment to the Bancroft Collection of the University of California Library at Berkeley; to the California State Library at Sacramento; to the California Historical Society, the Society of California Pioneers, and the Wells Fargo Bank and Union Trust Company, at San Francisco; and to Mr. Henry A. Brown, assistant treasurer of the Abbot-Downing Truck & Body Co. at Concord, New Hampshire, for transcriptions of orders, descriptions and other data concerning Concord stages that have long since rolled over the divide. Thanks are also extended to Wells Fargo Bank for the use of photographs.

MANUSCRIPTS

BALLOU, WILLIAM T., "Adventures." Dictated 1878. Bancroft Collection, University of California Library.

BURNETT, PETER H., "Recollections of the Past." 2 volumes. Dictated 1878. Bancroft Collection.

CONWAY, JOHN, "Early Days in California." Dictated 1880. Bancroft Collection.

GARNISS, JAMES R., "The Early Days of San Francisco." Dictated 1877. Bancroft Collection.

GWIN, W. H., "Memoirs on History of United States, Mexico and California." Dictated 1878. Bancroft Collection.

HODGKINS, PILSBURY, "Life." California State Library.

McCONNELL, W. J., "The Idaho Inferno." Dictated 1873. Bancroft Collection.

RANDOLPH, W. C., "Statement." Dictated 1877. Bancroft Collection.

SOULE, FRANK, "Statement." Dictated 1878. Bancroft Collection.

TODD, ALEXANDER H., "Statement." Dictated 1878. Bancroft Collection.

WILLIAMS, HENRY F., "Statement of Recollections on Early Days of California." Dictated 1878. Bancroft Collection.

PAMPHLETS

SHEARER, F. E., "The Pacific Tourist." New York, 1879.
A guide-book popular with travelers in the early years of the Pacific Railroad.

WELLS, HENRY, "Wells, Fargo & Co. Sketch of the Rise, Progress and Present Condition of the System." New York, 1864.

WELLS, Fargo & Co., "Instruction to Agents and Employes." San Francisco, 1882.

MISCELLANEOUS

DAGGETT, JOHN. Scrapbooks. California State Library.

HUME, JAMES B. Scrapbooks and personal files, preserved by Wells Fargo Bank & Union Trust Company, San Francisco.

SCHAEFFER, JOHN G., "The Early History of the Wells Fargo Express." MS. thesis, University of California Library, 1921.

WARD, HENRY. Scrapbook. California State Library.

Among books dealing with this theater of action that have been published in recent years the author has found the following unusually enjoyable:

BANNING, CAPT. WILLIAM, AND BANNING, GEORGE HUGH, "Six Horses." New York, 1930.

BREWER, WILLIAM H., "Up and Down California." New Haven, 1930.
    The journal, 1860–64, of the field commander of the California Geological Survey, edited by Francis P. Farquhar.

CHALFANT, WILLIE ARTHUR, "Outposts of Civilization." Boston, 1928.

CLOUD, ROY W., "On the Trails of Yesterday." San Francisco, 1931.

DAVIS, SAM P., ED., "The History of Nevada." 2 vols. Reno and Los Angeles, 1913.

EGAN, W. M., ED., "Pioneering the West, 1846–1878." Richmond, Utah, 1917.

FARISH, THOMAS EDWIN, "History of Arizona." 2 vols. Phoenix, 1915.

FULTON, ROBERT LARDIN, "Epic of the Overland." San Francisco, 1924.

GLASSCOCK, CARL BURGESS, "The Big Bonanza: The Story of the Comstock Lode." Indianapolis, 1931.

HAFEN, LE ROY R., PH.D., "The Overland Mail, 1849–1869: Promoter of Settlements, Precursor of Railroads." Cleveland, 1926.

HARLOW, ALVIN F., "Old Waybills: The Romance of the Express Companies." New York and London, 1934.

HUNT, ROCKWELL DENNIS, AND AMENT, WILLIAM SHEFFIELD, "Oxcart to Airplane." Of the series *California*. Los Angeles, 1929.

LYMAN, GEORGE D., "The Saga of the Comstock Lode." New York and London, 1934.

ROBINSON, WILL H., "The Story of Arizona." Phoenix, 1919.

ROOT, F. A., AND CONNELLEY, W. E., "The Overland Stage to California." Topeka, 1901.

STELLMAN, LOUIS J., "Mother Lode." San Francisco, 1934.

WILTSEE, ERNEST A., "The Pioneer Miner and the Pack Mule Express." San Francisco, 1931.

INDEX

A

Abbot, Downing & Co., coach builders, 30, 175, 184, 191

Abilene, 198

Adams & Co., bankers and expressmen, 22, 32, 35, 67; spectacular plans of, 69; opulent days of, 70; failure of, 73

Adams, Alvin, express magnate, 21, 22, 23, 70

Adams, Sheriff, 135

Almer, "Red Jack," stage robber, 205–209

Alpha, Nev., 241–2

American Eagle, steamboat, 63

American Express, 25

Angels Camp, 89

Antelope, steamboat, 153

Apache Indians, 148, 198

Apache Pass, 149

Applegate, Jesse, Oregon pioneer, 77

Applegate, Lindsay, Oregon pioneer, 76

Arapahoe Indians, 156

Arizona, 198 *et seq.*; gold in, 114

Aspinwall, Panama, 179

Auburn, 80

Aurora, Mining Camp of Sixties, 268, 270

Austin, Nev., 89

B

Bakers Field, 256

Baldwin, Judge, stage coach passenger, 141

Ballard rifle, 283–4, 286

Ballou, W. T., 12

Bank of California, 144

Bannock Indians, 156

Barlow, Marshal, 240

Bartholomew, Charles A., shotgun messenger, 201–2

Batterton & Hickman, provision merchants, 57

Bell, "Captain" Tom, bandit, 56, 57; 95–97; 137; lynched, 97

Belle, steamboat, 65

Bender, Jacob, packer, 15

Bennett, W. P., mail man, Wells Fargo manager, 18

Berford, expressman, 33

Berry, Dr., stage robber, 43 *et seq.*

Berry, Eleanor, schoolmistress, romantic experiences of, 244 *et seq.*

Bessie, steamboat engineer, 62

Big Whiskyjug, Piute Indian, 267, 268

Birch, James E., expressman, stage-coach pioneer, 33, 37, 38

Bisbee, Ariz., 201

"Black Bart," bandit. *See* Boles

Black's Crossing, 111

Blackburn, farmer, 16

Blackmore, Bill, stage driver, 92

Blair, Eugene, Wells Fargo shotgun messenger, 227, 261–3

Blair, Ned, stage driver, 127–129

Bloody Tank, Ariz., 204

Blue Cut, 280

Bodie, Mining Camp, founded by W. S. Body (*q.v.*), 270, 271, 290

Body, Waterman S. ("Bill"), prospector, 270. *See also* Bodie

Boise, landlord, 224

Boles, Charles E., bandit known as "Black Bart," 137, 277–279

Boot, Joe, bandit, 211, 212

Boot Hill, 126

"Boston," Pony Express rider, 152

Bowen, Charles, Wells Fargo messenger, 65, 66, 100

Boyce, John, Wells Fargo stage driver, 280, 281

Bragdon, river steamboat, 34

Brannan, Sam, 2, 35

Brastow, Wells Fargo San Francisco Superintendent, 57, 58

Brickwood, Wells Fargo agent, 207

British Columbia, gold in, 114

313